The Challenge of Youth Employment
in Sri Lanka

The Challenge of Youth Employment in Sri Lanka

Ramani Gunatilaka, Markus Mayer, Milan Vodopivec

THE WORLD BANK
Washington, D.C.

1818 H Street NW
Washington DC 20433
Telephone: 202-473-1000
Internet: www.worldbank.org
E-mail: feedback@worldbank.org

ISBN: 978-0-8213-8117-5
eISBN: 978-0-8213-8118-2
DOI: 10.1596/978-0-8213-8117-5

Cover photo: © Studio Times, Ltd.
Cover design: Naylor Design, Inc.

Library of Congress Cataloging-in-Publication Data

Gunatilaka, Ramani.
The challenge of youth employment in Sri Lanka / Ramani Gunatilaka, Markus Mayer, and Milan Vodopivec.
    p. cm. — (Directions in development)
  Includes bibliographical references and index.
  ISBN 978-0-8213-8117-5 (alk. paper) — ISBN 978-0-8213-8118-2 (ebook)
  1. Youth—Employment—Sri Lanka. 2. School-to-work transition—Sri Lanka. 3. Labor market—Sri Lanka. 4. Youth—Sri Lanka—Social conditions. I. Mayer, Markus, 1960- II. Vodopivec, Milan. III. Title.
  HD6276.S682G86 2010
  331.3'4137095493—dc22

                                                                        2009043694

Contents

Box

Figures

Tables

Foreword

Sri Lanka has been regarded as a model of a country with successful social policies, yet for decades it has faced major challenges in providing employment and satisfying other aspirations of youth. Although the labor force has become more educated, and this trend is particularly marked for youth, the main source of employment for both youth and adults remains the informal sector. Moreover, the importance of the informal sector as a source of employment has increased since the mid-1990s. On the positive side, unemployment declined in last decades, particularly for youth.

The Sri Lankan government has continually acted on various fronts to address the youth unemployment problem. It has tried to improve and modernise Sri Lanka's general education system, which has long been criticised as too academic, and to increase the accessibility of training so as to promote the employability youth leaving school. Other actions included strengthening entrepreneurship programs and introducing career guidance and counseling and improving labor market information to help young people in their job searches and to guide human resource planning. Some of these interventions have been actively supported by the World Bank (for example, surveys and research on active labor market programs) and the International Labour Organization (ILO) (downstream capacity building interventions to boost youth employment and livelihood; for example, the Youth Employment Project [ILO/Japan]).

In 2007, the government developed the National Action Plan for Youth Employment, built, for the first time, on a coherent youth employment policy framework and deriving an encompassing and consistent set of policy recommendations. The plan was based on in-depth analysis of Sri Lanka's labor market, provided via a series of background papers undertaken under the auspices of the Youth Employment Network (YEN).[1] To provide the richness and comprehensiveness of this analysis in its totality, these papers, updated and revised, are collected in the present book. The papers adhere to the "4Es" conceptual framework developed by the ILO, World Bank and UN-sponsored Youth Employment Network initiative; that is, they cover the following four key labor market areas: employment creation, employability, entrepreneurship, and equal opportunity. In each topic, one or more papers were commissioned to renowned experts, with the intention that the papers identify and analyze key issues and constraints—both by reviewing existing studies and by performing original analysis—and produce relevant, concrete, and implementable policy recommendations.

While posing a challenge, current trends of population aging also offer Sri Lanka a unique opportunity: In the next several decades, Sri Lanka will have the largest absolute cohort of young people the country is likely ever to have—a unique opportunity for spurring economic growth if these young people are productively employed. This book offers a wealth of valuable advice to the government and other stakeholders to achieve this goal. By exploiting the full potential of the youth, not only will their talent, aspirations, and energy be harnessed to advance economic growth, but also the existing inequities will be reduced and, hopefully in the longer run, eliminated.

Naoko Ishii   Tine Staermose
Director   Director
World Bank Colombo Office   ILO Colombo Office

---

1. The Youth Employment Network (YEN) was created within the framework of the Millennium Declaration where Heads of State and Government resolved to "develop and implement strategies that give young people everywhere a real chance to find decent and productive work." YEN is a partnership between the United Nations, the World Bank and the ILO, with an objective to bring together stakeholders and policy makers to explore imaginative approaches to the challenges of youth unemployment.

About the Authors and Editors

Asha Abeyasekera is a doctoral student in development studies at the department of social policy sciences at the University of Bath. She holds a BA in English literature from Mount Holyoke College, U.S.A., and an MA in women's studies from the University of Colombo, Sri Lanka. She has worked for more than 10 years as a practitioner and researcher in the development sector in Sri Lanka, focusing mainly on gender-related issues and psychosocial work. She has also been a visiting lecturer in women's studies at the University of Colombo. She has contributed to a number of publications within the gender, youth, and psychosocial fields, and was editor of Options, a Sri Lankan feminist magazine, for a number of years. Her main research work has included developing a framework for understanding wellbeing in Sri Lanka and exploring issues of gender equality and equity. Her doctoral research is looking at women's agency within marriages and families.

Harini Amarasuriya is a doctoral student in social anthropology in a joint PhD program with the University of Edinburgh and Queen Margaret University. She has worked in the development and humanitarian sector for the past 12 years as a practitioner and researcher, with a focus on gender, youth, children, and psychosocial wellbeing. She is the co-author of Political and Social Exclusion of Youth in Sri Lanka, and Re-thinking the

Nexus between Youth, Unemployment, and Conflict: Perspectives from Sri Lanka. She has been a visiting lecturer at the University of Colombo for the post-graduate diploma in psychosocial work and counselling and a temporary lecturer at the Open University of Sri Lanka within the department of sociology. Her research interests include gender, youth, and children. She has also conducted research on globalisation and development issues.

Nisha Arunatilake is a research fellow at the Institute of Policy Studies of Sri Lanka (IPS), She holds a BSc in computer science and mathematics from the University of the South and a PhD in economics from Duke University. Her work at the IPS has focused on employment, labor markets and human resource development. She has published in these areas both locally and internationally.

Sunil Chandrasiri is professor of economics and the dean, Faculty of Graduate Studies, University of Colombo. He holds a BA (Honors) and MA in Economics from the University Colombo; an MBA from the University of Hartford, U.S.A; and a doctorate in industrial organization from Latrobe University, Australia. He has published in the areas of industry and trade policy, small- and medium-scale enterprises, tertiary education, and labor market issues in Sri Lanka.

Ramani Gunatilaka is an adjunct research fellow of the Faculty of Business and Economics, Monash University, and works as an independent consultant in Sri Lanka. She holds a BSc in economics from University College London, an MSc in development economics from the University of Oxford, and a doctorate in applied econometrics from Monash University. She has published in the areas of income distribution, poverty alleviation, rural development and labor market issues in Sri Lanka, and on the determinants of subjective well-being in rural and urban China.

Dileni Gunewardena is a senior lecturer at the University of Peradeniya. She holds a BA (Honours) in Economics from the University of Peradeniya and a doctorate from American University, Washington, D.C. She has worked on issues relating to the measurement of poverty, child nutrition, gender wage inequality and ethnic inequality in Sri Lanka and in Vietnam.

Siri Hettige is senior professor of sociology at the University of Colombo, Sri Lanka. He was the dean of the faculty of arts at the same university from 1999 to 2002. He also holds the post of director, Centre for Social

Policy Analysis and Research there and the head of the National Committee on Social Sciences at the National Science Foundation of Sri Lanka. He is a graduate of the University of Colombo and received his PhD from Monash University, Australia. His research and publications spanning more than 30 years deal with a range of topics, such as social stratification, migration, education, ethnic relations, youth, governance, and social policy.

Priyanka Jayawardena is a research officer and holds a BSc (Honours) in statistics from the University of Colombo, Sri Lanka. She is currently reading for a masters in economics from the University of Colombo. Her research interests are in econometrics and economic modeling, economics of education, health economics, labor economics, and demographic studies.

Markus Mayer is program manager for South Asia at International Alert and the former country director of International Alert in Sri Lanka. He has worked in Sri Lanka for more than 15 years on poverty interventions, youth unemployment, conflict sensitive development programming, conflict impact assessment, and the role of local business in peacebuilding and has published in these areas. He was attached as a lecturer and researcher to the South Asia Institute, University of Heidelberg in Germany as well as to the University of Colombo in Sri Lanka, where he coordinated a capacity-development program to improve the employability of social science graduates and to create stronger linkages between academics, practitioners, and policy.

Zindu Salih is currently heading the democratic governance programme at UNDP, Maldives. She holds a BA in social anthropology from the University of Waikato, New Zealand, and an MA in international development and management from Lund University, Sweden. She has more than 10 years of experience in the development and media sectors. She worked for more than 5 years as a television news producer, presenter, and journalist, during which time she compiled a number of documentaries on issues of social significance. Her development work experience involves national-level research projects contributing to policy and governance, and programme coordination. She has worked in the Maldives and Sri Lanka, with a focus on issues related to youth, gender, and governance.

Milan Vodopivec is a lead economist at the World Bank. He holds a PhD in economics from the University of Maryland, College Park. His work at the World Bank has focused on the labor markets and income support systems for the unemployed and education, and he has published widely in these areas. He has worked both in the World Bank's headquarters as well as in the field offices in Colombo, Sri Lanka, and Pretoria, South Africa (his current posting).

Nireka Weeratunge is a senior scientist (gender and social development) at the WorldFish Center, Penang. She holds a BA in sociology from Brandeis University, a MA in development anthropology from Binghamton University, and a PhD in anthropology from University of Toronto. Her work at WorldFish focuses on gender disparities in fisheries-related livelihoods and how these are influenced by wider structures/processes of markets, natural resource degradation, governance, and climate change.

Nimnath Withanachchi holds a PhD in economics from Kobe University and a MBBS from Colombo University. He is a chartered management accountant, U.K. He presently works as an economist (Health Financing and Financial Analysis) at the Japan International Cooperation Agency, Afghanistan. He has work experience with the World Bank, the Japan International Cooperation Agency, and the University of Liverpool on social protection, health financing, and health economics.

Abbreviations

A-level	advanced level (education)
BOI	Board of Investment
CEFE	Competency-based Economies for the Formation of Entrepreneurs (GTZ)
DCS	Department of Census and Statistics
DTET	Department of Technical Education and Training
EPF	Employees' Provident Fund
EPZ	Export Processing Zone
FTZ	free-trade zone
GDP	gross domestic product
GCE	General Certificate of Education
GTZ	German Development Cooperation
HYBT	Hambantota Youth Business Trust
IDA	Industrial Development Authorities
IDB	Industrial Development Board
ILO	International Labour Organization
IT	information technology
JVP	Janatha Vimukthi Peramuna
LFS	Labor Force Survey
LMIB	*Labor Market Information Bulletin*

LTTE	Liberation Tigers of Tamil Eelam
MFA	Migrant Forum Asia
MFI	microfinance institutions
MVTT	Ministry of Vocational and Technical Training
NAITA	National Apprenticeship and Industrial Training Authority
NGO	nongovernmental organization
NITE	National Institute of Technical Education
NYSC	National Youth Services Council
OECD	Organisation for Economic Co-operation and Development
QLFS	Quarterly Labor Force Survey
SEDD	Small Enterprise Development Division
SIYB	Start and Improve Your Business (ILO)
SLBFE	Sri Lanka Bureau of Foreign Employment
SLCPI	Sri Lanka Consumer Price Index
SLIATE	Sri Lanka Institute of Advanced Technical Education
SL R	Sri Lankan rupee
SME	small and medium enterprises
TEVT	technical education and vocational training
TEWA	Termination of Employment of Workmen Act
TVEC	Tertiary and Vocational Education Commission
UAE	United Arab Emirates
VTA	Vocational Training Authority of Sri Lanka
YESL	Young Entrepreneurs Sri Lanka

Introduction: The Problem of Youth Unemployment

Most young Sri Lankans find it hard to get good jobs: educated young people make up a third of Sri Lanka's unemployed, while young workers in informal employment account for a third of the total workforce.

Although unemployment levels in Sri Lanka have halved during the past decade, with the largest decrease among young people, nearly 80 percent of all unemployed in 2006 were youth. Of these, roughly a third had at least 10 years of schooling. Sri Lanka's youth unemployment rate in 2006—at 16.8 percent—was nearly eight times higher than the adult unemployment rate of 1.2 percent. This figure is high by international standards: for example, Thailand's ratio of unemployed youth (15–24 years) to unemployed adults was 6 to 1; Indonesia's, 5.6 to 1; and the Philippines', 3.4 to 1.[1] High unemployment is not the only labor problem facing Sri Lanka's youth: even among the employed, youth between ages 15 and 30 accounted for 45 percent of informal employment, or roughly 30 percent of total employment (Gunatilaka 2008). Informal employment typically offers no job security and little possibility for advancement in either pay or skills.

The acute shortage of good jobs has been blamed for contributing to the civil unrest that has plagued Sri Lanka for several decades. As Harini Amarasuriya argues in her chapter on discrimination and social exclusion of youth in Sri Lanka, rigid forms of social hierarchy and ingrained systems of social and political patronage create structures of exclusion and discrimination based on class, caste, gender, and ethnicity. That sense of exclusion, according to Amarasuriya, makes most young people who do not have the desired family and social connections reluctant to look for jobs in the formal private sector. Instead they seek public sector jobs to provide social legitimacy and validation. But public sector jobs are hard to get without access to patronage and political party networks. Resulting youth frustration has been at the heart of the three youth insurrections that Sri Lanka has experienced since the early 1970s. Those of the early 1970s and late 1980s involved Sinhalese youth in the southern parts of the country. That involving Tamil youth began in the late 1970s and then morphed into a secessionist conflict with regional overtones.

In turn, violence and conflict have left large numbers of young Sri Lankans even more vulnerable and more critically disadvantaged in terms of their human capital. A countrywide survey of internally displaced persons in 2002 found that 60.1 percent were age 30 or younger, with the largest age group—22 percent—ages 11–20 (Hingst, Schoenfelder, and Willborn 2002). The physical and psychological trauma of being caught up in violence aside, conflict causes displacement, and repeated displacement leads to impoverishment and disrupted and discontinued schooling. Literacy rates among displaced young adults have been found to be lower than the national average, indicative of disrupted schooling caused by conflict (Health Policy Research Associates (Pvt) Ltd. 2006).

In this context, emerging demographic trends present both opportunities and challenges. While Sri Lanka's working–age population expanded during the past few decades and contributed to the labor force growth, this trend is now coming to an end. The country now has one of the fastest-aging populations in the world: its share of youth is declining, the adult share is rising, and it has been estimated that Sri Lanka's labor force may begin to shrink around 2030 if the labor force participation rates of 2006 remain unchanged (Vodopivec and Arunatilake 2008). If participation rates decline, as they have in recent years, then opportunities for economic growth with an expanding labor force will disappear much faster.

In fact, to maintain robust economic growth, Sri Lanka will require a combination of increased labor force participation, expanded employment opportunities, and higher rates of productivity growth. The economic implications of producing these necessary conditions are serious. It has been estimated that in the baseline scenario of a continued decline in participation rates and historical productivity growth rates, per capita gross domestic product (GDP) in 2020 would stand at 164,000 rupees (in 2002 prices), 41 percent higher than in 2008. In the increased participation and productivity scenario, per capita GDP would be 229,000 rupees, 40 percent higher than in the baseline scenario in 2020 and nearly double the level in 2008 (Ministry of Labour Relations and Manpower and others 2009).

In any case, until the labor force starts shrinking, Sri Lanka will have the largest absolute cohort of young people the country is likely ever to have (Abeykoon 2006). This one-time demographic bonus will present the opportunity for a last spurt in economic growth if these young people are engaged in productive employment. If they are not equipped with the necessary skills, however, and if the economy is unable to generate sufficient numbers of good jobs, the next decade may usher in an era of more intense and prolonged youth unrest and violence.

The Context

Sri Lanka has posted a healthy economic growth rate in recent years despite the long-standing secessionist conflict that ended in May 2009. Between 1999 and 2008, the Sri Lankan economy grew at an average annual rate of 5.1 percent. In the more recent period of 2002–08, the economy grew even more rapidly, at an average rate of 6.3 percent a year, resulting in a 45 percent increase in real GDP since 2002. Economic growth has been accompanied by a structural transformation in the composition of Sri Lanka's GDP, which has shifted away from agriculture and into higher value-added service-oriented activities. In 1999 the agricultural sector accounted for 15 percent of GDP, but by 2008 the sector's share had declined to 12 percent. The share of the industrial sector in total GDP has remained stable at approximately 28 percent over the past decade. The services sector has grown the fastest and contributes the most to GDP (58 percent in 2008).

Economic liberalization in 1977, which paved the way for export-oriented growth, has also transformed the composition of exports: agriculture's share in total exports declined sharply from 79 percent in 1977 to 23 percent in 2008, while manufacturing's share rose from 14 percent to 76 percent.

The labor market has transformed more slowly. In 1980 agriculture accounted for 46 percent of all employed (all island), but by 2008 this share had dropped to 33 percent (excluding the north and east). Manufacturing now accounts for a fifth of all employed, while the services sector accounts for roughly half. Unemployment rates declined to 3.6 percent for males and 8 percent for females in 2008 (Ministry of Labour Relations and Manpower and others 2009), but the nature of employment created is cause for concern. Formal sector job creation rates are relatively low other than in the public sector, which accounted for 15 percent of employment in 2008. Roughly two-thirds of the employed workforce was found to be informally employed in 2006, with males, young people, older workers, and the less educated more likely to be informally employed. Better education and skills are poorly rewarded in informal employment, signaling that Sri Lanka has been unable to reap the full benefits of its sound education policies because the economy has failed to generate the kind of jobs that can pay educated workers a good wage (Gunatilaka 2008).

Sri Lanka has invested heavily in social welfare since even before independence in 1948 (Anand and Kanbur 1991). It provides education services free of charge to its citizens from primary to tertiary levels. The country is on track to achieve the United Nations' Millennium Development Goals related to primary education enrollment and completion rates and gender equity ratios of 100 percent in primary, junior secondary, and senior secondary education (Department of Census and Statistics 2009).

As a result of these policies, Sri Lanka's labor force is becoming increasingly better educated. For example, between 1998 and 2008, the share of the total employed having only a primary-level education or lower declined sharply, from 32.5 percent to 20.3 percent. Conversely, the share of the total employed with lower secondary education rose from 39.1 percent to 47.9 percent. Similarly, the share of those with GCE (General Certificate of Education) Ordinary levels—the 10th year qualifying examination—declined marginally, from 17.4 percent to 15.8, while those with GCE Advanced-level qualifications—the 12th year qualifying examination that is also the university entrance examination—rose from 8.7 percent to 12.6 percent. The proportion of labor force participants with tertiary education rose only slightly, from 2.3 percent of the total employed to 3.4 percent (Ministry of Labour Relations and Manpower and others 2009).

There is no significant gender imbalance between the educational attainment of males and females that places females at a disadvantage. Indeed, 4.6 percent of employed women in Sri Lanka have a tertiary degree compared with 2.7 percent of men. Among employed women, 16.5 percent have GCE A-level qualifications, compared with 10.6 percent of men. As a result, in 2008, although women made up only 35 percent of the total workforce, nearly 48 percent of workers with a degree in the country were women, while more than 45 percent of workers with A-level qualifications were women (Ministry of Labour Relations and Manpower and others 2009).

As Sri Lanka's employed population has become significantly better educated, so too has the unemployed population. Areas of particular concern are the high levels of unemployment among higher educated young people and the high rates of female unemployment. Youth unemployment accounts for more than half of total unemployment, in which the largest share of the total unemployed (37.5 percent for males and 39.1 percent for females) is made up by the cohort ages 20–24. The share of the unemployed with at least A-level qualifications was 31.9 percent in 2008, up 8.8 percentage points since 1998. More than half of the unemployed have O-level education or more, whereas less than 32 percent of the employed population is similarly educated. Hence, the educated are found in disproportionate numbers among the unemployed.

One obstacle preventing employment among educated youth is poor English language skills—skills that are hard to acquire through the publicly provided general education system. The polyethnic class that has grown up with English as one of their home languages has been able to access English and monopolize the superior economic opportunities it has enjoyed, while most Sri Lankans have long viewed English as the language of privilege and look on it as the sword that divides society between the haves and the have-nots (Gunesekera 2005).

A significant minority of the youth labor force has migrated abroad for work, encouraged by government policy that depends on foreign remittances from migrant workers to manage the balance of payments. Nisha Arunatilake and Priyanka Jayawardena, in their chapter on labor market trends and outcomes in Sri Lanka, cite data from the Sri Lanka Bureau of Foreign Employment to show that 37.7 percent of the total number of Sri Lankans who migrated for work abroad in 2006 were youth, a number equivalent to 5.9 percent of the youth labor force. But for those looking for suitable work at home, the process of job search can be a frustrating, demoralizing process, particularly when they lack the social markers such as English language skills and class connections that open doors in the formal sector. Inevitably, other life decisions such as marrying and starting families need to be put on hold until suitable employment is found; until that time these young people are also forced to live at home with their parents and tolerate attendant curbs on their independence and sense of freedom.

One reason why Sri Lanka has not been able to create enough jobs in formal employment or to absorb greater numbers of its educated unemployed workforce is infrastructure constraints, which hold back greater investment and growth of businesses. Connectivity and accessibility are impeded by poor transportation and communication networks, and delayed implementation of power generation projects has given rise to some of the highest electricity tariffs in the region. Moreover, extreme vulnerability to macroeconomic shocks and political instability retard investment and restrict job creation rates in the formal sector. In fact, the country's score of 79 in the Global Competitiveness Index in 2009–10—the best in South Asia bar India—is based on the good performance of Sri Lanka in the areas of business sophistication, goods market efficiency, innovation, financial market sophistication, health, and higher education. Infrastructure scores poorly, along with labor market efficiency, institutions, and macroeconomic stability (Ministry of Labour Relations and Manpower and others 2009).

Underlying Factors of Unemployment and Social Exclusion

Sri Lanka has been grappling with the problem of youth unemployment for nearly four decades. Many theories have been advanced about the economic reasons underlying the phenomenon, and almost all are based on analyses of Sri Lanka's labor market. Other evidence points to shortcomings in the education system as a significant underlying factor explaining unemployment among youth. The youth unrest that led to decades of violent conflict in Sri Lanka has often been attributed to lack of employment and educational opportunity as well as to poor attitudes about work among youth. Young people have been seen by some analysts as lazy and unwilling to meet the demands of the job or their employer. Underlying both labor market institutions and the education system are social and cultural issues of exclusion and discrimination that deny some Sri Lankan youth access to both education and jobs.

Theories of Unemployment

Three broad hypotheses concerning imbalances in the labor market have been offered to explain the high youth unemployment in Sri Lanka. The skills mismatch hypothesis maintains that a mismatch between what the education system teaches and what the labor market requires produces educated youth who have few marketable job skills but who nonetheless aspire to "good" jobs—jobs that are secure, well-paid, and offer higher social status—and who spend a fair amount of time looking for such jobs. The queuing hypothesis, formulated in relation to the public sector, argues that the unemployed wait for an opportunity to take up good jobs in the public sector characterized by job security, generous fringe benefits, low work effort, and high social status. Political compulsions driving unending recruitment into an already bloated civil service have only reinforced the incentives for job aspirants to queue for these jobs. Some analysts have extended this queuing hypothesis to good jobs in the formal private sector. The institutional hypothesis, also called the slow job creation hypothesis, argues that labor market institutions raise the costs of formal job creation, thereby creating a counterproductive duality by depressing job creation rates in the formal sector and forcing the majority of workers into informal employment. In particular, highly restrictive employment protection legislation and high wages resulting from strong bargaining power of workers under conditions of virtually complete job security raise labor costs and impede job creation.

Many previous empirical analyses have attempted to verify these hypotheses and have reached conflicting conclusions. Several chapters in this volume look at various aspects of these three hypotheses. In chapter 3 Nisha Arunatilake and Priyanka Jayawardena examine these hypotheses again and find support for all three—at least among unemployed youth who have turned to the job placement service offered by Jobsnet to find employment. The authors find that most job seekers are waiting for white-collar occupations, where there are few vacancies, and that most available jobs are for blue-collar workers, which more educated youth are unwilling to take. This finding supports both the slow job creation and skills mismatch hypotheses. The authors also found some evidence that job aspirants queued for jobs with more social status, no matter what the occupation. Gender, experience, location, and employment status are minor sources of imbalance between jobs seekers and available jobs.

Employment Creation

Labor market institutions—the labor rules, organizations, and relationships that underlie the working of the labor market—can importantly contribute to job creation and efficient labor allocation at the same time that they protect fundamental worker rights. But, as Ramani Gunatilaka and Milan Vodopivec report in chapter 2, if these institutions are unbalanced and provide undue protection to certain groups, they may adversely affect labor market outcomes. Their analysis finds evidence that Sri Lanka's wage-setting and employment protection laws not only discourage job growth in the formal private sector but contribute to maintaining the sharp distinction between good jobs in the formal sector and bad jobs in the informal sector. About two of every three workers are informally employed and do not enjoy social security benefits such as participation in pensions or provident funds.

In particular, the authors find that the Termination of Employment of Workmen Act of 1971, which severely constrains private employers' ability to lay off workers during slow periods, not only depresses job flows but discourages small businesses from expanding and becoming subject to the law. They also find that formal wage-setting mechanisms have contributed to a wage gap between public sector and private formal sector workers and informal workers that is not fully explained by the productive characteristics of the workers. The gap is quite high: other things equal, returns to public sector workers are 40 percent higher than returns to informal employees, while returns for formal private sector workers are 20 percent higher.

Finally, Gunatilaka and Vodopivec find that civil service recruitment policies create perverse labor incentives and contribute to unemployment, particularly among educated workers. Especially distorting are the massive "recruitment campaigns" that sometimes take place in conjunction with pending elections, when all or most unemployed university graduates are given public sector jobs. As a result, jobless graduate students tend to wait for another recruitment campaign to give them a secure job in the public sector rather than seek employment elsewhere.

Employability

Technical education and vocational training can be important in enhancing the employability of new entrants to the labor markets by providing jobs skills that are not taught in the general education system. Appropriate training can reduce job search time and offer higher returns. But in chapter 4 on job training efforts in Sri Lanka, Sunil Chandrasiri finds that too often these programs have not performed up to expectations. Although training tends to increase employability among jobseekers with higher levels of education, overall training has not improved employability much. One reason may be that the training programs are concentrated in Western Province, where jobless rates are already relatively low. Another reason might concern the training itself. The author found that many of the training programs were hampered by outdated study programs, inadequate teachers and teaching aids, irrelevant industrial training, and insufficient practical work. Interestingly, although most training programs were targeted at school leavers who had completed their O-level examinations, a significant number of trainees had A-level or higher qualifications, indicating that their formal schooling had still left them unprepared in important ways for the labor market. A significant number of these students took courses in English and in information technology in an effort to improve their prospects for a good job—a further indication of shortcomings in the formal education system.

The finding that better educated youth had trouble finding work was amplified in chapter 5, in which Nimnath Withanachchi and Milan Vodopivec looked at the school-to-work transitions for a sample of state university graduates. They found that four years after graduation, nearly half had still not found job. The study confirmed the importance of social status and networks in securing a job in the formal private sector, putting rural graduates lacking such contacts at a disadvantage. The precise reasons for this could not be determined, but the authors suggested that there could be validity to the claims of some young Sri Lankans that privileged, elite families use their social and political networks to promote their children's employment.

In addition, despite a government program aimed at redirecting graduates' career aspirations toward the private sector (by providing a subsidy to private employers who hired them), the graduates seemed to prefer working in the public sector, where the pay was lower but job security and nonwage benefits were higher. As it turned out, all the unemployed graduates in the sample ultimately obtained public sector jobs as part of a government recruitment campaign directed at university graduates, confirming that queuing for a public job makes good sense.

The study also found support for the other two hypotheses regarding unemployment. The finding that graduates of certain fields of studies faced longer durations of unemployment, and lower wages when they did get a job, confirmed the skills mismatch theory, while it is plausible to believe that the employers use their social networks to help make hiring decisions in an effort to overcome costs imposed by rigid employment protection laws. To hedge against the risk of hiring bad workers, formal sector employers rely on their social networks when hiring young, inexperienced workers. Other things equal, graduates who lack social networks thus have a lower probability of being hired. Because that lowers their expected returns from school, students who lack social networks also have fewer incentives to participate in higher levels of education. In short, by lowering expected returns from schooling, Sri Lanka's restrictive labor laws help reduce school participation for the less privileged, thus creating a cadre of less educated workers and perpetuating a vicious cycle of poverty.

Migration for work is one strategy for improving one's employability. Until recently internal migration from rural areas to urban areas in Sri Lanka was limited because of pro-rural government policies. But roughly 1.5 million Sri Lankans migrate internationally for work—the equivalent of one-fifth of the domestic work force. With globalization and the liberalization of trade, international migration for work has become a permanent characteristic of the labor force. For most individuals, including young people, migration is temporary, undertaken to support themselves and their families. Parents often encourage their children to migrate as a way of learning job skills that they can use to find employment at home. However, most migrants work in informal, low-paying, and low-skilled jobs. Roughly half of Sri Lanka's international migrants are women, most of whom work as housemaids.

And, as Asha Abeyasekera writes in chapter 6, while the Sri Lankan government encourages international migration because of the foreign exchange and increased consumption it brings into the country, it does little to create employment opportunities for returning migrants. Abeyasekera also observes that politicians and society also take a paternalistic attitude toward female migrants—proposing, for example, that married women with young children be barred from migrating for work to protect the children—while doing little to protect migrant workers, both male and female, from abuses they sometimes suffer in host countries and at the hands of unscrupulous domestic employment agencies.

Entrepreneurship

Another recognized employment strategy for youth is entrepreneurship training that can lead to business creation and expansion. Several public, nonprofit, and private entrepreneurship training programs are available to youth in Sri Lanka. But relatively few young people use these services, and even fewer start or expand a business after receiving the training. In her investigation of entrepreneurship training, Nireka Weeratunge argues in chapter 7 that changing sociocultural attitudes about the value of business ownership is as important as improving the training and adopting regulatory and economic incentives to spur entrepreneurship.

Although more research needs to be done in this area, Weeratunge notes that surveys show that youth generally have negative attitudes toward self-employment and business ownership. The failure to pursue long-term strategies for creating an enabling sociocultural and regulatory environment to support business in general and entrepreneurship in particular has been a serious gap in Sri Lanka, she writes, one that especially affects youth, because their perceptions of, and decision making about, training and careers are largely influenced by their families and peers. Moreover, available impact studies show that too often youth who have no intention of engaging in self-employment or starting businesses are selected for entrepreneurship training programs. While all youth need to have enterprising attitudes to find and pursue their livelihoods, training all of them in full-scale programs for entrepreneurship development is an inefficient use of both resources and time.

Equal Opportunity

Linking past youth unrest in Sri Lanka to the frustrations young people feel when they are unable to find work is a simplistic reading of a far more complex problem involving systemic exclusion and discrimination that many youth in Sri Lanka experience. Often youth are said to be too lazy to take jobs in the private sector where they would be expected to work hard, or the education system is blamed for being unable to meet the demands of the labor market. But these views ignore the ways in which rigid forms of social hierarchy and an entrenched system of social and political patronage shape the experiences of youth as they pass through the education system and enter the labor market. Youth also experience class and caste discrimination across gender and ethnic groups. For example, low rates of private sector job creation have led to a system of rationing based on certain class-based skills and social assets that young people from rural backgrounds conspicuously lack. Addressing the issue of youth unemployment is important, but, as Harini Amarasuriya writes in chapter 8, a broader understanding that locates the issue of unemployment within systemic forms of exclusion and discrimination is necessary if policy makers and practitioners are to respond meaningfully.

In chapter 9 Dileni Gunewardena examines one form of discrimination—wage differentials based on gender and ethnicity. Women in Sri Lanka today have education attainments similar to those of men, and their employment opportunities have also expanded, suggesting that the traditional gender wage gap might have narrowed. Although women's wages have increased in Sri Lanka, gender wage gap decompositions show that in all sectors and for all ethnic groups, not only are women underpaid, but because women as a group have better productive characteristics than men as a group, women on average would earn more than men in the absence of gender discrimination. This finding was true even for women in the public sector, where they appear to benefit from gender-specific policies. Ethnic wage gaps among women were largely explained by difference in productive characteristics. Among men, Tamils were underpaid compared with Sinhalese in the same regions. The decomposition found larger wage gaps between Tamil and Sinhalese men in the public sector compared with the private and agricultural sectors, which could be related to language ability or patronage. Overall Sinhalese males appeared to be the primary beneficiaries of labor market policies and civil service hiring practices, which seemed to work against Tamil males. The author found no unfair disadvantage in wage determination for Moor men and women.

In a final chapter Siri Hettige and Zindu Salih look at the effects of Sri Lanka's conflict on its youth and their economic prospects. Particularly in those areas most affected by the fighting, families have been uprooted, education suspended, and job prospects diminished. Many children and teenagers have never known life without conflict. The fighting has also taken a tremendous toll on those youth directly affected, including those who were combatants as well as those who were physically injured. Psychological trauma can be devastating, with anxiety, distrust, grief, uncertainty about the future, and feelings of persecution and distress all common emotions among youth caught in the conflict. Although the conflict was rooted in ethnic differences, youth of all ethnicities cite the lack of jobs as a main concern. Failure to provide these young people with work, the authors observe, could easily lead to a vicious cycle of unemployment, poverty, and conflict.

Policy Directions

As the contributors to this volume have observed, the links that are drawn between youth frustrations and violence, unemployment, and education often overlook broad structural issues that perpetuate discrimination in Sri Lanka. Many of the factors that give rise to discrimination are themselves linked to particular sociocultural aspects of Sri Lankan society that are resistant to change. Nonetheless, the authors' findings suggest several concrete policy directions both for helping youth become more employable and for creating more employment opportunities. Even more will eventually need to be done if Sri Lankan youth are to realize their full potential, but the policy steps discussed below, if planned and implemented widely and equitably, will be a good start.

Creating More and Better Jobs

Well-functioning labor market institutions can contribute importantly to favorable labor market outcomes. To that end, the government should phase out ad hoc civil service recruitment practices and replace them with recruitment through competitive examinations and long-term hiring schedules based on government needs. Such policies will facilitate the smooth functioning of the labor market, reorient young job seekers to search for work in the private sector, and ultimately improve the productivity of the public sector as well as the overall capacity of the economy.

To expand employment creation and enhance access to decent work opportunities for youth, rigid job protection measures in the formal sector need to be revised. One strategy would replace job protection with worker protection, through mechanisms such as unemployment insurance. Worker protections would offer some security to workers while freeing up employers to expand and contract their employee base as opportunities arise. Before such revisions are made, however, their feasibility must be studied and a larger consultation process initiated with key stakeholders, including trade unions, to determine what will work best in the Sri Lankan setting.

Basic infrastructure has to be developed to spur growth and employment in underprivileged areas. Infrastructure development would facilitate private sector investment in these areas, as well as spur both the creation and expansion of firms—among other things, by enabling established, formal sector firms to outsource some of their work to informal businesses.

A reform that takes a two-pronged approach to entrepreneurship training could also lead to greater job creation, particularly in the private sector where the need for jobs is greatest. The first prong would aim to turn around existing negative attitudes about business by actively promoting an enterprise culture among youth. The second prong would focus on improved training, financial support, and improved regulatory environment for those young people who aspire to start their own businesses.

Increasing Employability

The first step in improving youth employability is helping children and youth improve their education outcomes. Education is a critical component in addressing not only youth employment but also many of the inequities than underlie it. While much of the concern about youth unemployment in Sri Lanka focuses on better educated youth who cannot find jobs, it should not be forgotten that the majority of unemployed young people have 10 years or school or less. Both the quantity and quality of their schooling must be improved if Sri Lankan youth as a group are to become the productive work corps that will drive the nation's future.

In particular, educational outcomes must be improved for poor and excluded children and youth. To that end, more resources should be allocated to schools in poor and rural areas, so that they have the teachers, materials, and facilities necessary to educate children. Development of an incentive scheme that can draw more qualified teachers into disadvantaged areas should be considered, with the goal of increasing participation of children in school and reducing dropouts. Innovative approaches to tailoring schooling and training to the needs of school dropouts or children who work may also be needed (for example, conditional cash transfer payments to keep children ages 11–14 in school).

Although most school curriculums include English language teaching, the quality of instruction is often poor and should be improved to give Sri Lankan youth not only a marketable skill but a measure of social inclusion. The education syllabuses currently include Sinhala as a subject for Tamil students and vice versa. But teaching methods need to be modernized, to emphasize communication and to include audio and video equipment, not just blackboard-based teaching. Broader knowledge of the Sinhala and Tamil languages can promote ethnic harmony through greater appreciation of each ethnic group's literature, lyrics, films, and drama—even jokes and cartoons. Information technology and basic business and economics are also subjects that could be more widely taught in school.

Employment prospects for youth can also be improved by strengthened job counseling in school and by improved and more widely disseminated information about the labor market and available jobs. Such counseling and information could help better align youth aspirations with opportunities in the labor market by guiding youth away from careers in areas either where there are few openings or where their skills do not match those required by the career.

Improved vocational training programs will be key to better aligning job aspirations with the job market. Promoting private sector participation in planning and conducting training programs and establishing a self-regulating mechanism through an association to standardize training programs can improve their quality and the relevance of the training. Training programs should be voucher-based and demand driven (through revitalizing the Skills Development Fund, for example), with subsidies for the youth in disadvantaged settings. Relaxation of eligibility restrictions on enrollment should be reconsidered with the aim of reaching the least educated youth. The portfolio of technical education and vocational programs should be expanded to include short-term courses, and the number of courses conducted in Tamil should be increased. Programs specially targeted to young women, disabled youth, and poor youth living in remote rural areas should be piloted.

Opportunities to increase the value-added created by migrants should be considered. At the government level, forging bilateral agreements with appropriate countries to secure short-term assignments for skilled and semiskilled labor, coupled with development of relevant training programs, can increase the revenue generation for youth. Concurrently, non-residential saving plans could be promoted for migrants to ensure higher economic gains. Care should be taken to ensure that youth (and other migrants) are protected from exploitation both at home and abroad, and returning migrants should be given support in reintegrating into society and finding work at home. The government should also find ways to encourage migrants with management or entrepreneurial skills to return and invest in Sri Lanka. That is already happening to some extent, but a more welcoming business climate could help increase those numbers and the jobs they bring with them.

Leveling the Playing Field

Programs aimed at improving youth employment should be aimed at helping all youth, no matter their ethnicity, caste, class, or gender. In some limited situations, affirmative action programs, such as scholarships for specific individuals, may prove effective in promoting equity. In the long run, though, more equitable distribution of education and training resources is likely to be most helpful in smoothing out imbalances.

A particular challenge for policy makers will be meeting the needs of conflict-affected youth. The introduction of special programs to reintegrate vulnerable groups of youth—such as ex-combatants, former soldiers, young widows, the displaced, and the disabled—should be considered. Such programs could offer psychological assistance, counseling, training, and employment or self-employment. Similarly, facilitating pilot projects for first-time employment of disabled youth may stimulate expansion of employment opportunities for young people with disabilities. To that end, existing training institutions need to improve their capacity to train disabled youth: specialized training institutions need to be upgraded and modernized, while regular training institutions need to make adjustments so they are able to provide training to persons with disabilities. Wherever possible, disabled people should be trained alongside able-bodied people.

Conclusions

The three broad policy directions outlined above are critical to addressing the problem of youth unemployment in Sri Lanka: creating more jobs, improving employability, and especially leveling the playing field. Efforts up to now have tended to be too parochial, and this volume espouses the need for a concerted, multidimensional, cross-sectoral approach.

These policy directions require actions in two interlinked arenas. One is education and training, and the other is the labor market. The first arena must prepare young people to be able to participate productively in the economy, be it as salary workers or as self-employed and entrepreneurs, taking into account that the labor force of the future needs to be not only better skilled but also more creative and adaptable. But producing a highly skilled workforce is not enough: to make the most of Sri Lanka's human resources, a supportive, effective labor market, coupled with effective institutional arrangements of tripartite (government, employers' organizations, and trade unions) social dialogue, must ensure that enough decent employment opportunities and good jobs are created so that such resources are optimally used and that adequate signals are produced to guide young people when deciding about their education paths and careers. Much remains to be done in both arenas, and the volume provides detailed recommendations on how to proceed.

Going beyond education and training and the labor market, the volume also focuses on the impact of privileges, social connections, and political patronage on young people's chances and aspirations for employment. Such practices can be altered by changes in the regulatory environment that promote and reward merit and competence, but in the short run, leveling the field for the socially unprivileged may require special actions both in education and the labor market. Indeed, the reforms implied above cannot be value free. In light of Sri Lanka's recent history, a nonnegotiable value has to be that of commitment to equity and inclusion—in offering quality education and decent employment opportunities—for all Sri Lanka's young people. That young people are a heterogenous group is evident from the discussions on class, caste, gender, ethnicity, and even geographical location. Coming to grips—in policy and practice—with the social, economic, and political consequences of exclusion and discrimination is all the more important in light of Sri Lanka's current struggle to reintegrate all those affected by the recently ended armed conflict.

The country is indeed at a critical juncture in its economic and policy history. In 2009 Sri Lanka saw the end of the three-decade-long armed conflict. At the same time, the growth rate of Sri Lanka's working-age population is showing signs of decelerating, and the country now has one of the most rapidly aging populations in Asia. To maintain robust economic growth and raise living standards, Sri Lanka requires a combination of increased labor force participation, expanded employment opportunities, and higher rates of productivity growth. The country therefore needs to address its long-standing problem of youth unemployment before the currently open window of opportunity shuts. In this context, institutions—whether in the private or public sector, whether concerned with labor, the economy, education, or employment—need to review policies and practices for their broader social and economic impact and to do so with a longer-term view of the country's prosperity.

Note

1. http://mdgs.un.org/unsd/mdg/SeriesDetail.aspx?srid=671. Comparable data are unavailable for other South Asian countries.

References

Abeykoon, A. T. P. L. 2006. "Fertility Transition in Sri Lanka: The Determinants and Consequences." Presented at a seminar on Fertility Transition in Asia: Opportunities and Challenges, sponsored by the United Nations Economic and Social Commission for Asia and the Pacific, Bangkok.

Anand, S., and R. Kanbur. 1991. "Public Policy and Basic Needs Provision: Intervention and Achievement in Sri Lanka." In *The Political Economy of Hunger: Endemic Hunger*, ed. J. Dreze and A. K. Sen, 59–92. Oxford: Clarendon Press.

Department of Census and Statistics, Sri Lanka. 2009. *MDG Indicators of Sri Lanka: A Mid-Term Review.* Colombo.

Gunatilaka, R. 2008. *Informal Employment in Sri Lanka: Nature, Probability of Employment, and Determinants of Wages.* New Delhi: International Labour Organization.

Gunesekera, M. 2005. *The Postcolonial Identity of Sri Lankan English.* Colombo: Katha Publishers.

Health Policy Research Associates (Pvt) Ltd. 2006. "The Living Situation of Refugees, Asylum-Seekers and IDPs in Armenia, Ecuador, and Sri Lanka: Millennium Development Indicators and Coping Strategies." Sri Lanka Country Report. Colombo.

Hingst, T., A. Schoenfelder, and S. Willborn. 2002. *Statistical Handbook: Survey of the Internally Displaced (IDPs) Sri Lanka.* Colombo: Ministry of Rehabiliation, Resettlement, and Refugees, United Nations High Commissioner of Refugees.

Ministry of Labour Relations and Manpower, Central Bank of Sri Lanka, and Department of Census and Statistics. 2009. *Labor and Social Trends in Sri Lanka 2009.* Colombo.

Vodopivec, M., and N. Arunatilake. 2008. *The Impact of Population Aging on the Labor Market: The Case of Sri Lanka.* IZA Discussion Paper 3456. Institute for the Study of Labor, Bonn.

CHAPTER 1

Labor Market Trends and Outcomes in Sri Lanka

Nisha Arunatilake and Priyanka Jayawardena

For youth who leave school and enter the labor market, a quick transition to productive employment is increasingly being recognized as important for reducing poverty in later life, improving well-being, and optimizing returns to investments in education and health (World Bank 2007). A speedy school-to-work transition can also provide work experiences and help develop interpersonal skills, improving individuals' productivity and employability in later life. A better understanding of the challenges youth face in finding productive employment is a key to improving youth labor market outcomes in Sri Lanka.

The Sri Lankan labor market is currently experiencing several changes that affect youth employment in the country. First, the country has one of the fastest-aging populations in the world—the youth share of the population in the country is declining, while the adult share is rising. As a result, the labor force has aged and its rate of growth has declined. If current participation rates remain constant, the Sri Lankan labor force is expected to begin to shrink around 2030 (Vodopivec and Arunatilake 2008). How are these changes affecting the labor market? Is Sri Lanka making optimum use of its diminishing labor resources?

Second, Sri Lanka has grappled with the problem of high unemployment rates among youth over several decades (Rama 1999). In recent times overall unemployment rates in the country have come down steadily. Has that decline led to a corresponding improvement in youth employment prospects? Finally, globalization and technological change have fueled the demand for better-skilled workers in information technology (IT) and IT-enabled services both internationally and domestically. At the same time, demand for skilled migrant workers is growing globally (Lewin and Caillods 2001). To take advantage of these emerging opportunities, the country needs to have a skilled, globally competitive workforce. Is the education sector in the country preparing young workers to meet the skill demands of these emerging labor markets?

To find answers to these questions, this chapter examines the trends in labor market indicators over time for Sri Lanka, with international comparisons, where appropriate. It begins with a description of the major data sources and definitions used in the study. It then looks at trends in the size of the labor force, employment, unemployment, and earnings distribution before offering some concluding thoughts.

The chapter finds that the youth labor force in Sri Lanka is shrinking, in part because of the slow growth of the youth population, but also because of declining labor force participation rates among youth. A higher proportion of youth than in the past is engaged in studies and thus delaying entry into the labor force. But the proportion of youth who are neither in the labor force nor engaged in studies has also increased. The ability of the country to encourage youth employment—measured by the employment-to-population ratio—is low compared with world regional averages. The main source of employment for both youth and adults is the informal sector, and its importance as a source of employment has increased over time. Despite a movement away from employment in agriculture, the proportion of workers in wage or salaried employment has not increased, leaving the informal sector to take up the slack. At the same time, the growth in earnings enjoyed by all population groups and economic sectors in the late 1990s deteriorated in the first six years of the new century. These adverse impacts are more pronounced for youth than for adults.

Sri Lanka's economy will prosper in the future only if the country encourages greater labor force participation and makes productive use of its available labor resources. To do this, the country urgently needs to encourage employment creation in the formal sector, where working conditions and remuneration levels are better and more stable. At the same time, access to and the quality of the secondary and tertiary levels of education need to be enhanced, so that the country can attract investments in the emerging global employment markets.

Data and Definitions

The main source of data for this chapter is the Labor Force Survey (LFS) data published by the Sri Lankan Department of Census and Statistics (DCS). The study covers trends in labor market indicators from 1992 through 2006. When information is lacking for 1992, later years are used as reference points, as indicated. Because of ongoing ethnic conflict, the LFS surveys did not cover Northern and Eastern provinces from 1990 to 2002 or for 2006. The survey covered some parts of Northern and Eastern provinces in 2003 and 2004, but only in 2005 did the survey cover all the administrative districts. To keep data comparable across different years, most of the analysis is conducted for the country excluding these two provinces. Where appropriate, information for these two provinces is provided using 2005 data. The study supplements LFS data with other sources of data as indicated.

Revisions made to the LFS survey schedule in 2006 make comparisons difficult for some labor market indicators. The main indicators affected by this change are the unemployment rate and type of employment. The differences in definitions are indicated in the annex as well as in the analysis where appropriate.

In this chapter, the term *youth* refers to persons ages 15 through 29, while *adults* are defined as persons age 30 and over. Some studies define youth differently. When making international comparisons, the analysis uses the same definitions as used by these studies, to enable meaningful comparisons. These definitional changes are noted in the paper. The analysis is conducted for three categories of age groups for youth, namely, 15–19, 20–24, and 25–29. The paper mostly uses internationally standard indicators for the analysis. Specific definitions used by the paper are provided in the annex.

The Size of and Trends in the Youth Labor Force

Over the 1992–2006 period, growth of the overall labor force slowed, while the youth labor force contracted. In 2006, 7.6 million Sri Lankans were in the labor force, a gain of 1.8 million since 1992. The rate of growth was slowing, however, from an annual average of 2.3 percent in 1992–99 to 1.9 percent in 2000–2006. In 2006 some 2.3 million youth were in the labor force, accounting for 29.8 percent of the labor force. Youth participation in the labor force was largely unchanged over the period (an average rate of change of 0.01 percent a year), and the youth labor force actually contracted over the 2000–2006 period compared with the 1992–2000 period. This decline was faster for youth ages 15–24 years.

The contraction in the youth labor force is explained by demographic changes as well as by a declining participation rate. Despite a marginal increase in the labor force participation rates for the overall population, the youth labor force as a share of that total declined by 2.9 percentage points during the period. (The adult rate increased by 3.4 percent, allowing the overall participation rate to rise.) At the same time, the youth population grew only marginally, at an annual average of just 0.4 percent. These trends are more pronounced for youth ages 15–24: for this age group, the youth population has remained more or less stagnant while the labor force participation rate has declined by 4.1 percent (tables 1.1 and 1.2).

These youth labor force trends for Sri Lanka are more similar to trends experienced by developed economies, Central and Eastern Europe, and East Asia than those experienced in the rest of South Asia and other developing countries. As in Sri Lanka, youth labor force participation was declining in the first set of countries, and the decline in the youth labor force was faster than the decline in the youth population (ILO 2006) (table 1.3).

Changes to the Structure of the Labor Force

Overall, the Sri Lankan labor force aged and became more female over the 1992–2006 period. In 2006 the labor force comprised 4.8 million working-age males and 2.8 million working-age females. Slightly more than three-fourths of all males were in the labor force, compared with just under two-fifths of all females. The share of females in the youth labor force (38 percent) was comparable to that in the total labor force. Compared with their adult counterparts, however, participation rates for youth were lower—less than two-thirds (65.5 percent) of all young males and 37.8 percent of all young females were in the labor force. The number of females in the labor force grew by an average rate of 3.4 percent a year, while the number of males grew by only 1.8 percent a year. The greatest increase to the labor force came from the 30 and over female population, which grew at an average annual rate of 5.9 percent over the period (table 1.4).

Labor Force Participation Rates

Part of the decline in labor force participation rates results from an increase in the proportion of youth who are engaged in studies. Most young males

Table 1.1   Youth Labor Force and Population Trends, Selected Years

Category	1992 (000s)	2000 (000s)	2006 (000s)	Percent change 1992–2006	Annual average percent change		
					1992–2006	1992–2000	2000–2006
Household population (15 years and above)							
All	10,303	11,989	13,265	28.75	2.05	2.05	1.77
15–19	1,597	1,681	1,564	(2.08)	(0.15)	0.65	(1.16)
20–24	1,418	1,475	1,433	1.12	0.08	0.50	(0.47)
25–29	1,148	1,233	1,408	22.58	1.61	0.92	2.37
30 and over	6,140	7,601	8,860	44.30	3.16	2.97	2.76
Youth (15–29)	4,163	4,388	4,405	5.81	0.41	0.68	0.06
Youth I (15–24)	3,015	3,156	2,998	(0.58)	(0.04)	0.58	(0.83)
Labor force							
All	5,731	6,799	7,579	32.24	2.30	2.33	1.91
15–19	427	433	373	(12.69)	(0.91)	0.16	(2.30)
20–24	998	999	921	(7.72)	(0.55)	0.02	(1.31)
25–29	829	869	963	16.18	1.16	0.60	1.80
30 and over	3,477	4,498	5,322	53.05	3.79	3.67	3.05
Youth (15–29)	2,254	2,301	2,257	0.13	0.01	0.26	(0.32)
Youth I (15–24)	1,425	1,432	1,294	(9.21)	(0.66)	0.06	(1.61)
Employed							
All	4,902	6,280	7,086	44.6	3.18	3.52	2.14
15–19	250	331	287	14.8	1.06	4.05	(2.21)
20–24	655	769	727	10.9	0.78	2.17	(0.92)
25–29	673	774	857	27.4	1.96	1.89	1.79

(continued)

Table 1.1 Youth Labor Force and Population Trends, Selected Years (*Continued*)

Category	1992 (000s)	2000 (000s)	2006 (000s)	Percent change 1992–2006	Annual average percent change		
					1992–2006	1992–2000	2000–2006
30 and over	3,324	4,406	5,216	56.9	4.07	4.07	3.06
Youth (15–29)	1,578	1,874	1,871	18.6	1.33	2.35	(0.03)
Youth I (15–24)	905	1,100	1,014	12.0	0.86	2.69	(1.31)
Unemployed							
All	830	518	493	(40.6)	(2.90)	(4.69)	(0.82)
15–19	177	102	86	(51.4)	(3.67)	(5.32)	(2.56)
20–24	342	230	194	(43.4)	(3.10)	(4.11)	(2.61)
25–29	156	95	106	(32.2)	(2.30)	(4.91)	1.95
30 and over	154	92	107	(30.5)	(2.18)	(5.04)	2.74
Youth (15–29)	676	426	386	(42.9)	(3.07)	(4.62)	(1.58)
Youth I (15–24)	520	332	280	(46.1)	(3.30)	(4.53)	(2.59)

Source: Authors' calculations, based on DCS, 1992–2006.

Note: In 2006 the survey added a new category: "expected to be employed." To maintain comparability from year to year, these people were considered unemployed.

Table 1.2   Labor Force Participation Rates, Employment-to-Population Ratios, and Unemployment Rates, by Age
Percent

Age group	Labor force participation rate			Employment-to-population-ratio			Unemployment rate		
	1992	2000	2006	1992	2000	2006	1992	2000	2006
All	55.6	56.7	57.1	47.6	52.4	53.4	14.5	7.6	6.5
15–19	26.8	25.7	23.9	15.7	19.7	18.3	41.5	23.5	23.1
20–24	70.4	67.7	64.2	46.2	52.2	50.7	34.3	23.0	21.0
25–29	72.2	70.5	68.4	58.6	62.8	60.9	18.9	10.9	11.0
30 and over	56.6	59.2	60.1	54.1	58.0	58.9	4.4	2.0	2.0
Youth (15–29)	54.1	52.4	51.2	37.9	42.7	42.5	30.0	18.5	17.1
Youth I (15–24)	47.3	45.4	43.2	30.0	34.9	33.8	36.5	23.2	21.6

Source: Authors' calculations, based on DCS 1992–2006.
Note: For 2006 those persons who said they expected to be employed are considered as unemployed.

Table 1.3   International Comparisons of Youth Labor Force and Population

Category	Youth labor force (000s)		Percent change 1995–2005	Youth population (000s)		Percent change 1995–2005
	1995	2005		1995	2005	
World	602,188	633,255	5	1,023,228	1,158,010	13
Developed economies and European Union	67,740	64,501	–5	126,434	124,404	–2
Central and Eastern Europe[a]	30,430	29,661	–3	64,453	70,941	10
East Asia	176,137	154,511	–12	234,364	229,488	–2
Southeast Asia and the Pacific	56,703	61,490	8	97,548	108,909	12
South Asia	118,278	136,616	16	233,818	289,160	24
Latin America and the Caribbean	53,738	57,149	6	95,303	105,468	11
Middle East and North Africa	25,086	33,174	32	62,651	82,915	32
Sub-Saharan Africa	74,077	96,153	30	108,658	146,726	35
Sri Lanka	**1,410**	**1,294**	**–8**	**3,083**	**2,998**	**–3**

Source: For Sri Lanka data, authors' calculations based on DCS 1996, 20006; for other countries, constructed using ILO 2006, table 2.2.
Note: Youth is defined as persons ages 15–24. The Sri Lankan data are for 1996 and 2006.
a. Does not include European Union members but does include members of the Commonwealth of Independent States.

Table 1.4   Labor Force Status of the Household Population 15 and Over, by Age Group and Gender, 1992 and 2006

Age group	Population 15 years and over (000s)	Labor force — Total labor force (000s)	Labor force participation rate (%)	Employed — Number (000s)	Employed — Rate (% to total labor force)	Unemployed — Number (000s)	Unemployed — Rate (% to total labor force)	Total (000s)	Not in labor force — Engaged in studies — Number (000s)	Not in labor force — Engaged in studies — As % of population
1992 Female										
All	5,164	1,867	36	1,450	78	417	22	3,297	560	11
15–19	770	162	21	87	54	75	46	608	476	62
20–24	696	380	55	207	54	173	46	316	66	10
25–29	568	284	50	196	69	88	31	285	8	1
30 and over	3,130	1,041	33	961	92	81	8	2,089	10	0
Youth (15–29)	2,034	826	41	489	59	337	41	1,208	550	27
Youth (15–24)	1,466	542	37	293	54	249	46	924	542	37
Male										
All	5,139	3,864	75	3,452	89	412	11	1,275	572	11
15–19	827	265	32	163	62	102	38	562	492	62
20–24	722	618	86	449	73	169	27	104	68	10
25–29	580	545	94	477	87	68	13	35	9	1
30 and over	3,010	2,436	81	2,363	97	73	3	574	3	0

Youth (15–29)	2,129	1,428	67	1,089	76	339	24	701	569	27
Youth (15–24)	1,549	883	57	612	69	271	31	666	560	37
2006ª Female										
All	6,975	2,755	39	2,488	91	267	10	4,220	612	9
15–19	764	141	18	103	73	38	27	623	504	66
20–24	738	360	49	257	72	103	29	378	87	12
25–29	765	356	46	291	82	64	18	409	13	2
30 and over	4,708	1,898	40	1,837	97	61	3	2,809	7	0
Youth (15–29)	2,267	857	38	651	76	206	24	1,410	605	27
Youth (15–24)	1,502	501	33	359	72	141	28	1,000	591	39
Male										
All	6,290	4,824	77	4,598	95	226	5	1,466	577	9
15–19	800	232	29	184	80	48	21	568	492	62
20–24	696	561	81	470	84	91	16	135	76	11
25–29	642	607	95	566	93	42	7	35	7	1
30 and over	4,152	3,424	82	3,378	99	46	1	728	3	0
Youth (15–29)	2,138	1,400	65	1,220	87	80	13	738	575	27
Youth (15–24)	1,496	793	53	654	83	139	17	703	568	38

Source: Authors' calculations, based on the DCS 1992–2006.

a. For 2006 those persons who said they expected to be employed are considered as unemployed.

who are not in the labor force are studying (84.5 percent), whereas their female counterparts are either studying (46.2 percent) or engaged in housework (47.3 percent). Of the economically inactive youth, the proportion engaged in studies has grown marginally over the 1996–2006 period. This increase is largest for 15–19-year-old females (with a corresponding decline in the proportion of females engaged in household work). For economically inactive young males, the rise in the proportion not working because of illness or disability is noticeable. Although a higher proportion of youth are engaged in studies, it is not clear whether this education will lead to greater employability in later life. Results of a study by Arunatilake and Jayawardena (chapter 3) that analyzed Jobsnet data show that many job seekers in the market have high levels of both formal and vocational training.[1] However, many have obtained training from institutions whose quality is unknown and have received qualifications that are not recognized by any national body. Further, most seem to be filling gaps in their formal education by improving their general skills such as in English language and computer literacy, rather than acquiring specific skills that would lead to a career (see table 1.4).

Compared with world and regional averages, youth labor force participation rates as a proportion of all youth are low in Sri Lanka: in the regional averages for 2005 only those for Central and Eastern Europe and the Middle East and North Africa were lower (table 1.5). These largely reflect the labor force participation rates of young males. For young females, the labor force participation rates in Sri Lanka were slightly better than those for South Asia, but slightly worse than those for Central and Eastern Europe. In keeping with worldwide trends, the youth labor force participation rates have declined for Sri Lanka for both young males and females.

Quality of the Labor Force

The labor force was more educated in 2006 than it was in 1992, and this difference is more marked for youth. In 2006, almost a third (32.5 percent) of the labor force had completed at least O-level examinations,[2] while another 46.5 percent had between 6 and 10 years of schooling. The proportion of the labor force with at least O-level qualifications grew by 5.9 percent over the 1992–2006 period and included an increase in those who were A-level qualified or degree holders. At the same time, the proportion of employed with an education attainment of primary level or below decreased markedly (from 26.8 percent to 21.0 percent). For youth ages 20–29, the proportion

Table 1.5   International Comparisons of Employment-to-Population Ratio and Unemployment Rates, 1995 and 2005

	Labor force participation rates		Employment-to-population ratio		Unemployment rates	
	1995	2005	1995	2005	1995	2005
World	58.9	54.7	51.6	47.3	12.3	13.5
Developed Economies and European Union	53.6	51.8	45.4	45.0	15.2	13.1
Central and Eastern Europe (non EU) and CIS	47.2	41.8	38.0	33.5	19.6	19.9
East Asia	75.2	67.3	69.5	62.1	7.5	7.8
South East Asia and the Pacific	58.1	56.5	52.8	47.5	9.2	15.8
South Asia	50.6	47.2	45.6	42.5	9.9	10.0
Latin America and the Caribbean	56.4	54.2	48.3	45.2	14.4	16.6
Middle East and North Africa	40.0	40.0	28.5	29.7	28.7	25.7
Sub-Saharan Africa	68.2	65.5	56.2	53.7	17.5	18.1
Sri Lanka	**45.7**	**43.2**	**31.2**	**33.8**	**31.7**	**21.7**

Sources: Sri Lanka: authors' calculations based on DCS 1992–2006; other countries, constructed using ILO 2006, table 2.2.
Notes: Youth is defined to be persons ages 15–24. The Sri Lankan data are for 1996 and 2006.

that was at least O-level qualified was larger compared with their older counterparts, and it has risen over time. This indicates that part of the gain in education attainment is at the lower levels of education—more children are staying in school longer.

Although the number of students enrolled in studies at the upper-secondary and tertiary levels was increasing, the proportion of employed with these levels of education is still low (only 15 percent of job holders have education higher than A-level). To be competitive in the global labor market, workers are required to have higher-level skills that are typically acquired at the upper-secondary and tertiary levels. They are also required to have other qualifications such as foreign language literacy and IT skills. The LFS does not collect detailed information on the competencies in these skills. However, information from Jobsnet data suggests that the English competency of job seekers is very low: only 3 percent of job seekers claimed to have "very good" competencies in English (see chapter 3). Although Sri Lanka has made inroads into improving primary-level education, these statistics suggest that the access and relevance of education at the upper-secondary and tertiary levels need to improve if Sri Lanka is to take advantage of the emerging global employment markets—both for migrant workers and for domestic workers in the IT-enabled services sector—and to make Sri Lankan businesses more competitive globally (table 1.6).

Summary: Labor Force

This analysis shows that overall growth of the labor force has slowed in Sri Lanka and the youth labor force is contracting. The contraction results mainly from the slow growth of the youth population coupled with declining participation rates. Moreover, compared with world regional averages, youth labor force participation rates in Sri Lanka are low. On the plus side, the lower participation rates are partly explained by a higher proportion of youth engaging in studies, but the proportion of youth neither in studies nor in the labor force has also increased. The labor force has become more educated over time, but a large part of the gain is at the primary level. Although the proportion of employed with upper-secondary or higher levels of education attainment has also increased, this proportion is still less than 15 percent of the total labor force.

Table 1.6   Composition of Sri Lankan Labor Force by Level of Education, 1992 and 2006

Percent

Age group	Primary or below	Secondary[a]	O-levels	A-levels	Degree and above
1992					
15–19	19.7	65.4	13.3	1.7	0.0
20–24	14.5	52.7	21.7	10.9	0.2
25–29	19.1	45.1	20.9	13.3	1.5
30 and above	33.0	42.8	16.6	5.4	2.1
Youth (15–29)	17.2	52.3	19.8	10.0	0.6
Total	26.8	46.6	17.9	7.2	1.5
2006					
15–19	5.7	70.9	19.0	4.5	0.0
20–24	6.4	50.5	23.1	19.5	0.5
25–29	7.8	50.8	19.3	18.0	4.0
30 and above	27.0	43.3	16.0	10.4	3.3
Youth (15–29)	8.3	56.7	19.3	14.2	1.9
Total	21.0	46.5	17.4	12.2	2.9

Source: Authors' calculations, based on DCS 1992 and 2006.
a. Individuals with 6 to 10 years of schooling.

To compete for emerging global employment opportunities in the IT and IT-enabled services sectors, the country needs to improve education attainment at the upper-secondary and tertiary levels, where students are taught higher-order skills that enable them to learn new technologies fast and to perform complex tasks. The progress at these levels of education has been marginal over the period. In addition, evidence from other studies shows that most youth engaged in studies are filling gaps in their formal education, rather than getting trained in higher-order skills.

Employment

The employed labor force in 2006 was 7.1 million, representing an employment-to-population ratio of 53.4 percent.[3] Of the employed, 1.9 million, or 25.4 percent, were youth.

The growth in employment numbers is explained largely by the increase in the number of employed females, especially in the 30 and above age group. The number of employed females in this age group rose at a pace of 6.5 percent a year over the 1996–2006 period, compared with the overall annual average of 2.9 percent. In contrast, the number of employed youth grew at an annual pace of only 0.9 percent a year over the period.

By geographic sector, the distribution of employed coincided with the distribution of the working-age population. The great majority of workers were in the rural sector (83.3 percent), followed by the urban (11.3 percent) and estate (5.4 percent) sectors. Most of the overall growth in employment occurred in the rural and estate sectors, where the number of employed grew by 3.0 and 6.4 percentage points, respectively.

From 1996 through 2006, the urban share of employed decreased marginally (from 13.2 percent to 11.3 percent), while rural and estate shares of employment increased. Although the percentage of all age groups employed on estates increased, the increase in the rural sector was largely for those in the 30 and over population. The rural share of employed in the 20–24 and 25–29 age groups decreased over time.

Employment-to-Population Ratio

The ability of the economy to create jobs, measured by the employment-to-population ratio, increased overall, rising 5.8 percentage points during the 1992–2006 period. However, much of this rise (4.8 percentage points) took place between 1992 and 2000. For youth, the employment-to-population ratio declined over the 2000 to 2006 period, and this decline was particularly high for youth ages 15–24 (see table 1.2).

The employment-to-population ratio is lower in Sri Lanka than the world regional averages, except for the Middle East and North Africa, and Central and Eastern Europe. However, although all regional averages of employment-to-population ratios have declined across the globe, they have increased in Sri Lanka over the 1995–2005 period. This anomaly is partly attributable to a decline in the youth population in Sri Lanka over the period in contrast to an increase in youth population across the world. Nevertheless, the increase in youth employment in Sri Lanka was above the world average, although it was far below the rates of South Asia, the Middle East and North Africa, and Sub-Saharan Africa (see table 1.5).

Sources of Employment
This section describes employment along five different fronts: status in employment, that is, wage or salaried employment as opposed to other types of employment; industrial sector of employment; emigration for employment; type of employment; and formal versus informal types of employment.

Status in employment. The International Labour Organization (ILO) defines three main categories measuring status in employment: wage and salaried workers, self-employed workers (also referred to as own-account workers), and contributing family workers (also referred to as unpaid family workers). Typically as countries develop and economies become more dynamic, there is a shift in employment from agriculture to the industry and services sectors and a corresponding increase in wage and salaried workers (ILO 2007). This section examines those trends in Sri Lanka.

The overall status in employment has shifted away from wage and salaried workers; however, this shift is less pronounced for youth. Of the total employed, 55.7 percent (numbering 3.9 million) were in salaried or wage employment in 2006. The rest were divided among own-account workers (30.9 percent), unpaid family workers (10.3 percent), and employers (3.1 percent). During the 1996–2006 period, the proportion of wage and salaried workers declined by 5.3 percentage points, mainly giving way to an expanding share of own-account workers. The proportion of unpaid family workers and employers also rose, albeit marginally. Compared with the share of youth in overall employment (26.4 percent), the share of youth in wage or salaried employment was higher (32.2 percent) in 2006. The higher share of young females in the manufacturing sector, particularly the garment industry, accounted for part of this difference. The share of youth in wage or salaried employment decreased over the 1996–2006 period, but by a smaller proportion compared with adults. The proportion of youth who work as contributing family workers also decreased, in contrast to adults (table 1.7).

Foreign employment. On average, in the 1992–2006 period, an additional 211,000 persons entered the labor force annually, but only an additional 156,000 persons found employment. At the same time, the number of unemployed persons dropped by about 26,000 a year, on average. This suggests that foreign employment was a main source of work for Sri Lankans. Information on the stock of Sri Lankans working abroad is available only for 2006. According to the Sri Lanka Bureau of Foreign Employment (SLBFE), 1.4 million Sri Lankans were overseas contract workers in 2006, which is equivalent to 20 percent of the

Table 1.7   Composition of the Employed, by Age Group and Type of Employment, 2006

Percent

Category	15–19	20–24	25–29	30 and over	All	Youth (15–29)
Number (000s) distribution	287	727	857	5,216	7,086	1,871
By type of employment						
Employee, public	2.0	6.2	13.4	15.1	13.5	8.8
Employee, private[a]	63.2	65.3	52.5	36.2	42.2	59.1
Employer	0.3	1.1	2.1	3.7	3.1	1.4
Own-account worker	8.8	15.3	22.1	35.7	30.9	17.4
Unpaid family worker	25.6	12.1	10.0	9.2	10.3	13.2
By sector of employment						
Formal	22.2	32.5	36.9	30.4	31.1	33.0
Informal	77.8	67.5	63.1	69.6	68.9	67.0
By status in employment						
Wage or salaried workers	65.2	71.5	65.8	51.3	55.7	67.9
Other workers	34.8	28.5	34.2	48.7	44.3	32. 1
Change in distribution, 1996–2006						
Employee, public	–48.2	–39.1	–9.4	28.3	15.4	–21.8
Employee, private[a]	–0.9	17.2	16.5	20.8	18.0	13.5
Employer	–44.7	83.0	44.7	76.2	71.9	45.3
Own-account worker	4.4	27.2	36.2	51.4	47.8	30.0
Unpaid family worker	3.0	–12.0	–5.7	75.1	35.7	–5.7
All	**–1.6**	**8.4**	**13.6**	**37.5**	**28.6**	**9.0**

Source: Authors' calculations, based on DCS 2006.

a. Individuals with 6 to 10 years of schooling.

workforce in domestic employment. On average, the departures for foreign employment increased by 4.5 percent a year over the 1992–2006 period to 201,948 persons a year.[4]

In 2006, 76,167 Sri Lankans who migrated for work were youth (37.7 percent of all migrants that year), a number equivalent to 5.9 percent of the youth labor force. Most migrants (94 percent of females and 46 percent of males) were unskilled workers.

Sector of employment. By industrial sector, employment patterns have shifted noticeably away from agriculture. In 1992, 41 percent of those employed were working in agriculture; by 2006 this share had dropped to 32 percent. Both services and industry sectors gained over the period, with industry enjoying the largest gain (an expansion of 6 percentage points). However, the service sector employed the most people (41 percent). These shifts in shares of employment are also apparent for youth. In 2006 only 24 percent of youth were employed in agriculture, down from 36 percent in 1992. Both industry and services sector shares in youth employment have gained over time, with industry enjoying a larger increase. Compared with youth, a noticeably larger share of adults was employed in agriculture in 2006, while a smaller share was employed in industry (table 1.8).

By industrial subsector, the largest gain in the share in employment during the period was for manufacturing workers, followed by the wholesale, retail trade, and hotel workers categories. The main losers were in agriculture and forestry and in public administration, defense, and other services. In all the sectors that gained over time, the youth share in employment rose by a larger margin than the adult share. In the two sectors that lost, the decrease in youth share in employment was greater than the decrease in adult share.

Employment by type. In 2006 the LFS data classified employment into six types: public sector, private sector, employer, own-account worker, unpaid family worker, and a new category called workers without a permanent employer. Careful examination of the data shows that workers in this new category were largely captured by the private sector category in the pre-2006 classification of employment types. In 2006 workers without a permanent employer accounted for 9.9 percent of all those employed.

By type of employment, the largest share in 2006 was in the private sector (32.4 percent), closely followed by own-account workers

Table 1.8   The Employed by Sector and Age Group

Percent

Sector	1992					2006				
	15–19	20–24	25–29	30+	All	Youth (15–29)	15–19	20–24	25–29	30+	All	Youth (15–29)
Agriculture	43.6	34.9	33.1	44.1	41.3	35.5	30.5	21.2	23.9	35.1	32.1	23.8
Industry	30.4	29.4	23.8	17.3	20.5	27.2	40.4	38.9	32.2	23.4	26.7	36.1
Services	26.0	35.7	43.1	38.6	38.2	37.3	29.1	39.9	43.9	41.5	41.2	40.1

Source: Authors' calculations, based on DCS 1992 and 2006.

(26.9 percent) (see table 1.7). Own-account workers increased their employment share (by 4 percentage points) over the 1996–2006 period, while shares for workers in the public and private sectors declined. Employment shares in unpaid family work and employers have increased marginally over time.

The main source of youth employment is the private sector, where around 60 percent of employed young males and females were working. Other significant sources of employment were own-account workers and unpaid family workers, where a quarter of all employed youth worked. A quarter of all employed youth ages 15–19 work in unpaid family employment, but that proportion gradually decreases for older age groups. Thus, for younger workers, unpaid family work appears to be a stepping-stone toward other types of work. As workers age, the share of private sector workers also decreases, while the shares of own-account and public sector workers increase gradually.

The share of females, especially young females, working in the private sector is higher than the corresponding share for males. Excluding workers without a permanent employer, the share of females in the private sector is marginally higher than the share of males working in the sector (34.0 percent compared with 31.5 percent). However, for younger age groups, there are large gender differences in the share of workers in the private sector. Almost two-thirds of young females in the 15–24 age group are in the private sector, compared to half of the young males in this age group. For workers age 25 and over a similar share of males and females are in the private sector. These patterns in employment are largely explained by the high incidence of employment in the manufacturing sector, particularly among young women.

The greatest gender difference in employment was for unpaid family work, followed by own-account work. More than a fifth of all females (21.2 percent) were employed as unpaid family workers, compared with just 4.2 percent of males. The share of females employed as own-account workers was 22.8 percent compared with 35.3 percent for males. The male-female differences in these categories of workers are more pronounced for adults than for youth.

A higher share of females than males also work in the public sector. The largest difference is in the 25–29 age group, where one-fifth of the females but only one-tenth of the males are employed in the public sector. In absolute terms, however, more males than females work in the public sector.

Formal and informal types of employment. The Department of Census and Statistics defines formal and informal employers and enterprises but not formal and informal workers. According to the DCS, the formal sector includes the public sector and private sector enterprises that are registered, keep formal accounts, and employ more than 10 workers. The residual private sector enterprises are considered to be informal. To differentiate informal and formal workers in formal enterprises, we examined whether they receive two types of benefits, namely, paid annual leave and retirement benefits.

Following definitions used by the DCS, in this study formal sector workers are defined to be "persons employed in a registered organization keeping formal written accounts and having more than 5 regular employees" who receive either retirement benefits or paid annual leave. Informal workers are all public and private formal sector employees who are not formal workers, all workers in private informal sector enterprises, all unpaid family workers, and all workers without a permanent employer. Only the 2006 LFS provides information that enables us to differentiate formal and informal workers according to this definition. Hence, the following analysis applies only to 2006.

Almost 7 of every 10 employed Sri Lankans work in the informal sector, and the share of informal sector workers has increased over time. Almost all of the annual employment growth since 1996 has been among informal workers. Largely informal types of employment—such as own-account workers and unpaid family workers—have expanded at a faster pace than the overall average annual employment growth rate of 2.9 percent.[5] Those classified as employers have increased by an average annual rate of 7.2 percent; however, they start from a low base. These shifts in employment patterns are partly explained by the demographic shifts of the employed toward older females, who are more likely to work in the informal economy. Employment in the public and private sectors has also risen over the period, but at a slower rate.

These general trends in employment patterns are somewhat different for youth. Similar to the overall trends, employment as own-account workers and employers rose for youth at a faster rate than growth in total youth employment; unlike for the overall trends, however, the share of employment in unpaid family work decreased and the share of employment in the private sector increased (see table 1.7).

The proportion of informal workers is comparable for youth and adults. Most male informal workers worked either in the private sector

(43.9 percent, which includes 17.3 percent who were without a permanent employer) or were self-employed (45.8 percent). Female informal workers were divided about evenly among private sector workers (31.0 percent, including 8.2 percent who were without a permanent employer), own-account workers (33.3 percent), and unpaid family workers (33.5 percent). The share of informal sector workers is larger for youth in the 15–19 age group, compared with adults.

A higher proportion of males than females are informal sector workers. Three-fourths of young males but just slightly more than half of young females worked informally. The share of informal work is highest for males and females in the 15–19 age group; the share decreases gradually for older youths and then increases again in the older age groups.

The main difference in formal-informal employment across gender was in the private sector. Seven of every ten male workers in the private sector held an informal job, fewer compared with less than four out of every ten female workers. Nearly one-fifth (17.3 percent) of the young male private sector workers did not have a permanent employer. This gender difference was largely attributable to the recent expansion of formal employment in the manufacturing sector aimed at young females.

Underemployment Trends
High levels of employment do not necessarily indicate productive labor usage—some workers may be underemployed. The underutilization of workers can occur for several reasons, including putting workers in jobs that do not require all their skills or that provide fewer hours of work than the employee would like. LFS survey data allow us to measure only time-related underemployment, defined as those who have worked fewer than 35 hours a week and are prepared and available for additional work if provided.[6] We use that definition in the following profile.

In 2006 around 300,000 workers were underemployed. That amounted to 4.3 percent of the employed. For comparison, 6.4 percent of the labor force was unemployed. About a third of the underemployed (35.0 percent) were males ages 30 and over, and a little more than a third (37.0 percent) were females ages 30 and over, and the rest were young men and women. Twice as many young males were underemployed as young females.

In absolute terms, the number of underemployed increased, by about 125,000, between 2000 (the earliest year for which underemployment information is available) and 2006. Correspondingly, the share of underemployed in the total labor force also grew (from 2.6 percent in 2000 to

4.0 percent in 2006). The youth share of the underemployed declined noticeably (from 40.4 percent to 28.8 percent) over the period.

Ninety percent of the underemployed resided in the rural sector. This rural share of underemployment increased from 80.6 percent in 2000 for all workers as well as for different age groups considered. The greatest increase was among adults. At the same time, the share of underemployed in both urban and estate areas decreased.

About half (50.9 percent) of the underemployed had 6 to 10 years of education. The remaining half was equally divided among those with a primary or lower education attainment and those who were at least O-level qualified. These shares of underemployed across different education levels remained constant over the 2000–2006 period.

The youth share in underemployment decreased over the 2000–2006 period for both young males and young females. This decrease is most prominent for young people in rural and estate sectors and for those with lower educational attainment (O-level qualified or lower).

Summary: Employment

The analysis on employment shows that in general, the ability of the country to create employment, measured by the employment-to-population ratio, has slowed over the 2000–2006 period. The employment-to-population ratio has worsened for youth and is low compared with those for youth in other countries. The employment opportunities available in Sri Lanka are not very attractive: main sources of employment are in the informal sector, which has become more important as a source of employment over time. Although the proportion of those employed in agriculture has decreased, there has been no corresponding expansion in wage and salaried employment. Overall, most of the gain in employment share is in self-employment at the expense of workers in the public and private sectors. By type and sector of employment, the statistics are somewhat better for youth. A higher proportion of youth have moved away from agriculture and, although the share of youth in the public sector has decreased over time, the share of employment in the private sector has increased. The share in unpaid family work has also decreased. At the same time, underemployment remains high in the country relative to unemployment.

Unemployment Trends

This section describes the unemployment trends in the country (excluding Northern and Eastern provinces). The definition of *unemployed* changed slightly in the 2006 LFS. First, the 2006 survey defined *unemployed* more stringently, compared with previous years. Second, persons who were not employed but had already made arrangements for a job or were about to be self-employed were no longer considered to be unemployed but instead were classified separately as *expected to be employed*. In 2006, 23,163 persons (0.3 percent of the labor force) fit this new definition. To be consistent with data from earlier years, the following analysis considers these individuals to be unemployed. However, 2006 data do not provide sufficient information to correct for the definitional change of *unemployed*. As a result, the unemployment statistics provided for 2006 in the following analysis are likely to be marginally lower than they would have been according to the earlier definition of unemployment.

The unemployment rate is higher for females, the more educated, and younger age groups. In 2006, 493,000 persons, amounting to 6.5 percent of the labor force, were unemployed. From 1992 through 2006, the number of unemployed almost halved and the unemployment rate came down steadily. The majority of the unemployed were youth. Among these, 39.3 percent were in the 20–24 age group in 2006. Roughly a similar number of males and females were unemployed. About a third of the unemployed had an education attainment of O-levels or above. A further 41.8 percent had 6 to 10 years of schooling.

The overall unemployment rate for females was more than double the rate for their male counterparts (9.7 percent compared with 4.7 percent). More than a quarter of females in the 15–24 age groups were unemployed, while around a fifth of males in these age groups were without a job. In comparison, the unemployment rates are below 5 percent for both males and females in the 30 and over age group. By education level, the unemployment rate for persons who had O-level qualifications or higher was 10.7 percent, more than seven times the jobless rate for persons who had a primary or lower education attainment (figure 1.1).

The unemployment rate decreased 8.0 percentage points from 1992 to 2006, with the greatest decrease for youth. The largest decrease was for the 15–19 age group, where the jobless rate decreased by 18.4 percentage points. The jobless rates for the 20–24 age group and the 25–29 age group also decreased by large margins (see table 1.2).

Nearly four out of every five unemployed persons (78.3 percent) were young people. At 17.1 percent, the youth unemployment rate was more than eight times higher than the adult unemployment rate of 2.0 percent. The unemployment rate for young females was almost twice that for young males. Youth unemployment rates were in double digits in all

Figure 1.1   Unemployment Rate and the Number of Unemployed, by Age, Sex, and Education Level, 2006

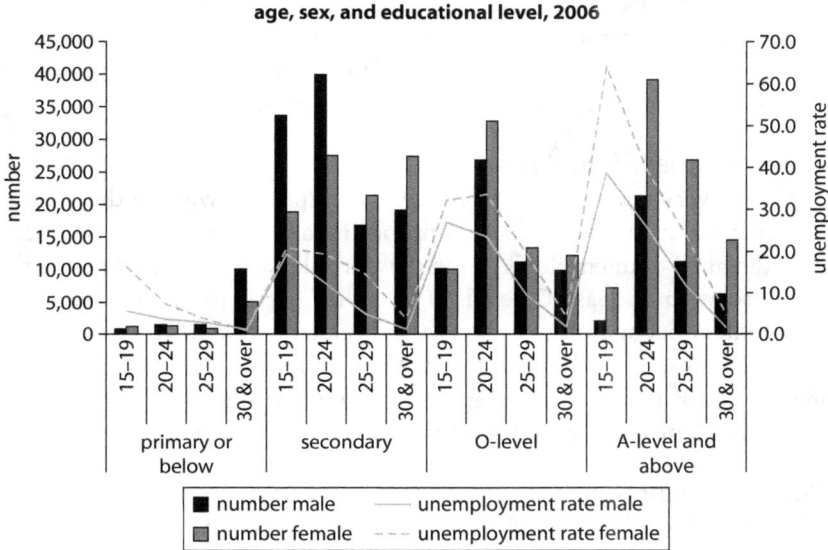

age, sex, and educational level, 2006

number male —— unemployment rate male
number female --- unemployment rate female

Source: Authors' calculations based on DCS 2006.

three sectors, with the highest rate (18.1 percent) in rural areas, where 81.8 percent of the youth labor force resided. The ratio of youth to adult unemployment is highest in the estate sector (13 to 1) and lowest in the urban sector (5 to 1).

Unemployment rates follow similar patterns for both males and females across age and education groups; they are higher for younger age groups and for the more educated. However, unemployment rates are higher for females than males, for all age groups and for all levels of education. These patterns are largely consistent in 1996 as well as 2006 (see figure 1.1).

In absolute terms, the number of unemployed is highest for 15–24-year-olds with a secondary level (6 to 10 years) education. At lower education levels, more males are unemployed than females, while at higher education levels, more females are unemployed. The number of unemployed by age and education groups has decreased for males, except for males with A-level qualifications or higher. The number of unemployed by age and education level has also decreased for females, except for females 25 and over with a secondary-level education and for females 15–19 with A-level qualifications or higher. This decrease is larger for lower levels of education and for younger age groups (see figure 1.1).

Despite the decline in unemployment, the jobless rate for youth in Sri Lanka was high compared with world regional averages. Except for the Middle East and North Africa, the youth unemployment rates in Sri Lanka were higher than all other world regional averages.

Expected Types of Employment

Three of every ten jobless persons were searching for work in the "clerks" occupational category. Of those, a proportionally larger share was female, including half of unemployed females with at least A-levels and two-fifths of those with at least O-levels. Two other occupational categories— "elementary occupations" and "craft and related workers"—were popular with the less-educated unemployed. More males than females were looking for work in the elementary occupations, while a similar share of males and females were expecting employment in craft and related jobs.

Unemployment Duration

Close to half of the unemployed (or 3.2 percent of the labor force) had been unemployed for more than a year in 2006. A slightly higher proportion of females (53.1 percent) than males (43.1 percent) fell into this category. Across age groups, males and females ages 25–29 were most likely to be unemployed for more than a year. Across education levels, more than half of those with O-level qualifications or higher were unemployed for more than a year.

Summary: Unemployment

Although unemployment declined over the period, particularly for youth, the youth unemployment rates were still high compared with those in other countries. The main reasons for the decline in unemployment were the slow growth of the youth population, greater participation in education, and foreign employment. Youth employment levels also declined in the country over the 2000–2006 period. Almost half the unemployed, especially females and those who were at least O-level qualified, were unemployed for more than a year. Most of these were expecting to be employed in the "clerks" occupational category, the white-collar occupation requiring the lowest level of skills. This finding indicates that although most of the unemployed have high levels of formal education, they probably do not have the skills required for many of the better white-collar jobs.

Patterns and Trends in Labor Earnings

Overall, average real monthly earnings rose by 19.8 percent from 1996 through 2006, with adults and males gaining more from the increase. Average monthly earnings for adults grew by a larger margin (20.4 percent), compared with those for youth. The earnings growth (9.0 percent) was lowest for youth ages 15–24. By gender, real earnings rose 21.8 percent for males and 17.2 percent for females. Youth ages 25–29 were the only age group in which male earnings did not rise more than female earnings.

Real earnings grew faster over 1996–2000 (3.8 percent) than over 2000–2006 (0.7 percent). This decline in real earnings growth was similar for males and females and for private sector workers. However, the real earnings in the public sector grew at a higher rate in the latter period. Real earnings showed positive growth in all occupational categories in the 1996–2000 period but slowed substantially or turned negative in the later period for all but three categories—"legislators," "professionals," and "skilled agriculture and fishery workers." By industrial classification, real earnings growth rates continued to grow only for "public administration, defense, and other services." In all other industries, the earnings either declined or showed very low growth.

These trends are largely explained by the poor performance of the garment and tourist sectors, which was largely attributable to increased competition and to the years of conflict. At the same time, high inflation and interest rates over the 2000–2006 period crowded out private investments. The ability of the country to attract foreign investments in the post-2000 period was also low (with the exception of the post-tsunami period), because of the unstable macroeconomic environment in the country.

On average, public sector employees earn more than private sector employees, and the public-private gap in earnings is wider for adults than for young people. Public sector monthly earnings, on average, were higher than private sector earnings for all age groups, with the highest public-to-private ratio (of 2:1) observed for adults. Over the 1996–2006 period, the public-to-private gap in average monthly earnings narrowed for youth groups. Real earnings rose for workers in both the public and private sectors—by 17.6 percent for private sector workers, and by 24.1 percent in the public sector. Real earnings also grew across age groups and sectors of employment, except for youth ages 15–24 in the public sector. Real earnings for this group fell by 5.1 percent over the period.

Table 1.9 Earnings Trends, by Age Group

Category	Mean monthly earnings (2006) All	Share in employment (2006), (%) All	Average annual change in labor earnings (%) 1996–2000 Y-I	Y-II	Adlt	All	2000–2006 Y-I	Y-II	Adlt	All	1996–2006 Y-I	Y-II	Adlt	All
All	8,379	100	3	4	4	4	0	0	1	1	1	2	2	2
Gender														
Male	9,051	65	3	4	4	4	0	0	1	1	1	2	2	2
Female	7,105	35	3	4	4	4	-1	1	0	1	1	2	2	2
Economic sector														
Public	12,660	14	5	2	2	2	-4	1	3	3	-1	1	2	2
Private	6,995	42	3	6	6	5	0	0	-1	0	1	2	2	2
Occupation														
Legislators and senior officials	22,488	10	5	8	4	6	2	0	1	2	3	3	2	4
Professionals	15,326	5	5	1	0	1	0	5	3	3	2	3	2	2
Technicians and associate professionals	12,851	5	9	13	3	5	-2	-2	1	0	2	3	2	2
Clerks	10,425	4	0	1	2	2	-2	0	1	0	-1	1	2	1
Service workers, shop and sales workers	7,507	7	3	1	3	4	-3	0	0	0	0	1	1	1
Skilled agriculture and fishery workers	5,973	22	16	13	8	9	3	0	1	2	10	5	4	5
Craft and related workers	6,869	17	2	2	5	3	-1	0	-1	-1	0	1	1	1
Plant and machine operators & assemblers	7,979	7	-1	2	3	2	-1	-1	0	0	-1	0	1	1
Elementary occupations	4,977	22	4	4	4	4	0	0	-1	-1	2	2	1	1

Source: Authors' calculations based on DCS 1996 and 2006.

Note: Y-I and Y-II refer to young people ages 15–24 and 25–29, respectively, and Adlt refers to persons ages 30 or more. Trends are calculated for real earnings in 2006 prices.

The distribution of monthly average earnings, measured by the Gini coefficient, became more unequal for the country during the ten-year period. Earnings were more equally distributed during the 1996–2000 period but grew more unequal in the later period. This trend held for all geographical sectors except the urban sector, where the dispersion of earnings became more unequal throughout the entire study period.

Conclusions and Policy Recommendations

This chapter examined labor markets trends in Sri Lanka over the 1992–2006 period, giving particular attention to youth. The analysis shows that the labor force growth slowed and that the youth labor force stagnated over the period and contracted over the 2000–2006 period. Both demographic changes and the lowering of labor force participation rates have contributed to this decline in the youth labor force. The decline is of concern because youth labor force participation rates were already low compared with those for other world regional averages, indicating that the ability of the market to attract workers is low.

As labor resources grow scarcer, it is essential to make optimum use of them. However, the ability of the economy to create employment has been low. The available sources of employment in the country are not very attractive. The major source of employment is the informal sector, and its importance as a source of employment has grown over the period. Although employment shows a movement away from agriculture, there is no corresponding increase in the share of wage or salaried employment. For youth, most of the job growth has been in the self-employment and employer categories, along with a marginal increase in employment in the private sector. Earnings growth deteriorated over 2000–2006, compared with 1996–2000. Youth have been more affected than adults by this deterioration. The ability of the economy to make use of opportunities opening up in the global employment markets is also low, given the fairly low proportion of the labor force with higher education.

Although unemployment rates have come down, particularly those for youth, the current rates are still relatively high compared with those in other countries. The decline in the unemployment rates is largely explained by demographic changes, emigration of workers, and increased education participation, rather than improved employment prospects in Sri Lanka. Close to half the unemployed have been unemployed for over a year. Most of them, despite having high levels of formal education, are expecting jobs requiring low skill levels, indicating that despite high levels of formal education, the market is demanding low competencies in skills.

The analysis shows the urgent need to encourage labor force participation rates by creating attractive employment opportunities, especially in the formal sector, where working conditions and remuneration levels are better and more stable. Several studies have highlighted the need to develop the investment climate in the country and relax labor laws to encourage the creation of more formal sector jobs (World Bank 2006).

Although the labor force has become more educated over time, a major part of the improvement has been at the primary level. The need is to improve not only education attainment at the upper-secondary and tertiary levels but also the relevance of education so that the workforce is competent in IT and English skills necessary for securing employment in the emerging global employment markets. In this regard, special attention should be paid to improving the quality and relevance of education, especially for rural youth from outside Western Province. The access to good-quality training programs is also low for youth, in part because these programs are costly and available only in and around Western Province (Colombo) and other urban areas. Further, many good training programs are conducted only in English, which is a further barrier to access. A concerted effort should be made to improve access to these better-quality training programs for all Sri Lankans by encouraging the training providers to offer these programs outside Western Province and by making financial assistance available.

At the same time, there is a need to improve English and IT education at the secondary level, so that youth do not spend time filling those gaps in their secondary education when they should be working or engaging in more advanced education programs. Although several initiatives have been introduced to improve the quality of English and IT education offered at the school level, progress has been slow. New innovative ways are needed for improving education in these areas quickly, so that the country does not lose out on the emerging opportunities.

Annex

Definition of Labor Market Indicators Used in the Analysis

The analysis uses standard labor market indicators as defined below:

Population (P): Economically active population 15 years and over.

Employed (E): Household members, who during the reference period, worked as paid employees, employers, own-account workers, or unpaid workers. This includes persons with a job but not at work during the reference period.

Employment-to-population ratio: The number of employed persons as a percentage of working-age population.

Expecting to be employed (EE) (2006): Persons who are not currently employed but already had a job or had made arrangements for self-employment are not considered to be employed.

Unemployed (U) (before 2006): Persons who were available and/or looking for work but who did not work during the reference period.

Unemployed (U) (2006): Persons available and/or looking for work, and those who did not work but took steps during the last four weeks to find a job and who are ready to accept a job given work. (The Department of Census and Statistics data do not consider those who are expecting to be employed as unemployed.)

Labor force (LF): Economically active population 15 years and over. (LF = E + U.)

Not in the labor force: A person who is neither employed nor unemployed.

Unemployment rate (UR): Unemployed as a percentage of the labor force.

Labor force participation rate (LFPR): Persons in the labor force as a percentage of the working-age population.

Reference period: Week preceding the week of data collection.

No permanent employer (2006): Employees who do not have a permanent employer.

Notes

1. Jobsnet is an Internet-based employment sourcing and delivery system for matching job vacancies with jobseekers who register with Jobsnet. The information store is updated on a real-time basis from all parts of the country.

2. At least O-level qualified includes A-level qualified and degree holders.

3. These statistics exclude Northern and Eastern provinces.

4. These figures are not adjusted for arrival of temporary workers after completing their work contracts.

5. More than 90 percent of own-account workers and all unpaid family workers are in the informal sector. Around half of all employers were also informal sector workers. Exact time trends in formal-informal employment cannot be estimated, because these two types of employment cannot be distinguished in surveys conducted before 2006.

6. As defined by the Department of Census and Statistics in Sri Lanka.

References

DCS (Department of Census and Statistics), Sri Lanka. 1992–2006. *Labor Force Survey.* Colombo.

ILO (International Labour Organization). 2006. "Global Employment Trends For Youth." Geneva.

———. 2007. "Key Indicators of the Labour Market." Geneva (www.ilo.org/kilm).

Lewin, Keith, and F. Caillods. 2001. *Financing Secondary Education in Developing Countries: Strategies for Sustainable Growth.* Paris: UNESCO-IIEP.

Rama, Martin. 1999. "The Sri Lankan Unemployment Problem Revisited." Policy Research Working Paper 2227. Washington, DC: World Bank.

Vodopivec, M., and N. Arunatilake. 2008. "The Impact of Population Aging on the Labor Market: The Case of Sri Lanka." IZA DP 3456. IZA (Institute for the Study of Labor), Bonn.

World Bank. 2006. "Sri Lanka: Strengthening Social Protection" http://site resources.worldbank.org/INTSOUTHASIA/Resources/Strengthening _Social_Protection.pdf (November 13, 2009).

———. 2007. *World Development Report 2007: Development and the Next Generation.* Washington, DC: World Bank.

CHAPTER 2

Labor Market Institutions and Labor Market Segmentation in Sri Lanka

Ramani Gunatilaka and Milan Vodopivec

Sri Lanka has devoted much attention to worker protection. Extensive legislation covers various aspects of working conditions, and the government has ratified eight International Labour Organization (ILO) conventions on core labor standards (although weaknesses in monitoring and enforcement of labor standards remain). It has also put in place several programs protecting children against exploitation. Tripartite mechanisms for social dialogue among trade unions, employers, and the government have been in place for a long time, and these groups interact and collectively resolve critical issues in industrial relations in the labor market.

Labor market institutions—the rules, practices, organizations, and relationships under which the labor market operates—that strike an appropriate balance between labor market flexibility and worker protection can contribute importantly to job creation and efficient labor allocation while simultaneously protecting fundamental rights of workers. But if these institutions are unbalanced and provide undue protection to certain groups, they may adversely affect labor market outcomes. This chapter attempts to shed light on this question in the Sri Lankan context. Specifically, it examines whether Sri Lankan labor market institutions contribute to the segmentation of the labor market, whereby workers are divided into two groups—one consisting of well-protected and well-paid formally employed workers, and the other of unprotected and low-paid informal sector workers. This question is studied by analyzing determinants of informal employment and wages, as well as by examining the effects of Sri Lanka's restrictive severance pay legislation on job creation and destruction and on enterprises' incentives to increase employment.

The chapter first provides an overview of the extent of segmentation in Sri Lanka's labor market and presents an analysis of personal and community characteristics associated with the probability of being employed in the public, private formal, and private informal sectors. It then analyzes institutional factors responsible for the formation of wages and the resulting wage premiums associated with public and formal private work. The chapter describes employment protection and analyzes its consequences on job creation and destruction and firms' growth, before concluding by placing the analysis in the policy context.

Determinants of Informal Employment in Sri Lanka

Sri Lanka's labor market divides sharply along the informality margin: a small formal sector of public and private workers sits alongside a large informal sector where working conditions are precarious. In 2006, 66 percent of Sri Lanka's employed labor force was in informal work (in line with the definition approved by the 15th International Conference of Labor Statisticians). Public employment accounted for a sizable 13 percent and private formal employment for only 20 percent (table 2.1). Of those in

Table 2.1   Labor Market Segmentation in Sri Lanka 2006, All Employed

Category	Percent
Public employment	
As a share of total employment	13.4
As a share of total formal employment	39.8
Private formal employment	
As a share of total employment	20.3
As a share of total formal employment	60.2
Informal employment	
As a share of total employment	66.3

Source: Gunatilaka (2008) based on the Sri Lanka Department of Census and Statistics' Quarterly Labor Force Survey Data 2006.
Note: Definitions of formal and informal employment follow those developed by the 15th International Conference of Labor Statisticians and include own-account (self-employed) workers, unpaid family workers, employers and employees working in formal and informal enterprises and households. See Hussmanns (2001) for the international definitions that were modified in this analysis to include agricultural workers, domestic service workers, and workers under the compulsory school-going age. See Gunatilaka (2008) for details of the definition criteria used in the Sri Lankan analysis.

informal work, 45 percent were own-account (self-employed) workers, 29 percent were employees in informal enterprises, and 8 percent worked in formal enterprises where they received wages but not social security benefits (table 2.2). Of the employees working in informal enterprises or households, only 6 percent had permanent tenure; the rest were mainly temporary, casual, or without a permanent employer. Moreover, 45 percent of informal employees were in enterprises with fewer than five workers (Gunatilaka 2008).

Below we apply a sector participation choice model to investigate the determinants of employment status among Sri Lanka's workforce in 2006. The following four employment statuses are distinguished: unemployment; public employment; private formal employment; and informal employment, with unemployment considered as a baseline option.[1] The marginal effects from the multinomial logistic regression denote the effect of a unit change in each variable on the probability of being in the specified category of employment relative to the base category—that is, unemployment—in the case of continuous variables. For dummy variables, marginal effects are discrete changes in the quantities of interest as the dummy variable changes from 0 to 1.

The results of the analysis are presented in table 2.3. Compared with workers in public and private formal employment, informal workers are disadvantaged in terms of age, ethnicity, education, and skill levels. Among informal sector workers, both young and old workers are overrepresented, as are ethnic Moors in comparison with the reference category, Sinhalese. The more educated workers are less likely to be informally employed, with workers with junior secondary school being 16 percent, and workers with tertiary education 53 percent less likely to be informally employed than

Table 2.2   Structure of Informal Employment

Category	Percent of total informal employment
Informal employment in formal sector	**8.3**
Family worker in formal enterprise	0.8
Employee in informal job in formal enterprise	7.5
Informal employment in informal sector	**91.8**
Own-account worker in informal enterprise or household	44.7
Employer in informal enterprise	3.0
Family worker in informal enterprise	15.0
Employee in informal enterprise or household	29.1

Source: Gunatilaka (2008) based on the Department of Census and Statistics' Quarterly Labor Force Survey Data 2006.
Note: See table 2.1. Figures do not add to 100 due to rounding.

Table 2.3   Determinants of Probability of Employment in Public, Formal, and Informal Employment: Marginal Effects of Multinomial Logistic Estimates – All Employed

Employment categories	Public	Formal	Informal
Demographics			
Male (d)	−0.0032	−0.0305***	0.0337***
Married (d)	0.0152***	−0.0165***	0.0012
Age	0.0105***	0.0037***	−0.0142***
Age squared	−0.0001***	−0.0001***	0.0002***
Sri Lankan Tamil (d)	−0.0242***	0.0299**	−0.0056
Indian Tamil (d)	−0.0097**	0.0222	−0.0126
Moor (d)	−0.0278***	−0.0366***	0.0644***
Other (d)	−0.0251***	0.0838**	−0.0586
Education			
Junior secondary	0.0138***	0.0206***	−0.0344***
Senior secondary	0.0545***	0.1096***	−0.1641***
Tertiary	0.3291***	0.1990***	−0.5280***
Occupation			
Managerial (d)	−0.0339***	0.1032***	−0.0693***
Professional (d)	0.1560***	0.0974***	−0.2534***
Technical (d)	0.1299***	0.2239***	−0.3538***
Clerical (d)	0.1529***	0.2593***	−0.4121***
Service (d)	−0.0011	−0.0306***	0.0317***
Agricultural (d)	−0.0674***	−0.2641***	0.3316***
Elementary (d)	0.0249***	0.0927***	−0.1176***
Industry			
Manufacturing (d)	−0.0321***	−0.0111	0.0432***
Services (d)	0.0482***	−0.1293***	0.0811***
Spatial			
Rural (d)	0.0104***	0.0091	−0.0195**
Estates (d)	0.2361***	0.2349***	−0.4710***
Central (d)	0.0299***	−0.0684***	0.0385***
Southern (d)	0.0084***	−0.0646***	0.0562***
North Western (d)	0.0069**	−0.0933***	0.0864***
North Central (d)	0.0400***	−0.0345***	−0.0054
Uva (d)	0.0137***	−0.0103	−0.0034
Sabaragamuwa (d)	−0.0064**	−0.0606***	0.0670***
Pseudo R^2	0.4394	0.4394	0.4394
Number of observations	27,724	27,724	27,724

Source: Authors' estimation based on Department of Census and Statistics' Quarterly Labor Force Data 2006. See Gunatilaka (2008).

Note: The base category is unemployed. (d) indicates discrete change in dummy variable from 0 to 1. The omitted dummy variables are female, Sinhalese, primary and no education, production workers, agricultural sector, urban sector, and Western Province. Estimation of marginal effects are calculated at mean values using Bartus (2005).

***, **, and * denote statistical significance at the 1 percent, 5 percent, and 10 percent levels, respectively.

workers with primary or no education (other things equal). Managers and other skilled occupation categories are less likely to be informally engaged relative to production workers, the reference category. Informal workers are also more likely to be employed in the manufacturing and services sectors rather than in agriculture, the reference category. They are also significantly more likely to be urban rather than resident in rural or estate areas. Of the provincial dummies, residents of Central, Southern, North Western, and Sabaragamuwa provinces are more likely to be informally employed than residents of Western Province.

In contrast, public sector workers are typically married, of middle years, and Sinhalese. They are also more likely to have attained tertiary-level education than either formal private or informal workers. They are more likely than private formal workers to be professionals and to belong to technical, clerical, or elementary occupations. The typical public sector worker is also likely to work in the services sector and more likely to live in a rural or estate area than in the urban sector, and in the provinces outside Western Province.

Formal private workers are less likely than public sector workers and informal private workers to be male but more likely to be single and of middle years. Sri Lankan Tamils are more likely, and Moors less likely, to be employed in this sector than Sinhalese. The more educated an individual is, the more likely he or she is to be employed in this sector. Formal private workers are also in more skilled occupations but less likely to be in services than agricultural workers. Formal private workers are also more likely to be in Western Province.

The Operation of Wage-setting Institutions

Do wage-setting institutions contribute to Sri Lanka's labor market segmentation and reinforce queuing in the job market? If so, one would expect the existence of a premium above the observable characteristics that is associated with working in protected segments of the labor market—that is, in the public and formal private sectors. Before we examine this question, however, we describe the wage-setting arrangements in Sri Lanka.

In Sri Lanka three tiers of wages can be distinguished, each determined through a different mechanism—those related to the public sector, to the formal ("protected") private sector, and to the informal ("unprotected") sector. Public sector wages are governed by two key mechanisms: periodic recommendations by government-appointed pay commissions; and adjustments by the cabinet in the cost-of-living allowance. Formal private sector wages are determined in three ways: by tripartite wages boards, which determine minimum wages; through collective bargaining between trade unions and the employers represented by the Employers' Federation of Ceylon; and through independent, individual bargaining between more skilled employees and their employers. Wages of workers in the informal sector are by and large determined freely by the market; although many informal workers are covered by the wage-board legislation, they may earn less than mandated where monitoring and enforcement is weak. At the same time, because the wage increases mandated by the wages boards have hardly kept up with inflation, market-determined rates above the statutory minimums prevail in areas such as Western Province where the labor market is tight.

From this description, it can be seen that public sector workers are the beneficiaries of the prevailing wage-setting system and informal workers the losers. Unions wield considerable political and strategic clout in the public sector, and they are also present in the private formal sector, compelling greater compliance with protective labor legislation and engaging in collective bargaining. Indeed, as shown in table 2.4, public employees enjoy the highest mean wages overall and in every wage tercile (it should also be remembered that public sector workers enjoy other benefits such as tax exemptions, job security, and noncontributory pensions).[2] The mean hourly wage of formal employees is also substantially higher than that of informal employees.

Further empirical analysis shows that public and formal private sector jobs command an important wage premium that cannot be explained by the productive characteristics of the workers. Table 2.5 sets out the regression results of wage equations corrected for sample selection bias by including the conditional probabilities of different employment outcomes as additional regressors. The conditional probabilities are derived from a multinomial logistic model with five employment outcomes. The first three columns permit a comparison of the impact of the variables on

Table 2.4   Mean Hourly Wages of Public, Formal, and Informal Employees in 2006, SL Rs

Hourly wage	Public	Formal	Informal
Mean	72.4	43.7	31.5
Highest tercile	120.4	84.5	54.7
Middle tercile	67.3	30.4	26.6
Lowest tercile	29.5	16.0	13.0

Source: Gunatilaka (2008) based on Department of Census and Statistics' Quarterly Labor Force Data 2006.

Table 2.5   Determinants of Hourly Wages, Employees

Characteristic	Public (1)	Formal (2)	Informal (3)	All employees (4)
Demographics				
Male	0.0897	0.1749***	0.4272***	0.3216***
Age	0.0786*	0.0471***	0.0504***	0.0465***
Age squared	−0.0008*	−0.0006***	−0.0006***	−0.0005***
Sri Lankan Tamil	0.0839	−0.0395	0.0685	0.0101
Indian Tamil	0.3483**	−0.0032	0.0208	0.0381
Moor	0.1735	0.1068	0.0834	0.1020***
Other	0.3622	0.5106***	−0.6192	0.0080
Education				
Junior secondary	0.1264	0.0523	0.0477	0.0539**
Senior secondary	0.2035	0.2703**	0.1305	0.1489***
Tertiary	0.3438	0.8156**	0.4390	0.4468***
Occupation				
Managerial	0.1448	1.0773***	0.0739	0.6314***
Professional	0.0777	0.6206	0.8182	0.5746***
Technical	−0.1659	0.4403*	0.0453	0.2058***
Clerical	−0.2132	0.3332*	0.2141	0.1997***
Service	−0.163	−0.0689	−0.1304	−0.1151***
Agricultural	−0.3271	−0.3351	−0.1105	−0.0123
Elementary	−0.2361	−0.2427**	−0.2136	−0.1960***
Industry				
Manufacturing	0.4783**	0.2443	0.0655	0.1738***
Services	0.2249	0.142	0.0061	0.1519***
Job-related variables				
Firm size <4		−0.0611	0.0388	0.0370
5–9		−0.0265	−0.0248	−0.0148
16–49		0.0591	0.0127	0.0091
50–99		−0.0312	0.1469	−0.0133
100+		0.1421*	−0.1368	0.0154
No specific institution		0.3286**	0.0492	0.1218*
No regular employees		−0.1183	−0.1118	−0.0986
Temporary		−0.1819***	0.0661	−0.2670***
Casual		−0.1969**	0.0627	−0.2772***
No permanent employer		−0.0300	0.1383	−0.1132***
Public employee				0.4176***
Formal employee				0.1969***
Spatial				
Rural	−0.1227	−0.0497	−0.0774	−0.0877***
Estates	−0.9098***	0.0857	0.0907	−0.3203***
Central	−0.0464	−0.2215***	−0.0150	−0.0412
Southern	−0.0323	−0.1029	0.1334*	0.0546*
North Western	−0.0785	−0.3300**	−0.0609	−0.0831**

(continued)

Table 2.5   Determinants of Hourly Wages, Employees *(Continued)*

Characteristic	Public (1)	Formal (2)	Informal (3)	All employees (4)
North Central	−0.2896	−0.2055*	0.009	−0.1140**
Uva	−0.1148	−0.0898	0.1095	−0.0344
Sabaragamuwa	−0.1299	−0.2875***	−0.2572**	−0.1976***
Conditional Expected Values of Residuals				
Outcome 1	−0.4319	−0.1833	0.0772	
Outcome 2	0.1651	0.0738	0.2659	
Outcome 3	−0.0597	−0.2841	0.2718	
Outcome 4	0.1121	0.1410*	0.2888	
Outcome 5	0.7573	−0.7131**	−0.0245	
Outcomes 3, 4, and 5				−0.0460***
Constant	2.4310	1.5829***	2.0599***	2.3280***
R^2				0.202
Number of observations				15439

Source: Estimation is based on Department of Census and Statistics' Quarterly Labor Force Data 2006.
Note: Estimates generated using Fournier and Gurgand's (2002) SELMLOG.ado. Sample selection bias correction based on multinomial logistic model with five employment outcomes: (1) unemployment; (2) employment as own-account workers, contributing family workers, and employers; (3) public employees; (4) formal employees; (5) informal employees. The omitted dummy variables are female, Sinhalese, primary and no education, production workers, agricultural sector, firm size 10–15, permanent tenure, formal employee, urban sector, and Western Province. Models (1), (2), and (3) allow for full wage parameter heterogeneity across outcomes (3), (4), and (5). This formulation allows for separate market equilibriums and different payments for the unobserved characteristics determining selection. Model (4) imposes the constraint of homogeneity in parameters across the wage equation for the three outcomes but still treats them as different outcomes in the selection equation. The coefficients on the conditional expected values of the residuals derived from the multinomial logistic model estimate the covariance between the residual in the regression and the residuals (or some function of the residuals) from the multinomial logistic model. Standard errors are derived from 100 bootstrap replications, with ***, **, and * denoting statistical significance at the 1 percent, 5 percent, and 10 percent levels, respectively.

employees' wages in the public, formal, and informal sectors. The fourth column shows the impact of the sector of employment, among other explanatory factors, on the determination of wages across all employees. We comment only on some of the more interesting results in what follows.

The results shown in column 4 in table 2.5 suggest that wage-setting institutions have contributed to an artificial gap between better-paying jobs in the public and the protected private formal sector and low-paying jobs in the unprotected informal sector. Other things equal, returns to public sector workers are 42 percent more, and returns to formal private sector workers are 20 percent more, than returns to informal employees. There is some evidence of gender wage disparities other than in the public sector, but little evidence of ethnic-based disparities (see chapter 9 in this volume, which provides a more nuanced analysis of gender and ethnicity-related wage inequalities). While the regression estimates relating to education variables are significant only for formal employees, note that education is most highly rewarded in the formal sector and least in the informal sector. At higher levels of education, informal employees enjoy half the returns to education enjoyed by equivalently educated employees in the formal private sector. The variables related to firm size are by and large not significant other than for the 100 employees plus group, which earns significantly more than employees in microenterprises in the formal sector and significantly less than employees in microenterprises in informal employment. Temporary and casual workers earn significantly less than permanent employees in formal employment.

Impact of Employment Protection Legislation

Labor market segmentation can also be fueled by employment protection legislation. In particular, large firing costs and procedural obstacles to worker dismissals may contribute to the emergence of dual labor markets. Such costs and obstacles reduce job separations as well the hiring of new workers, with informal sector workers and vulnerable groups such as young workers and females being particularly hurt. Firms hire fewer workers following positive shocks that would otherwise encourage them to expand, because high severance payments make it costly for firms to lay off workers in the face of a negative economic shock (Bertola 1992). Thus dismissal costs act just like hiring costs, reducing job flows and the speed with which labor markets adjust to exogenous shocks and constraining the reallocation of labor from declining to expanding sectors.

Recent microeconometric analyses have shown that labor market regulations can produce important efficiency losses. For example, Heckman and Pages (2000) show that in Latin America, more stringent job security laws are associated with lower employment and higher unemployment, particularly among young workers. Similarly, Besley and Burgess (2004) find that labor regulations in India had important adverse effects on output and employment. Ahsan and Pages (2007) report that regulations concerned with labor disputes and job security hurt covered workers. Kugler and Saint-Paul (2004) show that restrictions on firing reduce incentives for firms to hire the unemployed and lengthen unemployment spells for workers in the United States. Bassanini and Duval (2006) find that changes in tax and labor policies explain about half of the 1982–2003 changes in unemployment among members of the Organisation for

Economic Co-operation and Development (OECD). Other studies using macroeconomic data, including Nickell and Layard (1999), Haffner and others (2001), and OECD (1999), have also found negative efficiency effects of severance pay.

But these negative findings from labor market regulations are not universal.[3] Bauer, Bender, and Bonin (2007) found no evidence that dismissal protection affected worker turnover in Germany. Schivardi and Torrini (2008) found only modest evidence that employment protection legislation reduced firm incentives to increase employment in Italian firms.

This section explores some possible links between Sri Lanka's restrictive and costly employment protection legislation, embodied in the Termination of Employment of Workmen Act (TEWA), and labor market outcomes. In particular, it explores possible links of TEWA to job flows (job creation and destruction) and to patterns of firm growth.

Description of TEWA

The Termination of Employment of Workmen Act of 1971 is one of the costliest and most restrictive severance pay systems in the world. TEWA requires employers with more than 14 workers to seek the authorization of the Commissioner of Labor for intended layoffs (for each individual case, not only for mass layoffs as in some other countries). It not only calls for employers to pay high compensation to the laid-off workers, but its discretionary nature and lengthy procedures further discourage employers from laying off workers.

Revisions to the compensation formulas, adopted in 2005, reduced nontransparency and arbitrariness in the firing process, but the separation costs remain extremely high by international standards, and the process of separation still involves "prior approval" by the Labor Commissioner. During 2002–03 (the period used in the analysis here), the severance pay averaged nearly twice the monthly salary for each year of service, and the multiple could rise as high as six times the monthly salary (figure 2.1). As shown in figure 2.2, in 2003 a Sri Lankan worker with 20 years of service received an average severance package equal to 25 months of wages. In contrast, the average severance was 16 months of wages in other Asian countries, 12 months in Latin American countries, 7 months in African countries, 6 months in OECD countries, and 4 months in transition countries. Laid-off Sri Lankan workers with shorter spans of service also received unusually generous severance pay. And when the system switched to a fixed formula for computing the severance package in December 2003, the program became even more generous (World Bank 2007).

Figure 2.1   Generosity of TEWA Orders, 2002–03

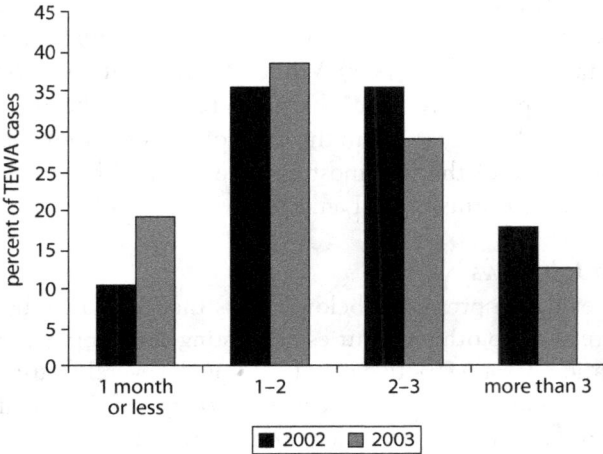

Source: Authors' computations based on the information provided by the Ministry of Labour and Social Affairs.
Note: The index of generosity is the multiple of the monthly salary per year of work service, computed from the
TEWA orders for firms.

Figure 2.2   International Comparison of the Generosity of Severance Pay

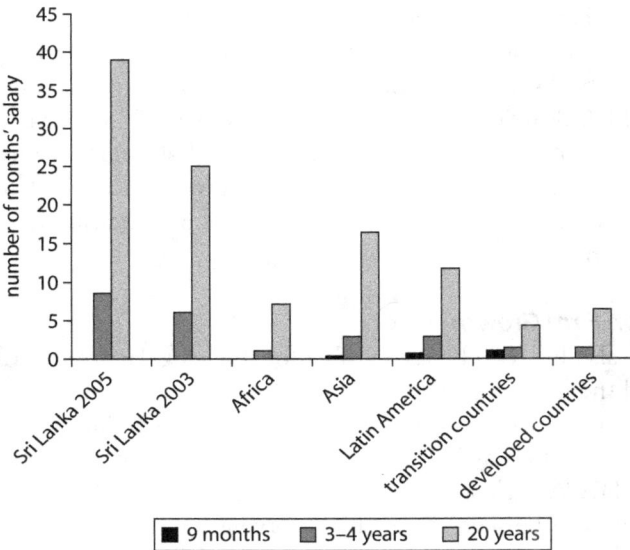

Source: World Bank 2007.
Note: Generosity is expressed as the multiple of the monthly salary paid to three types of workers: with 9 months,
3–4 years, and 20 years of tenure at the job from which they are laid off.

Firms may also try to sidestep TEWA obligations by contriving disciplinary grounds that would justify firing a worker or by harassing workers to make them quit. Alternatively, they could outsource work to avoid having to take on more workers. While it is difficult to assess how frequently these options are used, there are reasons to believe that firms have only limited ability to avoid the costs of TEWA. Inflexible labor regulations were one of the five most commonly cited business challenges reported by urban firms in Sri Lanka.[4]

Impact on Job Flows

Empirical evidence presented below shows that Sri Lanka has very low job flows relative to other countries, suggesting that employment protection legislation has a restrictive effect. Although several factors (exposure to macroeconomic and trade shocks, for example) can explain low job flows, the international comparison suggests that TEWA is likely to be a significant contributing factor.

According to the sample of firms used in our analysis, in the early 2000s job creation exceeded job destruction, with an average job creation rate of 7.9 percent and a job destruction rate of 4.1 percent (see box 2.1 for definitions and measurement of job flows). The resulting average gross job reallocation rate (the sum of jobs that disappeared in shrinking firms plus those that were generated in expanding firms) was 12 percent, and the excess job reallocation rate (a measure of the "job turnover") was 8.3 percent. Job flows of temporary workers, quite expectedly, strongly exceeded job flows of permanent workers (table 2.6). International comparisons presented in figure 2.3 show that in each dimension, job flow rates of other countries vastly exceed job flow rates of Sri Lanka (note that the comparison includes a range of developed, transition, and developing countries).

Impact on Firm Growth

TEWA is also likely to be responsible for the irregular size distribution of firms and the limited growth of firms with 14 workers. Surely, if TEWA is imposing additional costs on firms, firms must be trying to avoid them. One way to do so is by keeping their workforce below 15, thus benefiting from the TEWA exclusion. That firms actively avoid having a workforce of 15 or more can be seen simply by observing the distribution of firms by firm size, based on Employees' Provident Fund (EPF) data.[5] As figure 2.4 illustrates, each distribution in the period 2000–2003 has "a kink" at 14 workers. While the number of firms is reduced monotonically with the size of the firm for firms having more than 10 workers, there is an

Box 2.1

Measurement of Job Flows

We follow the usual conventions of job flow definitions (Davis and Haltiwanger 1999). Job creation is defined as the sum of increases in employment in all firms that expanded in a particular year, and job destruction is the sum of employment losses in firms that contracted in the particular year (note that net employment growth is equal to the difference between job creation and job destruction). We also use two summary job flow measures: job reallocation (the sum of job creation and job destruction) and excess job reallocation (the difference between the job reallocation and net employment growth). The latter measure is particularly interesting, because it reflects the intensity of enterprise restructuring (it measures the extent of job flows over and above what is needed to accommodate a needed change in net employment). For all variables, job flow rates are obtained by dividing job flows by the average of the stocks at the beginning and end of the period. More formally, job flow rates are defined as follows:

- *Job creation rate* between time $t - 1$ and t equals employment gains summed over all firms that expand between $t - 1$ and t, divided by the average employment at time $t - 1$ and t.
- *Job destruction rate* between time $t - 1$ and t equals employment losses summed over all firms that contract between $t - 1$ and t, divided by the average employment at time $t - 1$ and t.
- *Job reallocation rate* between time $t - 1$ and t is the sum of all plant-level employment gains and losses that occur between $t - 1$ and t, divided by the average employment at time $t - 1$ and t.
- *Excess job reallocation rate* between time $t - 1$ and t equals the difference between job reallocation rate and the absolute value of employment growth (the latter defined as the difference between employment at time t and employment at time $t - 1$, divided by the average employment at time $t - 1$ and t.

We use data from the Sri Lanka's 2003 Investment Climate Assessment survey of urban firms, reporting total employment as well as employment of permanent and temporary workers, for three years in the early 2000s.

irregularity for firms with 14 workers, with the number of firms this size being about the same as the number of firms with 13 workers, followed again by a reduced number of firms with 15 workers.

Moreover, TEWA also seems to affect the likelihood of firms reducing or increasing their employment. Among firms that are shrinking, firms

Table 2.6   Job Flow Dynamics, 2001–02 and 2002–03

Category	2001–02			2002–03		
	Total	Permanent	Temporary	Total	Permanent	Temporary
Rate of job creation and destruction						
Job creation	8.2	8.2	13.5	7.6	6.2	39.3
Job destruction	3.9	3.9	6.3	4.4	4.4	6.6
Job reallocation	12.1	12.1	19.8	12.0	10.6	46.0
Excess job reallocation	7.7	7.8	12.5	8.8	8.9	13.3
Memorandum items						
Employment	160,167	153,814	6,353	165,337	156,502	8,835
Number of firms		418			426	

Source: Authors' computations based on 2003 urban Investment Climate Assessment data (see the description of data in World Bank and Asian Development Bank 2005).
Note: See box 2.1 for the definition of job flows.

Figure 2.3   Job Creation and Job Destruction Flows

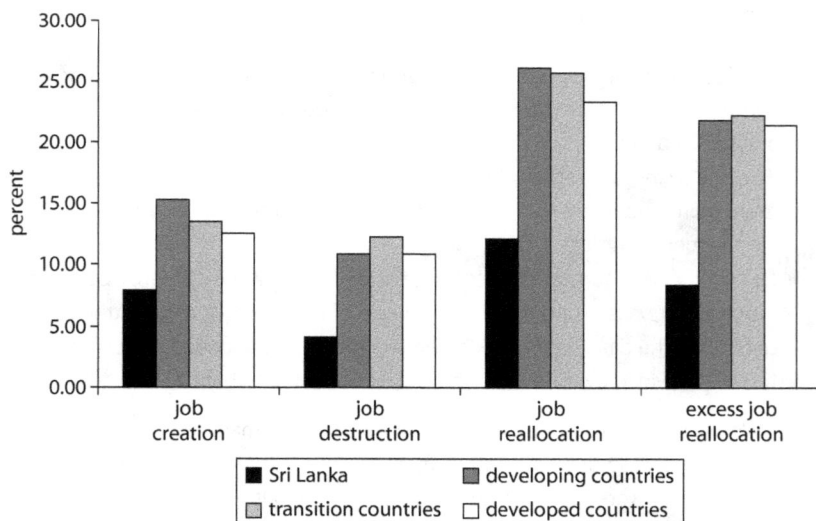

Source: World Bank 2007.
Note: Sri Lanka ICA 2003 urban survey (average for 2001/02 and 2002/03). Transition countries: Estonia 1997–2000; Hungary 1994–2000; Latvia 1994–99; Romania 1994–2000; Slovenia 1992–2000. Developed countries: Canada 1985–97; Denmark 1982–94; Finland 1989–98; France 1991–96; Italy 1988–93; Netherlands 1994–97; Portugal 1984–94; United Kingdom 1987–98; United States 1989–97; West Germany 1978–99. Developing countries: Argentina 1997–2001; Mexico 1987–2000.

Figure 2.4   Number of Firms by Size, 2000–2003

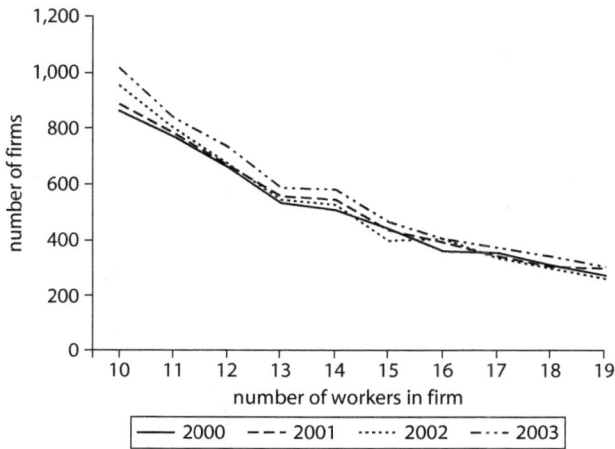

Source: Authors' computation based on EPF data, 2000–2003 (the panel of firms consisted of 43,838 firms in 2000 and 50,748 firms in 2003).

with 15 workers are shrinking more intensely than firms smaller or larger; analogously, growing firms with 15 workers are exceeding the intensity of growth of their immediate neighbors (figure 2.5). In other words, the firm size of 15 is found to be particularly "unstable," and the firm size of 14 particularly stable.

This pattern of growth is consistent with the hypothesis that firms subject to TEWA will tend to mass at the threshold of 14 workers while awaiting an atypically large productivity shock that would enable them to cross the threshold. Abidoye, Orazem, and Vodopivec (2009) tested this hypothesis more formally, by applying a difference-in-differences method to a somewhat longer EPF panel data set covering the period 1995–2003. The methodology also distinguished between firms in the Export Processing Zones (EPZs)—where enforcement of TEWA was said to be less stringent—and others. The study confirms the above results. It found that non-EPZ firms at or below the 14-worker threshold are less likely to increase employment compared with non-EPZ firms above the threshold. Above the threshold, non-EPZ firms are more likely to shed workers while EPZ firms are more likely to add workers. Moreover, at all sizes, EPZ firms are more likely to add workers than non-EPZ firms. These findings suggest that the TEWA policies that were designed to preserve employment have

Figure 2.5   Employment Growth of Firms (Deviations from the Common Growth Trend), 1995–2003

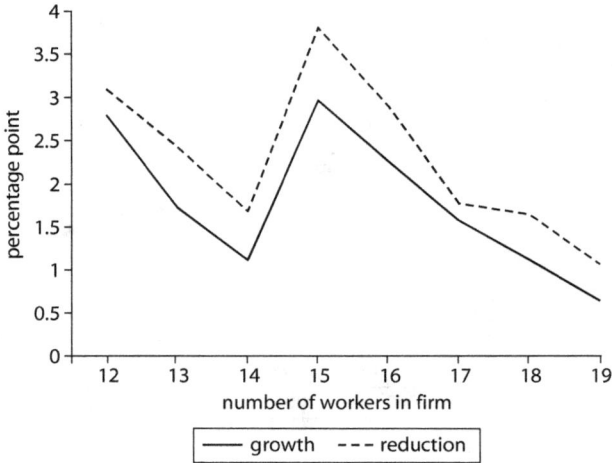

Source: Authors' computation based on EPF data, 1995–2003 (the panel of firms consisted of 34,655 firms in 1995 and 50,748 firms in 2003).
Note: The figure plots the coefficients—size-specific dummies—as follows. For each year during 1996–2003, we grouped firms into either a growing or shrinking group and then regressed growth (reduction) rates on firm size and year dummy variables. All size-specific dummies, reflecting deviations from the common growth trend, were found to be statistically significant.

exactly the opposite effect, depressing employment growth and inducing firms to seek sectors where they can avoid the law.

To summarize, restrictive employment protection legislation is likely to be an important determinant of both low job creation and low job destruction rates in Sri Lanka. If so, incumbent formal sector workers are clear winners, with the unemployed and those seeking formal jobs the biggest losers. While the first group has a strong formal representation, the workers of the informal sector have been without an effective voice and their interests continue to be inadequately represented. Moreover, by retarding growth of firms, the legislation limits overall employment growth (the above analysis does not allow us to quantify these effects).

Concluding Remarks

This chapter investigated whether Sri Lankan labor market segmentation is fueled by labor market institutions, in particular, by wage-setting mechanisms and employment protection legislation. Our policy-relevant findings are twofold. First, wage regressions show that public and "protected" private sector jobs carry a wage advantage unaccounted for by productive characteristics of workers. This finding is consistent with formal wage-setting mechanisms helping to increase returns to formal sector workers, thereby creating an artificial wage gap and contributing to labor market segmentation. As a corollary, higher labor costs reduce creation of formal sector jobs and thus deprive informal sector workers and unemployed access to jobs in the "protected" sector. Also, higher wages create incentives for queuing of the unemployed for public sector jobs rather than looking for work or taking a job in the formal or informal private sector (because government employment campaigns may prefer the unemployed).

Second, our analysis shows that in comparison with other countries, Sri Lankan job flows—both job creation and destruction—are depressed and that firms at or below the threshold of 14 workers are less likely to increase employment compared with firms above the threshold. These findings provide rather strong evidence that TEWA is inhibiting employment expansion of small firms (those below 15 workers) and offers suggestive evidence that TEWA, to the extent it is indeed responsible for depressed job flows, is discouraging employment growth of formal sector firms in general, thereby reducing job prospects for informal sector workers and vulnerable groups such as youth and women.

While one cannot draw strong policy conclusions from these findings, they do provide some considerations for policy makers. First, the government should consider reforming public sector recruitment practices. In particular, ad hoc government recruitment of unemployed graduates is counterproductive because it reduces incentives for youth to take non-government jobs (see also chapter 5). Second, government needs to refrain from interfering in wage setting for the private sector. It should restrict its involvement to the determination of minimum wages as a partner under the tripartite minimum-wage-setting mechanism, but it should not directly interfere in private sector wage setting, even in the form of "recommended" wage increases, because they, too, may introduce distortions in wage setting.

And third, the government may want to consider revising the generosity of severance pay. International experience shows that reducing job protection is best achieved by enhancing other aspects of social protection, for example, by introducing unemployment insurance, an explicit form of worker protection (see a broader discussion of this issue in Vodopivec 2004).

Notes

1. As explained in Gunatilaka (2008), choosing unemployment as the baseline option helps to correct for the selection bias (Maddala 1983). Following Heckman's (1979) seminal insight, economists routinely implement selectivity bias correction methods when estimating wage equations over an endogenously selected population. This is because only a subsample of all working-age persons are employed and able to report earnings, and selectivity bias could arise if analysis were based only on the observed earnings of this subset.

2. Rodrigo and Munasinghe (undated) have also shown that the pay advantage of civil service workers over their private sector counterparts applies particularly to lower-level occupations.

3. Recent reviews include Addison and Teixeira (2003), Baker and others (2005), and Freeman (2007).

4. The others were an unreliable supply of electricity, uncertain government policy, macroeconomic instability, and the high cost of obtaining external financing (World Bank and Asian Development Bank 2005).

5. The Employees' Provident Fund (EPF) provides an extremely rich database on the firm-level number of workers—all registered firms are required to pay contributions for their permanent workers—but the data are not free of problems. Above all, firms report only workers for whom EPF contributions are paid. If for whatever reason such contributions are not paid, the true number of workers of the firm deviates from the number reported to the EPF. Such deviations can have a prominent effect, particularly when computing growth rates. To improve reliability of the data, in the analysis of the growth of firms we therefore excluded firms with fewer than 10 workers (either in current or previous year), as well as firms with growth rates in the current year (positive or negative) exceeding 20 percent, because such large changes almost certainly reflected reporting inaccuracies (and firms going out of business are not of particular interest for this analysis).

References

Abidoye, B., P. Orazem, and M. Vodopivec. 2009. "Firing Cost and Firm Size: A Study of Sri Lanka's Severance Pay System." Social Protection Discussion Paper Series No. 0916. Human Development Network, World Bank, Washington, DC.

Addison, John, and Paulino Teixeira. 2003. "The Economics of Employment Protection." *Journal of Labor Research* 24, no. 1 (March).

Ahsan A., and C. Pages. 2007. "Are All Labor Regulations Equal? Assessing the Effects of Job Security, Labor Dispute and Contract Labor Laws in India."

Social Protection Discussion Paper 0713. Human Development Network, World Bank, Washington, DC.

Baker, D., A. Glyn, D. Howell, and J. Schmitt. 2005. "Labor Market Institutions and Unemployment: A Critical Assessment of the Cross-Country Evidence." In *Fighting Unemployment: The Limits of Free Market Orthodoxy*, ed. David R. Howell. Oxford, U.K.: Oxford University Press.

Bartus, T. 2005. "Estimation of Marginal Effects Using Margeff. *Stata Journal* 5: 309–29.

Bassanini, A., and R. Duval. 2006. "Employment Patterns in OECD Countries: Reassessing the Role of Policies and Institutions." Working Paper 486. Organization for Economic Co-operation and Development, Economics Department, Paris.

Bauer, Thomas K., Stefan Bender, and Holger Bonin. 2007. "Dismissal Protection and Worker Flows in Small Establishments." *Economica* 74 (296): 804–21.

Bertola, Giuseppe. 1992. "Labor Turnover Costs and Average Labor Demand." *Journal of Labor Economics* 10: 389–411.

Besley, T., and R. Burgess. 2004. "Can Labor Regulation Hinder Economic Performance? Evidence from India." *Quarterly Journal of Economics* 119 (1): 91–134.

Davis, S., and J. Haltiwanger. 1999. "Gross Job Flows." In *Handbook of Labor Economics*, ed. O. Ashenfelter and D. Card. Amsterdam: North Holland.

Fournier, M., and M. Gurgand. 2002. SELMLOG: Stata Module to Perform Selection Bias Correction Based on the Multinomial Logit Model" http://ideas.repec.org/c/boc/bocode/s428301.html (April 20, 2008).

Freeman, R. B. 2007. "Labor Market Institutions around the World." NBER Working Paper 13242. National Bureau of Economic Research, Cambridge, MA.

Gunatilaka, R. 2008. "Informal Employment in Sri Lanka: Nature, Probability of Employment and Determinants of Wages." International Labour Organization, Colombo.

Haffner, R., S. Nickell, G. Nicoletti, S. Scarpetta, and G. Zoega. 2001. "European Integration, Liberalization and Labour Market Performance." In *Welfare and Employment in a United Europe*, ed. G. Bertola, T. Boeri, and G. Nicoletti. Cambridge, MA: MIT Press.

Heckman, J. 1979. "Sample Selection Bias as a Specification Error." *Econometrica* 47: 153–61.

Heckman, J. J., and C. Pages. 2000. "The Cost of Job Security Regulation: Evidence from Latin American Labor Markets." NBER Working Paper 7773. National Bureau of Economic Research, Cambridge, MA.

Hussmanns, Ralf. 2001. "Informal Sector and Informal Employment: Elements of a Conceptual Framework." Paper prepared for the Fifth Meeting of the Expert Group on Informal Sector Statistics (Delhi Group), New Delhi.

Kugler, Adriana D., and Gilles Saint-Paul. 2004. "How Do Firing Costs Affect Worker Flows in a World with Adverse Selection." *Journal of Labor Economics* 22 (3): 553–84.

Maddala, G. S. 1983. *Limited Dependent and Qualitative Variables in Economics.* Cambridge, U.K.: Cambridge University Press.

Nickell, Stephen, and Richard Layard. 1999. "Labor Market Institutions and Economic Performance." In *Handbook of Labor Economics*, ed. O. Ashenfelter and D. Card, vol. 3, pp 3029–84. Amsterdam: Elsevier.

OECD (Organisation for Economic Co-operation and Development). 1999. *Employment Outlook.* Paris.

Rodrigo, C., and P. Munasinghe. Undated. "Outcomes of Wage-setting Mechanisms and Options for Wage Policy Reforms in Sri Lanka." International Labour Organization, Colombo.

Schivardi, Fabiano, and Roberto Torrini. 2008. "Identifying the Effects of Firing Restrictions through Size-contingent Differences in Regulation." *Labour Economics* 15 (3): 482–511.

Vodopivec, M. 2004. *Income Support for the Unemployed: Issues and Options.* Washington, DC: World Bank.

World Bank. 2007. "Sri Lanka: Strengthening Social Protection." Report 38197-LK, World Bank, Washington, DC.

World Bank and Asian Development Bank. 2005. "Sri Lanka: Improving the Rural and Urban Investment Climate." World Bank, Washington, DC.

CHAPTER 3

Explaining Labor Market Imbalance in Sri Lanka: Evidence from Jobsnet Data

Nisha Arunatilake and Priyanka Jayawardena

High unemployment among youth, mainly resulting from prolonged job search, has been of concern to policy makers in Sri Lanka for close to four decades. Numerous studies have explored the reasons for youth unemployment in the country and have offered several hypotheses that focus on job search behavior of individuals and hiring practices of employers. Many of these studies rely on household data sets, which collect information only from employers on availability of vacancies and their nature. We take advantage of newly available Jobsnet data, containing detailed information on job seekers and job vacancies, to test the validity of some of the existing explanations regarding unemployment in the country. Jobsnet data come from the information source of a web-based interface that facilitates job placement. Capitalizing on information available from both the demand and supply sides of the labor market, the study examines the excesses and shortages in Sri Lanka's labor supply. This study also evaluates the usefulness of Jobsnet as a source of labor market information.

Previous studies in the country have put forward three main arguments to explain unemployment. The first argues that "skills mismatch"— that is, the imbalances in the supply and demand sides of the labor market—creates unemployment. The second is the "queuing" hypothesis, which posits that unemployment is created as job seekers wait to get placed into more lucrative, secure jobs in the public and formal private sectors that pay more and have better benefits. The third set of studies argues that unemployment in the country is caused by slow job creation, which results in large part from restrictive labor laws that make it difficult for employers to expand their labor forces. Our study uses Jobsnet data to examine whether the main sources of labor market imbalance in the country result from some combination of these three factors or from other factors such as gender and location. Given that Jobsnet data do not allow us to distinguish between public or private formal and informal jobs, we are unable to test whether the labor market imbalance results from a skills mismatch or queuing. However, we are able to observe whether job seekers queue for permanent jobs, which are likely to be public or formal private sector jobs rather than informal jobs. We are also unable to examine slow job creation directly because we cannot isolate the factors affecting job creation. However, we are able to observe the quantity of jobs available in different occupation categories.

The results of the study support the slow job creation hypothesis and find some evidence to support the skills mismatch and queuing hypotheses. The results show that the majority of job seekers are educated but inexperienced youth who are new entrants to the labor market. Most job seekers are waiting for white-collar occupations, while most vacancies are for elementary occupations (domestic helpers, laborers, security workers, caretakers, and the like) and blue-collar workers. The main source of mismatch in the labor market stems from employment aspirations related to education, while gender, location, and employment status are minor sources of imbalance. We begin with a description of the conceptual framework for the study.

Framework for Analysis

Most studies that have tried to explain the unemployment problem in Sri Lanka focus on skills mismatch, queuing, and slow job creation as likely factors. The skills mismatch hypothesis was first proposed by Seers (1971), who theorized that the prolonged job search by educated youth was the root cause of youth unemployment. Job searches were prolonged, Seers suggested, because the education system taught little of relevance to the job market, leaving youth with high job expectations but without the skills to acquire jobs that met those expectations. Seers recognized that the higher-skilled jobs are characterized by greater job security, better pay, and better social protection, and that limited job creation also contributed to high unemployment; however, in his view the main reason for the labor market imbalance was the mismatch in the demand and supply of skills.

The validity of the skills mismatch hypothesis has been tested over the past several decades by numerous researchers using a variety of methods. Glewwe (1987) and Dickens and Lang (1991) examined the relationship between education and unemployment and came to different conclusions. Glewwe found support for the skills mismatch hypothesis among both men and women in rural and urban sectors, while Dickens and Lang found supportive evidence only for rural women. More recently, Rama (1999) compared the lowest wages acceptable to the unemployed with the actual labor earnings of the employed with similar characteristics, reasoning that if the skills mismatch hypothesis was correct, the difference between the actual earnings and lowest acceptable wage should increase with education attainment. He thus rejected the hypothesis when he found that education attainment increases earnings more than it increases wage expectations. Tan and Chandrasiri (2004) tested the skills mismatch hypothesis by examining the time to first job and found that the more educated and better trained found jobs faster than those with less education and training. Not only did their evidence yield little support for the skills mismatch hypothesis, it also indicated that the better educated did not queue for good jobs.

The queuing hypothesis takes two forms. One argues that the attractive remuneration and work conditions in the public sector, together with recruitment practices, give job seekers an incentive to wait for a public sector job. The second argues that the better job protection and attractive remuneration packages in the private formal sector give incentives for potential workers to queue for jobs there. This hypothesis was first implied by Seers (1971) when he suggested that youth tend to wait for good jobs that pay better, offer better job security, and have better social status. Glewwe (1987) and Dickens and Lang (1991) further elaborated this hypothesis for the public sector, arguing that the government's practice of periodically creating public service jobs as a means of reducing unemployment reinforced the incentives to wait for such jobs to open up. Rama (1999), testing the validity of these hypotheses by estimating earnings equations, accepted the queuing hypothesis. Tan and Chandrasiri (2004) also found support for the queuing hypothesis by showing a positive correlation between the share of public sector jobs and probability of being unemployed.

The slow job creation hypothesis argues that the inflexibility in labor regulations in Sri Lanka discourages employers from making investments that would expand the number of job openings. In particular, the Termination of Employment of Workmen Act (TEWA) of 1971 imposes high costs on firing or laying off employees, making employers reluctant to add workers that they might have to let go if business slows and thus limiting the number of formal sector jobs (Rama 1999, and chapter 2 in this volume).

Most of these studies tested these three hypotheses through indirect means, by looking at estimates of the probability of unemployment, for example, or earnings functions or time to first job. The results, therefore, only imply a relationship between unemployment and job search behaviors and job aspirations. In contrast, Jobsnet provides information on job aspirations of individuals as well as on available job vacancies, thus allowing a direct comparison of job aspirations with job vacancies. The same information can be used to assess whether individuals queue for a narrow or broad spectrum of jobs.

Data

Jobsnet is an "employment sourcing and delivery system" established under the National Employment Policy of Sri Lanka in 2003 and made up of an islandwide network of 19 job service centers; anyone in Sri Lanka can use the centers, which have access to information on vacancies around the world. Jobsnet matches job vacancies from employers with job seekers who register with Jobsnet. Each employer is required to pay a fee and become a member of Jobsnet before using its services, while job seekers are provided with the service free of charge. The jobs information is updated in real time from all parts of the country. In addition to matching job seekers to jobs, the service offers advice on improving employability through career guidance and further training. In 2005, 30,371 job seekers and 4,366 employers with more than 100,000 job vacancies registered with Jobsnet.

This study analyzes the information provided by job seekers and employers who registered with Jobsnet for the six months between January 1 and June 31, 2005. Detailed characteristics of the sample are shown in table 3.1.

Because registration with Jobsnet is voluntary, information obtained through the Jobsnet database, unlike a scientifically executed survey, is not representative of all job seekers and potential employers in the country. As a result certain caveats should be noted. According to information

Table 3.1   Characteristics of the Jobsnet Sample

Category	Number	Percent	Category	Number	Percent
Job seekers	11,550	100	**Vacancies**	23,448	100
By age group			*By age group*		
Under 16	48	0.4	Under 16	0	0.0
16–30	10,183	88.2	16–30	200	0.9
Over 30	1,319	11.4	Over 30	7,194	30.7
			Any age	12,420	53.0
			Age not specified	3,634	15.5
By gender			*By gender*		
Female	5,543	48	Female	7,210	30.7
Male	5,896	51	Male	7,418	31.6
			Either	8,820	37.6

Source: Authors' calculations using Jobsnet data.
Note: The breakdown of job seekers by gender was not available for all observations.

provided by Jobsnet officials, the job seekers and employers who register with Jobsnet tend to be the most desperate: job seekers who fail to secure jobs through traditional means such as newspaper ads and personal contacts; and employers who are unable to fill vacancies because the jobs are unattractive or the remuneration is inadequate. The data on vacancies tends to be particularly weak because Jobsnet centers have incentives to screen out those vacancies they think they may not be able to fill.[1] Hence we supplement the vacancy data with information available through the *Labor Market Information Bulletin* (LMIB) based on newspaper advertisements.[2]

Some information used in the analysis was not available for all individuals in the data set. For the most part, data were available for all but 1 to 2 percent of the total sample. The main exception was information on education qualifications, which was available for only 8,421 individuals; of this sample, information on English language skills was available for only 6,544 individuals. It is possible that the Jobsnet data used for our study period were affected by the December 2004 tsunami, which may have slowed subsequent Jobsnet activities in tsunami-affected areas. In addition, more job vacancies than usual during this period would have been open for construction workers and social workers.

Results

The following section provides a profile of the Jobsnet data records with comparisons with the LMIB information, where appropriate. The analysis is organized according to possible sources of mismatch to facilitate discussion on labor market imbalance.

Location

A majority of vacancies were not location specific, or they were jobs outside Sri Lanka. About 40 percent of the vacancies did not specify a location, that is, the job could be done from any geographic area in the country.[3] Another 23 percent were vacancies for jobs outside Sri Lanka. Close to 30 percent of the vacancies were located in Western Province (Colombo). Central, Uva, and Northern provinces each had less than 5 percent of the registered vacancies. (We note that, in addition to the caveats regarding coverage of job vacancies described above, the geographic distribution of job vacancies is influenced by efficiency of the field staff in obtaining information on job vacancies.) LMIB does not provide information on the geographic location of local jobs; however, LMIB data show that 73 percent of the job vacancies were advertised in the classified sections, which probably indicate that they are informal sector jobs.[4] More than 99.4 percent of the job vacancies were in the private sector.

Among local jobs that were location specific, a majority of the vacancies in most occupation categories were located in Western Province. More than half the vacancies for "legislators, senior officials and managers," close to half the vacancies for "elementary occupations," and more than 30 percent of the vacancies for "technicians and associated professionals" and for "clerks" were in Western Province. Job opportunities most available outside Western Province were in the "professionals," "craft and related workers," "service workers and shop and market sales workers," and "machine operators" occupational categories. "Skilled agriculture and fishery workers" are not considered in this analysis because the data set had only 12 observations for this category of workers.

Most job seekers were willing to migrate for work. Three-fourths of all job seekers were willing to work in any district within the country and 13.6 percent were willing to consider foreign job opportunities. A small proportion (2.1 percent) were looking only for foreign jobs, while 10.7 percent were looking for work in specific locations in Sri Lanka. Job seekers from Western Province, the most developed province in the country, were relatively more willing to consider foreign jobs (25 percent were open to international migration for work), but they were relatively less willing to migrate internally (only 54 percent were willing to work outside their home province).

Females were more willing to migrate internally for work and less willing to migrate internationally for work. The proportion of females who were willing to take jobs in any location within the country was 81.8 percent, compared with 69.4 for males. In contrast, 4.8 percent of females but 22.1 percent of males were willing to consider foreign jobs. These statistics are somewhat counterintuitive because most temporary migrant workers from Sri Lanka are unskilled females taking foreign employment as housemaids. It is possible that job seekers with the fewest skills, especially females, are not captured by Jobsnet data.

Job seekers looking for professional, associate professional, and clerical occupations were relatively more likely to be location specific in their job search, and they were relatively less willing to consider foreign jobs. Meanwhile, job seekers looking for work in less-skilled occupations were relatively less likely to be location specific and relatively more willing to migrate abroad for work. Among more-skilled occupational categories, managers were also relatively more willing to seek work overseas.

In summary, these statistics show that location does not seem to prevent job seekers from accepting jobs; most job seekers were willing to migrate—internally and often internationally—for work. The findings suggest a geographical imbalance in the distribution of job seekers and vacancies across the country. Many of the vacancies for high-skilled jobs and for elementary occupations were in Western Province, while a majority of people seeking jobs in those categories were from outside Western Province. It is possible that most job seekers know where the job opportunities are and are willing to migrate for them.

Gender

Overall, job vacancies were distributed equally across gender. For jobs within Sri Lanka, however, there were more vacancies for female workers. Of the 23,448 jobs available on Jobsnet; 31 percent were exclusively for men, and 32 percent were exclusively for women; the remaining 8,820 (37 percent) were for individuals of either sex. Even within different age categories, the number of vacancies was evenly divided between males and females. Within Sri Lanka, however, 36 percent of the vacancies were for female workers compared with 27 percent for male workers, while 37 percent of the jobs were for either gender. The LMIB data also show a similar share of gender-neutral job vacancies (36 percent). Unlike Jobsnet data, however, about 49 percent of the vacancies were exclusively for men, while only 15 percent were exclusively for women. The LMIB data further show that over time, the share of gender-neutral vacancies in the market has increased.

Overall, job seekers were divided evenly among males (51 percent) and females (49 percent). However, the gender of job seekers varied from province to province. In Western, Southern, Eastern, Uva, and Northern provinces, more than 55 percent of job seekers were male, while in Central and Sabaragamuwa provinces more than 55 percent of the job seekers were female.

In summary, these statistics imply a balance in job vacancies and job seekers across gender, according to Jobsnet data; however, LMIB suggests that job opportunities are more limited for females. Gender differences in job seekers across provinces should not pose a major obstacle in matching vacancies to job seekers because most job seekers are willing to migrate for work.

Age and Experience

The great majority of vacancies registered with Jobsnet were for inexperienced youth. Close to 80 percent of the listed jobs did not necessitate any previous experience; another 17 percent required less than two years of experience. The LMIB data somewhat reinforces this finding— 42 percent of job advertisements did not ask for previous experience, and the highest number of vacancies was for individuals in the 21–25 age group. Vacancies for individuals in the 26–30 age group and those in the 18–20 age group were also high.[5]

Only 2.5 percent of the job vacancies required more than five years of experience. Of those, 93 percent were open only to males, and 6 percent were open to both males and females, while less than 1 percent were open just to females. Close to two-thirds of these jobs were located outside Sri Lanka, while most of the rest did not specify the location of the job. Two-thirds of the jobs that required five years of experience did not specify any education qualifications, while 23 percent sought applicants who had passed their advanced level (A-level) examinations. By occupational category, the vacancies for more experienced workers were concentrated among "business professionals" (22 percent), "building frame and related trade workers" (21 percent), and "motor vehicle drivers" (12 percent).

Most of the job seekers are inexperienced youth. More than two-thirds of the job seekers are in the 18–25 age group. The age distribution does not change across provinces. Close to 80 percent of job seekers do not have any previous job experience; a further 10 percent have less than two years of work experience.

The proportion of first-time job seekers is particularly high, and this is more so in less-developed provinces. The percentage of first-time job seekers was highest in Uva Province (91 percent), followed by Southern (89 percent) and North Western (86 percent). The proportion of first-time job seekers was much below the national average of 78 percent only in Western Province (61 percent).

In summary, these findings show that experience is not a major problem in matching job seekers to vacancies: most job seekers are inexperienced youth, and a majority of vacancies are also for inexperienced youth. The high proportion of first-time job seekers supports the skills mismatch argument, which states that new entrants to the labor market engage in prolonged job search as they wait for jobs that match their skills.

Education, Skills, and Training

The greatest demand is for individuals with low levels of education. According to the Jobsnet database, 42 percent of job vacancies did not state the type of educational qualification needed, 25 percent required A-levels, 12 percent required only ordinary-level qualifications (O-levels), and 6 percent required less than O-levels. Slightly over 1 percent asked for any kind of degree or higher qualification. Most of these vacancies were for science graduates. According to LMIB data, 90.4 percent of job vacancies did not ask for any educational qualifications, while 4.3 percent asked for degree holders, 3.5 percent asked for applicants who had passed their A-levels and 1.8 percent asked for applicants who had passed their O-levels. Part of the difference between the two data sets may be attributable to small employers with low-skill jobs who might prefer cheaper newspaper ads to the higher costs of registering with Jobsnet.

A majority of the job seekers registered with Jobsnet are educated, having high levels of both formal and tertiary-level education. Close to 70 percent of the job seekers had passed their A-levels, while another 22 percent had successfully completed their O-levels. Of the individuals who had passed their A-levels, 8 percent had degrees or equivalent qualifications, a further 33 percent had obtained diplomas, and another 31 percent had obtained certificate-level qualifications. Of the individuals with O-levels, 20 percent had obtained diplomas and another 31 percent had obtained certificate-level qualifications.[6] These degrees, diplomas, and certificates were issued by various types of international, national, regional, and private job-training institutions. Information in Jobsnet is not sufficient to categorize these qualifications according to their quality, duration, and standards.

The data show limited vacancies for skilled workers, but information is unreliable because of a weakness in the software. The only specialized skill category for which there was a significant number of vacancies was skilled accountancy. Contrary to popular belief, the demand for general skills— such as English and computer literacy—was limited, but this finding could have resulted from missing information on job skills in the database. According to Jobsnet officials, the Jobsnet interface currently allows the capture of only one skill per job vacancy. LMIB does not provide information on specific skills sought by the market.

The majority of the job seekers were illiterate in English, with English literacy levels better in more developed and multiethnic provinces. Of the job seekers who provided information on English literacy, only 3 percent claimed a "very good" knowledge of English. Close to 80 percent said they had only a "fair" knowledge of English, while 18 percent reported "poor" English literacy. Job seekers claiming a "very good" knowledge of English were concentrated in Eastern, Western, and Northern provinces.

Job seekers with more educational attainment also appeared to have more training in general skills such as English and computer literacy. Less than 2 percent of individuals with less than O-levels obtained training in English language or computer skills. In comparison, 14 and 42 percent of individuals with A-levels and 4 and 11 percent of individuals with O-levels trained in English and general computer skills, respectively. This could indicate that individuals with higher educational attainments feel the need for computer and English language literacy when applying for jobs requiring high skill levels. Jobsnet data do not allow us to examine the quality of the training received. But data indicate that private institutions have provided much of the training, which suggests its quality is questionable.[7]

The data show few job vacancies in the computer field, which would seem to support the skills mismatch hypothesis. But it is possible that other types of high-paying jobs not captured in the Jobsnet data may require general skills in computers and English. The high incidence of general skills training among more educated individuals might also occur because individuals with higher formal education attainment are more likely to come from affluent families who can afford training in these types of skills even if the training does not lead directly to a job.

Individuals with higher levels of formal education were also more likely to obtain vocational training aimed at better-paying jobs. In addition to general skills in computer science and English language, individuals with A-level qualifications sought computer science, accountancy, and secretarial skills. More than 5 percent of individuals with A-levels also obtained various types of degrees. For individuals with O-levels and below, the most sought-after skills were in mechanics and construction, electronics and maintenance of electrical appliances, and sewing and related crafts.

Individuals with better English knowledge were more likely to obtain skills required for jobs at the higher end of the occupation ladder than those with only fair or poor English skills. A higher share of individuals with a good knowledge in English obtained training in specialized computer science courses and various types of accountancy, managerial, secretarial, and technical courses. Although the data do not allow for an assessment of the quality of training, this analysis suggests that English language literacy does make a difference in the types of vocational training one can undertake. This finding shows that skill gaps not only prevent individuals from taking up lucrative jobs but also from obtaining training aimed at high-paying jobs.

Most vacancies required low skill levels, while the jobs most preferred by job seekers required moderate to high skill levels (table 3.2). As the analysis of job seekers showed, individuals with more education seem to obtain further training in a diverse set of skills, especially computer and English language skills. However, the number of Jobsnet vacancies requiring these skills is low. If we assume that the Jobsnet data represent the demand for skills in the general market, this finding supports the skills mismatch hypothesis as well as the slow job creation hypothesis. It must be noted that at least part of this observed skills mismatch results from the limitations in information available in the Jobsnet database noted earlier.

LMIB data on labor demand largely correspond with the Jobsnet data. Except for two occupational categories, the distribution of jobs advertised by main occupational category, the location of the advertisement in the newspaper itself, and the experience requirement are largely consistent with Jobsnet data.[8] As with Jobsnet data, LMIB data show that the vacancies for low-skilled workers are high. Unlike Jobsnet data, LBIM data show a moderately high number of vacancies for professionals, senior officials, and managers in the formal sector. It is possible that employers seeking to fill vacancies for such jobs prefer to get wider coverage through newspaper ads and do not register these job vacancies with Jobsnet. These overall findings are again consistent with the skills mismatch hypothesis. They show that most job vacancies are in the informal sector or require low skills. Vacancies for high-skilled jobs are mostly in the formal sector,

Table 3.2 Top 10 Job Vacancies and Preference for Those by Job Seekers

Occupation category	Job vacancies		Job seekers		Labor surplus/shortage (as a percentage of job vacancies)
	Number	Rank	Number	Job ranked by preference	
Top 10 types of vacancies					
Textile, garment, and related trade work	2,968	1	864	11	−70.9
Domestic and related helpers, cleaners	2,317	2	90	55	−96.1
Finance and sales associate professionals	2,087	3	1,202	6	−42.4
Client information clerks	2,077	4	1,026	8	−50.6
Building frame and related trades workers	1,559	5	326	18	−79.1
Shop salespersons and demonstrators	1,215	6	901	10	−25.8
Housekeeping and restaurant services workers	999	7	252	26	−74.8
Textile, fur, and leather products machine operators	995	8	396	15	−60.2
Other laborers not elsewhere classified	796	9	232	30	−70.9
Physical and engineering science technicians	718	10	533	13	−25.8
Top 10 job preferences by job seekers					
Computer associate professionals	241	20	2,285	1	848.1
Administrative associate professionals	286	18	1,939	2	578.0
Numerical clerks	84	37	1,903	3	2,165.5
Secretaries and keyboard-operating clerks	137	28	1,449	4	957.7
Computer professionals	105	33	1,221	5	1062.9
Finance and sales associate professionals	2,087	3	1,202	6	−42.4
Cashiers, tellers, and related clerks	74	39	1,070	7	1,345.9
Client information clerks	2,077	4	1,026	8	−50.6
Accounts clerks	82	38	974	9	1,087.8
Shop salespersons and demonstrators	1,215	6	901	10	−25.8

Source: Authors' calculations using Jobsnet data.

and more than 80 percent of them require experience. The availability of formal sector jobs for first-time job seekers with education is low.

Occupation

Job vacancies are mostly for blue-collar occupations both within and outside the country. With only a few exceptions, both males and females preferred white-collar occupations requiring semispecialized skill levels (table 3.3).

Aspirations were low for manual jobs and for high-skilled jobs. The least preferred occupational category was "skilled agriculture and fishery workers," followed by "senior officials and managers." The low social status attached to agriculture- and fishery-related occupations and the low wages received by workers in these occupations make them unattractive to most job seekers.[9] In addition, fewer than 5 percent of job seekers said they were looking for work as "plant and machine operators and assemblers" and in "elementary occupations." The low skill levels required by these jobs may make them less attractive to more educated job seekers.

Table 3.3   Top 10 Occupation Preferences by Gender

Occupational category	All		Rank according to occupation preference		
	Frequency	Percentage	All	Male	Female
Computer associate professionals	2,285	19.78	1	1	1
Administrative associate professionals	1,939	16.79	2	2	3
Numerical clerks	1,903	16.48	3	3	2
Secretaries and keyboard-operating clerks	1,449	12.55	4	15	4
Computer professionals	1,221	10.57	5	6	7
Finance and sales associate professionals	1,202	10.41	6	4	9
Cashiers, tellers, and related clerks	1,070	9.26	7	11	6
Client information clerks	1,026	8.88	8	18	5
Accounts clerks	974	8.43	9	10	8
Shop salespersons and demonstrators	901	7.80	10	5	13
Textile, garment, and related trade work	864	7.48	11	12	10
Physical and engineering science technicians	533	4.61	13	7	30
Motor vehicle drivers	361	3.13	16	8	—
Machinery mechanics and fitters	358	3.10	17	9	—

Source: Authors' calculations, using Jobsnet data.
Note: More than 10 occupational categories are listed because the 10 most preferred categories are included for each sex.
— Indicates a rank lower than 30.

Job seekers also shied away from executive and management positions, perhaps because these high-skill jobs typically require job experience that the jobs seekers know they do not have.

For jobs within Sri Lanka, competition was highest for "clerks" positions, with 17 job seekers for each job vacancy. The competition for "professionals" and "associate professionals" was also high, with five and three job seekers, respectively, for each position. This distribution of competition for jobs was roughly similar in all provinces (table 3.4).

A large share of job seekers seem to queue for a small number of occupational categories (figure 3.1). More than 25 percent of individuals with A-level qualifications preferred just three occupational categories, all at the higher end of the occupational ladder. Although the frequency distribution of preference for occupational category was also skewed for individuals with less than O-level qualifications, it was not as pronounced, and the preferences were mostly in blue-collar occupations. The distribution of job preference across occupational categories was more uniform for individuals with O-level qualifications. Among these individuals, 4 percent or fewer preferred any single occupational category.

These findings coupled with the findings in the previous section show that a major source of mismatch between job seekers and job vacancies stems from aspirations formed on the basis of high education attainment: job seekers with more education are more likely to aspire to jobs at the high end of the occupation ladder where there are fewer vacancies. These findings support both the skills mismatch and the queuing hypotheses. As argued by the skills mismatch hypothesis, job seekers aspire for high-end office jobs but are not prepared to take on low-end jobs that are available in the market. Queuing occurs when job seekers wait for jobs with better benefits, no matter what the occupational category. Typically these more lucrative and secure jobs are found in the public and private formal sectors. Although the data do not allow us to identify formal and informal sector jobs, the findings on job preferences and job vacancies show that there is queuing for jobs with more social status.

Employment Duration
Many job seekers were indifferent about whether a job was permanent or temporary. Three-fifths of job seekers were willing to consider both types of jobs. Only 17.7 percent of job seekers were looking only for a permanent job. In Western Province, however, the share of job seekers looking only for permanent jobs was much higher, at 42.8 percent, while only

Table 3.4 **Ratio of Job Seekers to Job Vacancies, by Province and Occupational Category**

	Western	Central	Southern	Eastern	Sabaragamuwa	North Western	North Central	Uva	Northern	Sri Lanka
Managers	0.8	9.2	28.3	1.3	4.9	6.4	3.7	2.8	7.0	1.9
Professionals	5.4	45.5	4.1	7.2	5.3	4.1	0.9	40.4	8.7	5.2
Associate professionals	1.4	22.1	4.3	4.1	5.9	2.7	0.7	4.6	17.1	2.9
Clerks	6.7	52.3	22.4	33.5	16.5	20.3	12.6	19.0	—	17.1
Service workers	0.6	19.2	2.2	1.4	3.2	5.0	1.0	3.6	—	2.1
Craft workers	0.7	46.0	0.8	18.4	1.9	1.7	1.0	7.5	—	1.6
Machine operators	0.6	1.9	0.8	6.4	18.9	0.7	0.6	21.9	—	1.5
Elementary workers	0.2	5.6	0.7	4.2	1.0	2.0	0.5	14.3	—	1.1

Source: Authors' calculation using Jobsnet Data.
Note: The skilled workers occupational category is not shown because it had only 12 job vacancies.
— Negligible.

Figure 3.1   Frequency Distribution of Job Preferences by Education Level

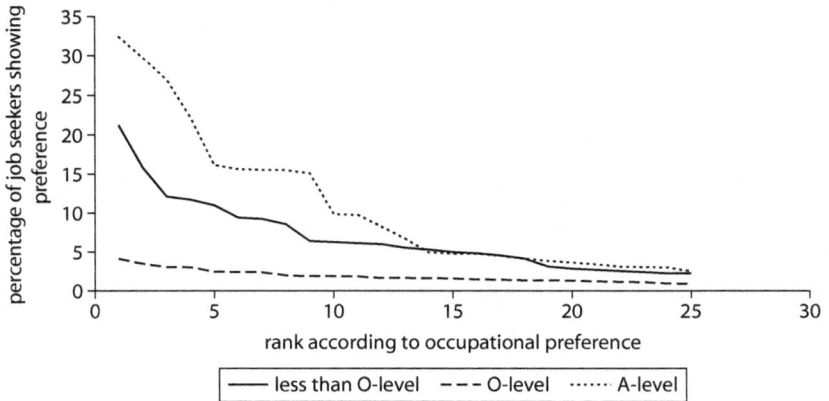

Source: Authors' calculations using Jobsnet data.
Note: The X axis ranks different occupation categories according to the revealed preference of job seekers by education level (job seekers may have more than one preference). For example, more than 30 percent of job seekers with A-level qualifications wanted work in a single occupational category (in this case "computer associate professionals").

one-third of job seekers there were willing to consider both temporary and permanent jobs.

Females were more flexible than males about duration of employment. Although both males and females were fairly flexible (65.6 percent of the females and 57.4 percent of the males were indifferent to duration), 21.0 percent of the males would consider only permanent employment, compared with 14.4 percent of the females.

Most job seekers in all skill categories were flexible about the duration of employment; however, the more-skilled seekers were more likely to look for permanent jobs. Not surprisingly, more-educated job seekers also were relatively more likely to look for permanent employment. The proportion of A-level-qualified job seekers looking only for permanent jobs was 9.2 percent, compared with 7.2 percent of O-level-qualified job seekers and 2.7 percent of job seekers with less than O-level qualifications.

These findings show that employment duration is not a major source of mismatch, with the possible exception of job seekers in Western Province. A majority of the job seekers were willing to accept jobs whether or not they were permanent. As indicated earlier, the job seekers who register with Jobsnet tend to be those who are unable to find jobs in more conventional ways. As a result, they may be more flexible about employment type than other workers.

Main Findings and Recommendations

This study analyzes Jobsnet data to explain labor market imbalances in Sri Lanka. The data results show that the main imbalance is the mismatch between the supply of jobs seekers with higher education levels and job aspirations and the demand for workers with those levels of education attainment. The data suggest that the inability of the education system to teach general skills essential for securing "good" jobs could be a source of inequality. Individuals with high levels of formal education were more likely to obtain general training in English language and computer skills, indicating a lack of competency in these skills among all school leavers. Most job seekers have obtained vocational training from private institutions that are not nationally recognized, suggesting that the training carries little weight in improving employability. Individuals with better English skills obtained training geared toward jobs at the higher end of the occupation ladder where vacancies were relatively scarce. Location is not a major source of labor market imbalance, mainly because of the willingness of most job seekers to migrate for work. However, most vacancies in all occupational categories are in Western Province. Age, gender, experience, and employment duration are also not main sources of imbalance.

These results support all three hypotheses—slow job creation, skills mismatch, and queuing. First, vacancies for "good" jobs are limited. Most vacancies are for inexperienced youth and in low-skill occupational categories.[10] LMIB data also suggest that the majority of the vacancies are in the informal sector. Second, the data show that most job seekers are educated, young, inexperienced, new entrants to the labor market who aspire to white-collar office jobs. However, such jobs are of limited availability, supporting the skills mismatch argument. The data also suggest that most of these job seekers need further learning to acquire the information technology (IT) and English skills demanded by the market. This finding points to limitations in the education system. Last, although the data do not allow us to identify formal and informal sector jobs and the remuneration levels attached to jobs, they do suggest that job seekers queue for jobs that have a higher social status.

There is a need to promote creation of jobs at the higher end of the occupation ladder and to improve working conditions for lower-skill occupations so that they are more attractive to job seekers. The demand for skilled workers is also increasing globally. However, these jobs call for English literacy with IT competencies—skills that are lacking in most Sri Lankan job seekers. To make the most of these opportunities, science, English, and IT education urgently needs to be improved at the secondary school level.

Vocational education in the country should be improved and modernized, so that potential workers do not waste time obtaining training that does not improve their employability. The current practice of obtaining training in English and IT skills after leaving school creates inequity and wastes valuable time that can be better used gaining job experience or obtaining higher-level vocational training. Special efforts should be made to improve formal education delivery aimed at poorer individuals. Children should be taught functional English in school, so that after they leave school they are able to obtain further training that prepares them for better jobs in the market. At the same time, scholarships or loan programs should be introduced, so that even individuals from poorer backgrounds are able to afford better-quality training.

Limitations of Jobsnet Data

Jobsnet data have several limitations as a source of labor market information. As highlighted earlier, Jobsnet data on job vacancies are particularly weak, partly because of the high fees required to post and screen job vacancies.

Jobsnet should be restructured to improve its role as a provider of information. Currently, its main focus is providing employment services. If Jobsnet is to take on the additional role of providing information on the labor market, it needs to be restructured. At a basic level, the current performance monitoring indicators should be changed to discourage Jobsnet centers from screening out job vacancies they do not think they can fill. At the same time, new monitoring indicators should be introduced to ensure wider and better coverage of information. Data should be categorized and systematized to facilitate analysis.

Revenue generation activities by Jobsnet should not impede information collection. To the extent possible, revenue generation should be separated from employment services, so that employers are not discouraged from registering information on job opportunities. For example, revenue generation through placement of advertisements on Jobsnet website can be seen positively in this regard because it is not linked to providing employment services.

The Jobsnet web interface should be modified so that it captures information on job seekers and job vacancies in an easy-to-analyze and comprehensive manner. Jobsnet has already recognized these deficiencies and has introduced modifications to improve data collection. These efforts should be further strengthened to enable periodic systematic analysis of information on job seekers, vacancies, and training needs of the market.

Jobsnet could be a valuable source of data on technical education and vocational training (TEVT) graduates. Currently, data on TEVT graduates are entered into the database on an ad hoc basis by officials at different Jobsnet centers. A system should be developed to categorize various vocational training courses and enter information on these to the database in a systematic manner. This information could then be analyzed periodically to obtain information on the TEVT sector. Ideally, sufficient information on each training episode by job seekers should be collected, so that TEVT courses can be classified according to standard classification codes that would allow cross comparisons (Perera 2007; UNEVOC 2006). Given that this information is provided by job seekers themselves, it is possible to obtain detailed information on training undergone by different individuals. On the one hand, specific information on training and individual competencies is necessary for making successful job matches, because such information will facilitate the job search. On the other hand, such data will provide valuable information on the TEVT sector in the country.

A system should be developed to trace job seekers who register with Jobsnet as they make their job search. Such information could provide not only valuable real-time information on the labor market, but also valuable information on the success of the Jobsnet and any shortcomings in its operation.

Notes

We thank Jobsnet officials, IPS staff, anonymous referees, and participants of Youth Employment Network consultant meeting for useful comments and suggestions, and Suwendrani Jayaratna and Indika Wijethunga for assistance with data analysis. This study was funded by the World Bank.

 1. To monitor performance and ensure financial viability, job centers are required to meet certain performance and revenue targets. Because these centers are better able to meet these targets when job matches are high, they customarily give preference to vacancies that are likely to result in a job match, and

employers whose vacancies are for workers with special skills or for skills in short supply or who offer poor remuneration are discouraged from registering. As a result, some types of jobs are underrepresented in the Jobsnet database.

2. The LMIB vol. 01/'05 collects data contained in 36,848 job advertisements published in the *Silumina* and *Observer* newspapers (the English newspaper with the widest circulation and its sister Sinhala newspaper) for the period from January to June 2005.

3. These mostly included jobs as marketing officials.

4. It is cheaper to advertise in the classified section, and the advertisers need not disclose their identity.

5. The stated percentages do not add to 100 because some jobs were open to individuals across several age groups.

6. Some individuals have obtained informal education in a variety of educational programs. For the purpose of this analysis an individual's highest informal education qualification was used. For example, if a person had a degree and a diploma, his level of informal education was considered to be a degree. The following hierarchy was used to categorize the various informal education programs: degree, degree-equivalent, diploma, and certificate.

7. Jobsnet data provide the name of the institutions providing training. In the absence of a registry of training institutions and their performance, it is difficult to ascertain the quality of training received by individuals. Lack of regulation has reduced the start-up costs of training institutions and increased their number. Anecdotal evidence suggests that only a few of these private institutions are effective providers of vocational training.

8. LMIB classifies advertisements placed under classified columns of the newspapers as advertisements for jobs in the informal sector, while advertisements placed by enterprises under their enterprise name are classified as advertisements for formal sector jobs.

9. According to Labour Force Survey data, the average private sector wage for agricultural and fisheries workers was SL Rs 4,598 a month, only slightly higher than the private sector average wage of SL Rs 3,768 for the elementary occupations category.

10. It is possible that at least some high-end jobs are not advertised in the newspapers or the Jobsnet.

References

Dickens, William T., and Kevin Lang. 1991. "An Analysis of the Nature of Unemployment in Sri Lanka." NBER Working Paper 3777, National Bureau of Economic Research, Cambridge, MA.

Glewwe, Paul. 1987. "Unemployment in Developing Countries: Economist's Models in Light of Evidence from Sri Lanka." *International Economic Journal* 1 (4): 1–17.

Perera, Vajora. 2007. "NVQ – New Qualification System for Vocational Training." *Daily News*, February 13. http://www.dailynews.lk/2007/02/13/fin06.asp (Nov. 10, 2009).

Rama, Martin. 1999. "The Sri Lankan Unemployment Problem Revisited." Policy Research Working Paper 2227, World Bank, Washington, DC.

Seers, Dudley. 1971. "Matching Employment Opportunities and Expectations." International Labour Office, Geneva.

Tan, H., and S. Chandrasiri. 2004. "Training and Labor Market Outcomes in Sri Lanka." World Bank Institute Working Paper, Washington, DC.

UNEVOC (UNESCO, International Centre for Technical and Vocational Education and Training). 2006. "Participation in Formal TVET Programmes Worldwide: An Initial Statistical Study." Bonn.

World Bank. 1999. "Sri Lanka A Fresh Look at Unemployment." Report 19609-CE, World Bank, Washington, DC.

CHAPTER 4

Effect of Training on Labor Market Outcomes

Sunil Chandrasiri

Unemployment of educated youth has been a key policy concern for Sri Lanka for the last three and half decades. Unemployment and underemployment are widely prevalent among the young, whether or not they have technical education and vocational training (TEVT). Youth unemployment, resulting mainly from prolonged job search, is of particular concern among the new entrants to the labor market. TEVT is part of the national education system and plays a vital role in promoting growth and development. It also promotes labor mobility, adaptability, and productivity by providing students with necessary academic, technical, and "soft" skills such as communications and leadership. This chapter examines the effects of training on labor market outcomes with a special focus on the school-to-work transition, the link between education and training, post-training job search, and employability of TEVT graduates.

The key findings of this chapter point to some useful policy recommendations on the effects of training on labor market outcomes in Sri Lanka. First, most of the TEVT programs provided by public sector institutions are targeted at school leavers with ordinary-level (O-level) qualifications. Female participation in training programs is relatively low, and TEVT programs are heavily concentrated in Western Province. Second, youth (ages 15 through 29) are receiving proportionately more training than adults, and the rising trend of training at higher levels of education irrespective of gender is apparent from time series data. Similarly, year-of-entry cohort effects on training were clearly evident after 1977 during the postliberalization regime that focused on promarket, probusiness policy reforms. Third, training tends to increase the probability of employment among individuals with higher levels of education. Fourth, several tracer studies point to low employability of TEVT graduates in general and to wide variations in employability across major public TEVT providers. The influence of socioeconomic factors on training is evident in low-income districts. The application of career guidance as a strategy to improve the labor market outcome of training is also noted in the assessment.

Evolution of TEVT Policies and Institutional Framework

Policy initiatives to promote TEVT activities in Sri Lanka date back to the early 1970s. The high jobless rate among youth and the youth insurrection of 1971 led the government to consider TEVT as an important strategic sector for reducing youth unemployment.[1] As a result, government provision of preemployment technical and vocational training was recognized as an important aspect of human resource development. Since the beginning of the promarket policy regime in 1977, several changes have been made in the TEVT sector. For example, private sector training has been explicitly recognized as part of a larger strategy to promote national competitiveness. An analysis of policy changes between 1995 and 2006 points to a strong policy support for the TEVT sector irrespective of ideological differences of successive governments.[2]

TEVT in Sri Lanka covers a plethora of public, private, and nongovernmental organizations. Currently, three cabinet ministries and seven noncabinet ministries provide TEVT.[3] Of these, the Ministry of Vocational and Technical Training (MVTT) is the key public institution responsible for technical and vocation education in Sri Lanka. The Tertiary and Vocational Education Commission (TVEC), established in 1992, is at the apex of the public TEVT sector and is responsible for policy formulation, coordination, and planning and development. Its responsibilities also include formulation of occupational skill standards, testing and certification procedures, registration of training institutions, standard setting, and accreditation of course programs.

In addition to the MVTT, the Ministry of Labor Relations and Manpower and the Ministry of Rural Industries and Self-employment Promotion also provide training and retraining for both employed and unemployed individuals. The latter ministry, for example, is actively engaged in promoting technical and entrepreneurial skills through the Industrial Development Board. The noncabinet ministries provide technical and vocational training through a different set of institutions. For example, the National Youth Services Council, functioning under the Ministry of Youth Affairs and Sports, provides a wide range of TEVT programs targeted at unemployed youth. Similarly, the Ceylon-German Technical Training Institute, under the Ministry of Skills Development and Public Enterprise Reforms, is a major TEVT provider. The TVEC has identified 21 public sector TEVT providers catering to the training needs of 26 industry sectors.[4]

Within the public sector, the key training providers include the Department of Technical Education and Training (DTET), National Apprenticeship and Industrial Training Authority (NAITA), National Institute of Technical Education (NITE), Vocational Training Authority of Sri Lanka (VTA), and National Youth Services Council (NYSC). The pioneer of TEVT in Sri Lanka, DTET, has been in existence for 108 years, and its delivery network currently includes 37 technical colleges and affiliated institutions in major provincial and district capitals. Using this regional network, the DTET offers about 60 courses, both on a full-time and a part-time basis, in management and commerce (32.5 percent), building and construction (29.7 percent), and electrical and electronics trades (17.9 percent). Most of its training is formal and institution based.

NAITA, the successor to the National Apprenticeship Board established in the early 1970s, has islandwide coverage through a delivery network of 86 regional and rural training centers in all nine provinces. It also has three national institutes: the Apprenticeship Training Institute, the Automobile Training Institute, and the Technician Training Institute. NAITA offers four major vocational training programs: enterprise-based apprenticeships, institution-based dual (theory and practical) training, in-plant training for other tertiary-level courses for workers and university students, and training of trainers. Together, these institutes offer about 140 courses representing 20 different trade groups or occupational categories.

The VTA was established in 1995 to provide training for rural youth. It operates through a network of 219 rural vocational training centers that are closely linked with rural development committees and local organizations. The VTA also offers certificate courses through 14 district vocational training centers, 3 national training institutes, and 9 special centers.

The National Youth Services Council, established in 1969, is another public institution that operates through 25 training centers in different parts of the country. In addition to training, it provides job market information and career guidance services to rural youth. The Sri Lanka Institute of Advanced Technical Education (SLIATE), established in 1995, conducts higher-level technical courses that were previously run by the DTET. It oversees six advanced technical institutions and three advanced technical centers. The National Institute of Technical Education, established in 1994, is mainly responsible for curriculum development, training of trainers, development of teaching materials, and provision of consultancy services for state and nongovernmental sector service providers.

The training mix of public TEVT providers is summarized in the annex table. The top five industry groups account for more than 57 percent of training programs and are concentrated in six industry sectors: metal and light engineering; textiles and garments; electrical; electronics and telecommunications; automobile repair and maintenance; and finance and management. The long-term, full-time programs leading to certificates and diplomas are predominantly targeted at school leavers, whereas the short-term programs are focused on working people. The pricing policy of public TEVT institutions is guided by both cost recovery and welfare considerations (see table 4.1).

An analysis of training by entry qualifications indicates that a majority of public TEVT programs (59 percent) are targeted at school leavers who have passed their O-levels. Seventeen percent of the programs are targeted at school leavers who have completed ninth grade, while 9 percent are focused on those who have completed their A-levels. The remainder are divided between programs targeted at other school completion levels (5 percent) and programs for which academic achievement is not an entry requirement (9 percent).

The growth and expansion of vocational training in Sri Lanka is associated with policy reforms in trade and industry and with the export-led growth strategies that have been adopted since the economy was liberalized in 1977. As a consequence, economic activities have expanded in the industrial and service sectors of the economy, creating additional demand for skilled, semiskilled, and unskilled labor. The traditional public vocational training program did not have the resources and the institutional flexibility to respond to market demand, which presented an opportunity for the private sector to emerge as an alternative service provider. Currently, private training providers are well established in several occupational areas such as machining; welding; radio repair; motor repair; electrical wiring; refrigeration and air conditioning; television, computers, and communications

Table 4.1   Training and Probability of Unemployment Last Week Using Pseudo-Cohort Data, 1992–2002

Dependent variable	Training status			
	With training		No training	
Unemployed last week (1,0)	Coefficient	t-statistic	Coefficient	t-statistic
Male	−0.4415	−17.22	−0.3728	−27.17
Level of education				
Primary	0.1124	0.16	−0.1113	−1.73
Lower secondary	−0.2166	−0.32	0.0760	1.20
Upper secondary	−0.1498	−0.22	0.3526	5.68
O-level	−0.0904	−0.13	0.4440	7.09
A-level	−0.1443	−0.21	0.4665	7.28
Degree	−0.1434	−0.21	0.2852	3.11
Postgraduate	0.0979	0.10	0.8098	1.41
Potential experience (pexp)	−0.1935	−12.06	−0.1489	−21.31
Pexp-2	0.0050	4.75	0.0019	4.45
Pexp-3	−0.00004	−2.15	0.000003	0.40
Year of entry cohort				
1950s	−0.6845	−1.19	0.0532	0.33
1960s	−0.9704	−1.51	−0.1919	−1.03
1970s	−1.1874	−1.79	−0.4279	−2.17
1980s	−1.5056	−2.28	−0.7637	−3.86
1990–94	−1.7345	−2.63	−0.9784	−4.92
1995–99	−1.7564	−2.64	−1.1836	−5.91
2000–02	−1.8134	−2.66	−1.3189	−6.25
Constant	2.6137	2.73	1.0518	5.04
Number of observations	1,081		2,009	
Adjusted R^2	0.5963		0.8007	

Source: World Bank 2005.

technology; tourism; and the hotel industry. Many of these private training programs—particularly those for bookkeeping and accountancy, computer technology, and office management—charge fees. Training providers sponsored by nongovernmental organizations (NGOs) include religious and voluntary organizations that offer craft-level training, either free of charge or for a nominal fee.

In 2005 about 351 training institutes were registered with the TVEC, including 246 public institutions, 91 private entities, and 14 in the NGO sector. In addition, a sizable number of private sector providers offer training without registering with the TVEC. Although registration with the TVEC is mandatory, only 105 out of an estimated 1,800 or more private and NGO training providers are registered with the TVEC. None of those registered, however, provide any information on enrollments, completion rates, or subsequent employment of the trainees. Consequently, virtually nothing is known about the training provided by the private sector and NGOs or about in-house training provided by employers themselves. Monitoring and evaluation of technical education and vocational training in Sri Lanka is thus essentially limited to key public sector providers.

Participation Trends

This section reviews participation trends in public technical education and vocational training programs in terms of enrollment, gender, administrative provinces, age, level of education, and year of entry cohorts. As can be seen from figure 4.1, the major public TEVT providers increased their student enrollment from 32,612 to 67,612 between 1990 and 2004, representing an average annual growth of 5.7 percent. The VTA enjoyed an increasing share of enrollment compared with the other major providers, mainly because of its penetration into the rural sector. In 2002 its rural centers, with 19,351 trainees, and its district centers, with 3,157 trainees, accounted for about one-third of total enrollment in programs operated by the major public TEVT providers.

Given the high the rate of unemployment among educated females, gender can be considered an important aspect of TEVT in Sri Lanka.[5]

Figure 4.1   TEVT Enrollment in Major Public Institutions, 1990–2004

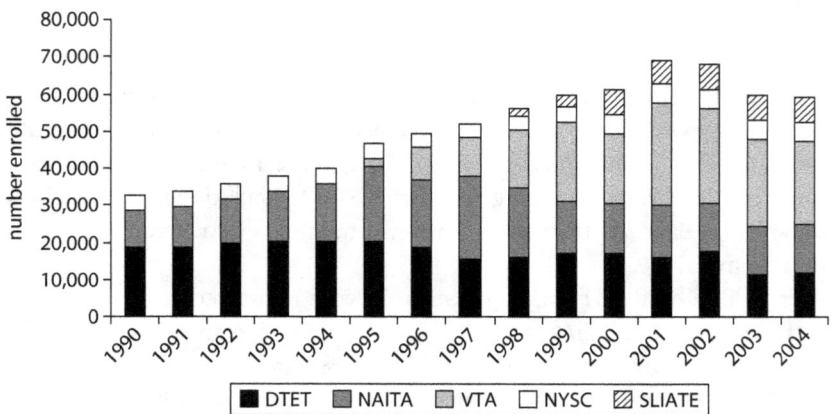

Source: TVEC, Labour Market Information Bulletin, various issues.
Note: The drop in DTET share since the mid-1990s is partly because the SLIATE has taken over some of its programs.

The proportion of female enrollment in TEVT appears to have remained stable at around 40 percent of total enrollment and is concentrated in a few areas traditionally considered to be female occupations (such as dressmaking, industrial sewing machine operator, and beautician and secretarial trades). Recently, however, female participation has expanded into several new areas such as computer applications (73 percent of all enrollees are women), English language (69 percent), accounting technicians (65 percent), and computer programmers and operators (57 percent). An analysis of gender differentials in training by level of education and province shows a high incidence of training among those with higher levels of education, especially those with O-levels or above. It also confirms earlier evidence that females receive less training than their male counterparts. The gender gap in training, however, is least pronounced at higher levels of education, especially for those at the tertiary levels.

An assessment of the incidence of training across the provinces by gender reveals two major findings directly relevant to policy makers: a relatively high incidence of training in Western Province for both males and females; and a wide gap between males and females who received any training. Figure 4.2 shows a heavy concentration of TEVT activities in Western, Southern, Sabaragamuwa, North Western, and Central provinces, which jointly account for about 84 percent of the country's gross domestic product (GDP) and 75 percent of public TEVT enrollments. Western Province alone accounts for about 30 percent of enrollments, while the other four provinces jointly account for more than 45 percent of all enrollments. The heavy concentration of TEVT activities in Western Province, where unemployment tends to be lower, is an issue that deserves special attention, particularly in view of the high rate of unemployment among educated Sri Lankans. For example, in 2006 the relative shares of total GDP for Western and Southern provinces were 50 and 10 percent, respectively. In the same year, the rate of unemployment among male O-level holders in Southern Province was twice that of the Western Province. Among females, unemployment was nearly two and a half times as high as in Western Province.

The school-to-work transition is an important aspect in analyzing the links between training and employment. In fact, this transition has rapidly become a "system" of partnerships among schools, businesses, community groups, and parents. Although the concept of transitioning from school to work is not new, it is of particular importance to Sri Lanka, given the high rate of unemployment among educated youth. The provision of

Figure 4.2   TEVT Enrollment by Province, 1990–2002

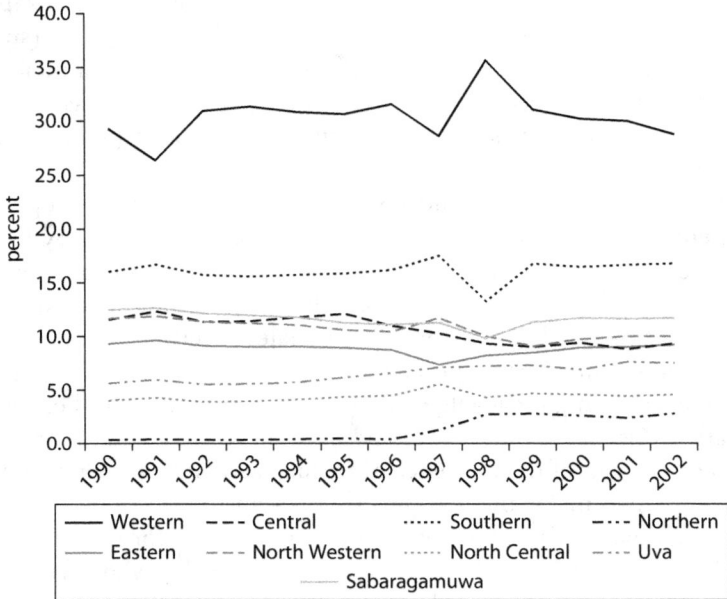

Source: TVEC, Labour Market Information Bulletin, various issues.

a comprehensive and effective school-to-work system could have a significant impact on employability of new entrants to the labor market. Such a system would ensure a continuous flow of information to the education sector on the labor market situation and training opportunities in the TEVT sector. It would also allow training providers to establish close links with the school sector and assist school leavers in selecting technical and vocational education options.

Empirical evidence based on time-series data from the government's quarterly Labor Force Survey (QLFS) reveals a rising trend in training related to economic factors between 1992 and 2002 with a decline in 2001 following a period of negative economic growth.[6] It also shows that a higher proportion of youth (ages 15–29) receive training than their adult counterparts. The greater likelihood of training for recent entrants to the labor market can stem from either supply-side or demand-side effects or a combination of both. Supply-side effects refer to the increasing number of private sector training providers and the introduction of new training programs. Demand-side effects refer to individuals' interest in acquiring job-related skills and to the increasing competitiveness in the labor market.

Evidence published by the World Bank (2005) confirms that the incidence of training among both youth and adults increased from 1992 to 2002. The findings also indicate significant increases in training for Sri Lankan youth with A-levels and above, but not for those with O-levels and below. Among adults, only university graduates showed an increased incidence of training.

As an alternative approach, training-experience profiles have also been analyzed using pseudo-cohorts (that is, 1–19, 20–21, 22–23 years)[7] constructed from QLFS data covering the 1992–2002 period. The regression estimates further confirm the earlier finding that males have a higher probability than similarly educated females of receiving training over their work life. It also reveals a high degree of variation in the incidence of training by level of educational attainment.

In any country, the TEVT sector functions as the intermediary between school education and the world of work. Technical and vocational training in fact facilitates youth transition from school to work and from unemployment to productive work. Table 4.1 examines the interval between unemployment and work for individuals with and without training. The evidence reveals that males are significantly less likely than females to experience a spell of unemployment with similar educational, experience, and year-of-entry cohort attributes. This gender gap in unemployment probability is 44 percent for the group with training and about 37 percent for those without training.

Interestingly, for the group without training, the probability of unemployment rises with the level of education. In this group, the probability of unemployment among A-level holders is 47 percent compared with 44 percent for those with O-level qualifications. For those with some training, the level of educational attainment is not significantly related to unemployment. Training also seems to make a difference for people with work experience. The findings show that the probability of unemployment drops by 19 percent for experienced workers with training but declines by only 15 percent for experienced workers without training. The lower panel of table 4.1 presents the year-of-entry cohort effects, which tend to take an interestingly negative value over the past five decades. It appears that promarket policy reforms and export-led growth strategies that came about after 1977 have created better employment opportunities for those individuals with training and a higher level of educational attainment than existed for similarly situated individuals who entered the labor market before 1977. In overall terms, these findings, particularly those establishing a close link between education and training, point to some useful policy interventions. The findings also highlight the relevance of promarket policy reforms in promoting training and labor market efficiency.

Sector Performance

This section looks at the effect of the TEVT sector on labor market outcomes based on findings of tracer studies and QLFS data. As stated earlier, hardly any information exists on the performance of private and NGO training providers, and so the labor market outcomes for these two sectors cannot be assessed separately. Using QLFS data, however, the overall performance of the TEVT sector, as measured by training and employment outcomes, can be examined. As can be seen from table 4.2, irrespective of the source of training, 67 percent of the employed persons with vocational training are wage employees and 24 percent are own-account workers (self-employed). In terms of gender, the share of female wage employees with training is higher (72 percent) than that for males (65 percent). In contrast, 27 percent of male self-employed workers have vocational training compared with 18 percent of female self-employed workers.

Among the unemployed with vocational training, 42 percent have completed their A-levels while another 25 percent have completed their O-levels (table 4.3). Fifty-five percent of the females with training and A-level education were unemployed compared with 31 percent of their male counterparts with similar education qualifications. An analysis of QLFS data for 2003–04 also reveals that the jobless rate among TEVT graduates in computer training (for data entry operators) and clerical-related training programs was 54 and 30 percent, respectively. In contrast, TEVT trainees in carpentry, masonry, printing, gem cutting, and plumbing had very low rates of unemployment (TEVC 2005).

The impact of training on the school-to-work transition is shown in table 4.4. The evidence shows some interesting and policy-relevant

Table 4.2   Status of Employed Persons with Vocational Training, 2004

Employment status	Male (%)	Female (%)	Total (number)	Total (%)
Employee	64.7	72.0	752,915	66.9
Employer	5.1	1.8	46,467	4.1
Own-account	26.5	17.5	267,301	23.8
Unpaid family worker	3.7	8.7	58,607	5.2
Total	100.0	100.0	1,125,289	100.0

Source: TEVC 2005.

Table 4.3   Educational Qualifications of Unemployed Persons with Vocational Training by Gender, 2003–04

Level of education	Male (%)	Female (%)	Total (number)	Total (%)
Year 1–10	37.6	15.0	52,642	28.4
Passed O-levels	28.1	21.8	50,614	25.5
Passed A-levels	31.4	55.4	89,485	41.9
University degree and above	2.8	7.9	11,131	4.3
Total	100.0	100.0	203,872	100.0

Source: TEVC 2005.

Table 4.4   School-to-Work Transitions with and without Training

Dependent	All youth		Without training		With training	
Time-to-employment	Coefficient	z-statistic	Coefficient	z-statistic	Coefficient	z-statistic
Lower secondary	−0.329	−15.6	−0.340	−15.8	−0.166	−1.7
Upper secondary	−0.471	−24.2	−0.492	−24.7	−0.294	−3.1
O-level	−0.434	−21.0	−0.448	−20.9	−0.284	−3.0
A-level	−0.454	−20.8	−0.445	−19.4	−0.350	−3.6
Degree	−0.340	−10.8	−0.276	−8.1	−0.459	−4.2
Formal training	−0.069	−6.0	—		—	
Informal training	−0.106	−5.2	—		—	
Male	−0.070	−8.1	−0.069	−7.3	−0.077	−4.0
Married	0.113	9.6	0.136	10.4	0.028	1.0
Urban	0.030	2.9	0.049	4.1	−0.040	−1.8
Province						
Central	0.027	2.1	0.017	1.2	0.059	2.1
Southern	0.177	13.1	0.169	11.1	0.190	6.5
North Western	−0.029	−2.0	−0.032	−2.1	−0.036	−1.0
North Central	−0.072	−4.4	−0.098	−5.5	0.026	0.7
Uva	−0.048	−2.9	−0.086	−4.6	0.111	3.0
Sabaragamuwa	0.114	7.9	0.099	6.1	0.161	5.1
Constant	1.964	54.0	1.979	50.2	1.771	14.7
Sample size	33,206		26,274		6,932	
Number finding jobs	24,605		19,678		4,927	

Source: World Bank 2005.
Note: — Indicates not available.

findings. The first column (all youth) indicates that formal and informal training are both associated with shorter job search time, with informal training appearing to have a larger impact (−0.10) than formal training leading to a diploma or certificate (−0.07). A comparison of the second and third columns indicates that those with training spend less time overall looking for a job than those without training. As can be seen from column 3, the duration of the job search reduces linearly with educational attainment TEVT and reaches a peak at degree level. For example, the impact on graduates without training is –0.445 compared with –0.350 for graduates with training. In the case of A-level holders it is –0.448 for those without training and –0.284 for those with training. Thus, a positive interaction between education and training is clearly established. The recognition of the significance of training is important for policy makers working on strategies to reduce unemployment among educated youth.

The impact of technical and vocational training on monthly wages and salaries has also been analyzed as an indicator of labor market outcomes. The results reveal that the returns to formal, certified training (7.0 percent) are usually higher than those to informal training (4.4 percent). One possible explanation is that most informal training is taken by those with the lowest levels of schooling attainment, while the more educated tend to favor formal training. However, the rewards to formal and informal training vary dramatically across sectors. In public sector employment, formal training is highly valued (returns of 7.6 percent) relative to the private sector (returns of 6.6 percent). In general, the private sector appears to value formal and informal training equally. The results also indicate that the returns to an additional year of general schooling (9.0 percent) are higher than a year of any technical or vocational training (6.6 percent).[8] In terms of regional variation, wage levels are higher in Western Province (the omitted category) relative to other provinces, and North Western and North Central provinces stand at the lowest end of wage levels.

The performance analysis presented so far covers public, private, and NGO providers. As stated earlier, information on private and nongovernmental TEVT providers is not available, so the rest of this analysis examines the performance of only the major state sector TEVT providers. Currently, the annual intake of these providers is about 67,000 students enrolled in certificate, diploma, and higher diploma programs. As table 4.5 shows, more than 80 percent of students enroll in certificate-level courses, where the completion rate is about 72 percent, compared with an overall completion rate of 65 percent.

The analysis presented in table 4.6 is an attempt to examine the performance of state TEVT providers based on selected efficiency criteria. The data show that NAITA has the highest demand (78 percent) and one of the lowest completion rates (46 percent). In contrast, demand for the NYSC is 51 percent, but its completion rate is 83 percent. The DTET has

Table 4.5 Enrollments and Completions in Selected Public Sector TEVT Institutions, 2004

	Certificate		Diploma		Higher diploma		Total	
Institute	Enrolled	Completed	Enrolled	Completed	Enrolled	Completed	Enrolled	Completed
VTA	22,267	17,921	207	191	—	—	22,474	18,122
DTET	11,758	8,166	108	174	—	—	11,866	8,340
NAITA	12,793	7,471	285	222	—	—	13,078	7,693
INGRIN[a]	975	804	109	94	—	—	1,084	898
NIBM	1,211	853	382	b	120	b	1,713	853
NYSC	—	—	—	—	—	—	5,100	3,315
Total	49,004	35,212	1,091	681	120	0	60,526	39,301

Level of training

Sources: TEVC 2004.
a. Sri Lanka Institute of Printing and Graphics.
b. Training in progress.
Note: — Indicates not available.

Table 4.6   Efficiency of TEVT Providers

Performance indicators	DTET	VTA	NAITA	NYSC
Enrollment in 1997	14,892	13,115	24,812	3,499
Completion number	6,132	9,919	11,447	2,886
Completion percentage	41.2	75.6	46.1	82.5
Instructor/trainee ratio	1:26	1:20	1:72	1:30
Unit recurrent costs (rupees)	11,361	9,259	8,524	5,974
External efficiency				
Social demand (Admitted % in 1997)[a]	26	47	78	51

Source: ADB 1998.
a. Social demand is total demand for a training program measured in terms of total number of applications received.

both the lowest demand and completion rates. The unit cost evidence given in table 4.6 indicates that NYSC is the least expensive of all four programs. However, one should be cautious in interpreting this informa-tion, because the operating costs of training programs can vary quite signif-icantly in duration, academic achievement (that is, diploma or certificate level), and subject coverage.

The analysis given in table 4.7 provides more specific details on labor market outcomes of TEVT providers based on tracer study evidence for 2000–2001. It clearly indicates that NAITA graduates have a higher rate of employment than DTET and VTA graduates. About 73 percent of NAITA graduates believe that the training skills they acquired were very relevant to their current job. The ratings for the DTET and VTA were 40 and 65 percent, respectively. Tracer study evidence also indicates that 30 percent of NAITA graduates found employment immediately after graduation while another 24 percent found jobs within the first six months. For the DTET and VTA, the share who found jobs immediately after graduation was around 38 and 3 percent, respectively.

Another tracer study conducted by the DTET (2005a) revealed that the unemployment rate was 28 percent among the graduates who fol-lowed the National Certificate Course in Engineering Draughtsmanship.[9] It also showed a marked decline between 1995–96 and 2000 in the pro-portion of graduates who found employment within the first six months. In overall terms, the labor market outcome of NAITA appears to be much better than DTET and VTA.

An assessment of enterprise-based craft apprenticeship programs con-ducted by NAITA (2005b) focused on the procedure for selecting trainees, delivery of training, and trade testing and certification procedures,

Table 4.7   Principal Outcomes of Tracer Studies of TEVT Graduates
Percent

Outcome	DTET[a]	NAITA[b]	VTA[c]
Employment status			
Wage employment	49.3	62.2	14.3
Self employment	6.1	9.6	14.3
Employed in other categories of work	10.7	0	0
Unemployed	33.9	28.2	62.7
Not seeking a job	0	0	8.7
Total	100.0	100.0	100.0
Relevance of training to the job			
Very relevant	39.8	72.7	65.4
Relevant	30.4	15.8	8.9
Not at all relevant	29.8	11.5	25.7
Total	100.0	100.0	100.0

Sources: DTET 2002, NAITA 2001, and VTA 2001.
a. Based on a sample of 2,732 graduates taking DTET courses in 1995 and 1996; the sample covers all but Northern Province.
b. Based on a sample of 706 apprentices graduated during 1996–99. The sample was drawn from the Western, Central, Southern, and North Western provinces.
c. Based on a sample of 973 trainees in 48 trades drawn from Central, Uva, and Southern provinces.

and the findings lend some useful insights on training and labor market outcomes.[10] With regard to the first criterion, the study found that the excessive time taken to select the trainees and start the training program, together with an inability to provide training in the chosen trade, were key factors affecting performance efficiency of training. Similarly, the study noted that irrelevant industrial training, nonavailability of basic training, insufficient practical work, inadequate time allocation for advice and guidance, poor communication between employer and apprentice, and relatively little monitoring and evaluation were major reasons for low completion rates. Long delays in holding the trade tests and issuing certificates were also identified as a factor affecting performance efficiency. According to the survey, only 19.3 percent of apprentices were able to collect their certificates within three months.

Another study by NAITA (2005a) looked at factors leading to low enrollment and high dropout rates in its programs.[11] The evidence revealed that 97 percent of the dropouts were living in rural areas and that the household income of 60 percent of them was less than 5,000 Sri Lankan rupees a month.[12] The VTA (2005a) also looked at the issue of high dropout rates at its rural training centers based on a sample drawn from

Badulla and Hambantota districts.[13] The findings lend further support to low household income as an important reason for high dropout rates. In fact, about 67 percent of dropouts were making some contribution to their family income. The average family income was less than SL Rs 3,000 a month for about 23 percent of the families, and another 60 percent had monthly income of SL Rs 3,001–5,000 a month. Program instructors also identified low income as a major reason for the high dropout rates. In addition, heavy emphasis on theory, use of poor-quality equipment, lack of facilities—such as classrooms, libraries, and workshops—at training centers, and lack of career guidance were also identified as key factors affecting high dropout rates. The evidence on teaching aids further confirms the poor learning environment that characterizes the VTA's rural vocational training centers. Among instructors, 56 percent cited inadequate resources and 25 percent cited lack of technical facilities as major constraints faced by these training centers. A recent study by the DTET (2005b) on engineering craft courses emphasized the need for introducing modern training methodology and training of trainers as remedial measures to enhance participation in training.[14]

A study by the NYSC (2005) of its Diploma in Computer Science program provides further evidence of links between training and employment.[15] The findings reveal that about 22 percent of the respondents remained unemployed after the training, while another 27 percent stated that training was not helpful in finding a job. Of those who were employed, about 42 percent found employment within one year, while another 17 percent had to wait for as long as two years. This study also reported that about 32 percent were employed in fields other than the field of training, and more than 57 percent of the employed were earning less than SL Rs 6,000 a month.

Career guidance is an important strategy for linking training and employment. This aspect has also been examined by the VTA based on a sample of students selected from Moneragala District.[16] About 40 percent of the sample was in the 15–20 age group, and three-fifths of them were females. At the end of the career guidance program, about 78 percent of the participants opted for wage employment, self-employment, or further training. Another study by NAITA (2005c) reveals some interesting evidence on employability of TEVT graduates in the private sector.[17] The findings show that only 37 percent of respondent companies were prepared to consider graduates from the public TEVT institutions when recruiting employees. Respondents cited insufficient practical skills, poor quality of programs, inadequate use of state-of-the-art technology, and inadequate industrial exposure as reasons for declining to consider these graduates. The findings of the study also reported that more than 85 percent of companies were reluctant to upgrade the skills of their employees through public TEVT providers.

Summary of Findings

The technical education and vocational training sector is strategically important, particularly in enhancing employability of new entrants to the labor market. It intermediates between the general education sector and the labor market by providing technical and vocational training not taught in the general education system. This is of vital importance for Sri Lanka, given the high rate of educated youth who are not employed. Governments since 1970 have in fact clearly recognized the importance of training by introducing several institutional and policy reforms to improve the labor market outcomes of TEVT. Despite these efforts, the overall performance of the TEVT sector has been far below expectations.

As noted earlier, about 67,000 students enter TEVT sector programs every year. Although most of the programs are geared toward school leavers with O-level qualifications, a significant number of school leavers with A-level and higher qualifications sign up for the programs. TEVT programs are heavily concentrated in Western Province, where educational attainment and wages are comparatively high and the jobless rate is relatively low. In addition, female participation in training is relatively low, although at higher levels of education both men and women were more apt to seek training. The year-of-entry cohort analysis suggests that over the past five decades, more and more Sri Lankans have been entering training programs and that the pace of entry has picked up since pro-market reforms were instituted in 1977.

In terms of labor market outcomes, evidence shows that training reduces job search time and that formal, certified training offers higher returns. In general, however, the sector performance analysis revealed low employability among TEVT graduates and wide variations in employability across major public TEVT providers. The evidence also revealed that training enrollees often encountered negative factors affecting their future employability, such as outdated study programs, inadequate teaching aids, irrelevant industrial training, insufficient practical work, and inadequate interaction with the relevant industry. The influence of low-household income over completion rates was also noted, especially in low-income districts such as Badulla and Hambantota.

Policy Implications and Recommendations

The analysis presented in this chapter indicates a remarkably consistent story about labor market outcomes of the technical education and vocational training sector in Sri Lanka. The positive interaction between education and training indicates the need for establishing a close link between school education and the TEVT sector. Policy makers in Sri Lanka have already recognized that training can smooth the transition from school to work and have come up with several policy measures, including the introduction of vocational subjects in school. The implementation of these policies, however, has been rather disappointing. The high incidence of training sought by youth with A-level or higher qualifications highlights an interesting policy issue given the limited access to university education in Sri Lanka. The experience of the Republic of Korea in reducing the heavy emphasis placed on university education and promoting TEVT at the school level is relevant in this regard. Similarly, the Japanese experience of improving labor market outcomes of training through close links with the industry, continuous curriculum development, and introduction of new programs focused on skill requirements of the job market can help meet the demand for skilled labor in domestic and foreign markets alike.

Because the private sector is the main beneficiary of TEVT services, it has to play an active role in developing the curriculum, providing practical training for apprentices and trainees, and familiarizing the training staff with the machinery and technologies used in industry. The responsibility of the state is to act as a facilitator, coordinator, regulator, and standard setter. Accreditation of private sector TEVT institutions is equally important, and that responsibility rests with the TVEC. In this regard, the experiences of Japan and Korea can provide a guide in maintaining close links between industry and training. These two countries use technological and human resources available within specific industries to improve performance efficiency of TEVT institutions.

Career guidance and sharing of labor market information is also important for guiding students to high-demand segments of the labor market. The information compiled by the labor market information units of the TVEC and the Ministry of Labour Relations and Manpower is very useful in this regard and needs to be fed into the entire network of TEVT providers. Similarly, more emphasis on career guidance activities by training providers would enhance the external efficiency of training. TEVT institutions in Bangladesh are already using such programs to help their students stay abreast of changing demands in the labor market. Policy makers' ability to monitor and evaluate the performance of the TEVT sector is yet another important aspect, which requires information sharing by public, private, and NGO providers. It also involves training of personnel in state and private training institutions on database systems relating to internal and external efficiency of the TEVT sector.

Policy makers have already addressed the issue of relatively low female participation in TEVT, and both policy makers and TEVT providers need to come up with new programs, particularly in computing, accounting, and English language skills, that broaden and enhance women's job opportunities. The heavy concentration of TEVT activities in high-income provinces is yet another issue that deserves the attention of policy-making bodies in allocating funds for TEVT. The presence of public TEVT providers with improved facilities in outer provinces may lead to more economic benefits in terms of equity and balanced growth. Building up training centers in the outer provinces is well in line with ongoing regional development programs and other efforts to reduce the high rate of unemployment among educated workers in these areas.

Annex TEVT Training by Type of Industry (Public Sector Only)

IC	Industry sector	Number of TEVT providers	Number of programs	Age	Duration	Fees (SL Rs)
1	Agriculture and livestock	6	12	17–30	6M–2 Y/FT	250–5,000
3	Art and media	6	37	17–35	2W–3Y/FT	Free–30,000
4	Automobile repair and maintenance	9	71	16–30	3W–3Y/FT	Free–19,000
5	Aviation, aeronautics and navigation	2	3	18–35	3M–3Y/FT	Free–17,750
6	Building and construction	8	58	16–30	5D–3Y/FT	Free–20,000
7	Computer and information technology	10	56	NAL	2D–Y/FT	Free–55,000
8	Electrical, electronics, and telecommunication	8	72	16–35	3D–3.5Y/FT	Free–9,500
10	Finance and management	6	61	NAL	2D–4Y/FT	Free–37,000
12	Gems and jewelry	5	24	16–30	2M–2Y/FT	Free–20,400
13	Handicraft and cottage industries	1	4	Adults	NS	NS
14	Hotel and tourism	5	39	16–25	4M–4Y/FT	Free–16,500
15	Leather and footwear	3	4	16–25	6M–2Y/FT	Free
17	Medical and health science	3	4	16–25	2–3Y/FT	Free
18	Metal and light engineering	8	80	16–25	5D–4Y/FT	Free–9,500
19	Office management	7	28	16–25	3D–1Y/FT	Free–6,250
20	Personnel and community development	3	14	16–30	4–6M	Free–4,600
21	Printing and packaging	5	24	16–30	4M–2Y/FT	Free–21,000
22	Rubber and plastics	1	1	16–25	2Y/FT	Free
23	Textile and garment	5	79	16–30	2D–1Y/FT	Free–70,000
24	Wood-related	4	22	16–30	6M–3Y/FT	Free–3,000
25	Language	4	32	17–35	4M–2Y/FT	Free–9,300
26	Teacher training	2	10	18+	5D–2Y/FT	30,000

Source: TEVC, Training Prospectus 2005.
IC = industry code; NAL = no age limit; NS = not specified; D = days; W = weeks; M = months; Y = year; FT = full time.

Notes

1. The 1971 insurrection began with an upheaval of educated unemployed youth organized under an extremist political party against the government. They were mainly concentrated in the rural sector.

2. Some of the major policy documents include "Industrialization Strategy of the Ministry of Industrial Development" (1989); "New Industrialization Strategy of the Ministry of Industrial Development" (1995); "Presidential Task Force on TEVT Reforms in Sri Lanka" (1997); and from the Ministry of Finance and Planning, "Vision 2010" (2001); "Regaining Sri Lanka" (2001); "Draft National Employment Policy" (2002); "The National Policy and Action Plan for the Development of Technical Education" (NEC, 2002); and "Budget Speech" (2006). For a detailed discussion on policy evolution of the TEVT sector in Sri Lanka, see Chandrasiri 2004 and World Bank 2005.

3. Ministry of Sports and Youth Affairs, Ministry of Samurdhi and Poverty Alleviation, Ministry of Textile Industry Development, Ministry of Mass Media and Information, Ministry of Foreign Employment Promotion, Ministry of Skills Development and Public Enterprise Reforms, and Ministry of Housing and Construction.

4. Major public TEVT providers as identified by the TEVC include Ceylon-German Technical Training Institute, Clothing Industry Training Institute, Department of Technical Education and Training, Gem and Jewelry Research and Training Institute, Institute for Construction Training and Development, National Apprentice and Industrial Training Authority, National Institute of Technical Education of Sri Lanka, National Youth Services Council, Sirimavo Bnadaranayake Institute of Tourism and Hotel Management, Sri Lanka Export Development Board, Sri Lanka Institute of Advanced Technical Education, Sri Lanka Institute of Printing, Sri Lanka National Design Centre, INGRIN Institute of Printing and Graphics, Vocational Authority, Sri Lanka Ports Authority, Department of Agriculture, Ministry of Health, National Institute of Business Management, Nursing School, and Sri Lanka Television Training Institute.

5. In 2006 the rate of unemployment among males with O-level and A-level and above qualifications was 26.6 and 18.3 percent, respectively, compared with 26.7 and 34.3 percent for females with similar qualifications.

6. It is important to note that term *training* used in the labor force survey captures the services provided by public, private, and NGO training institutions.

7. In essence, this pseudo-cohort approach involves collapsing the 1992–2002 labor force survey data into cells cross-classified by year, sex, level of educational attainment, two-year age intervals, and training receipt, with information on the weighted count of individuals in each cell.

8. One caveat is that participation in training may not be on full-time basis, so the returns to training may be underestimated.

9. This study was based on a sample of 269 graduates of the National Certificate in Engineering Draughtsmanship program. The program offered in 2000 was the revised version of 1995/96 program.

10. The study was based on a 2003 sample of 169 respondents representing 73 graduates, 67 in-training candidates, and 29 dropouts.

11. The study was based on a sample of 57 respondents representing 20 graduates and 37 dropouts. It was also based on interviews with 29 parents, 9 dropouts, 21 schoolteachers, and 20 NAITA instructors. Coverage was 1998 to 2004 and limited to Western Province.

12. US$ 1= 100.50 Sri Lankan rupees in 2005.

13. The study was based on a sample of 76 respondents representing 26 graduates, 30 dropouts, 16 instructors, and 4 business executives. Coverage was 2002 and limited to Badulla and Hambantota districts.

14. This study (DTET 2005b) was based on a sample of 285 respondents representing 7 technical school principals, 43 instructors, and 235 graduates of engineering craft courses.

15. The study by NYSC (2005) was based on a sample of 70 respondents, 97 percent of whom were under age 29 and 63 percent of whom had A-level qualifications. The sample covered students from course programs offered in 1997, 2000, 2001, 2002, and 2003.

16. The study by VTA (2005b) was based on a sample of 221 respondents representing 215 participants and 6 instructors.

17. The study by NAITA (2005c) was based on a sample of 200 companies representing micro (37 percent), small (28.5 percent), medium (13.5 percent), and large (21 percent) enterprises providing services, buying and selling, production and exporting, and production and selling.

References

ADB (Asian Development Bank). 1998. "Final Report of Skills Development Project." ADB/TA/3051-SRF. Colombo.

———. 2004. "Improving Technical Education and Vocational Training." Manila.

Chandrasiri, S. 2004. "Technical Education and Vocational Training in Sri Lanka: An Assessment" *IWE Journal* (Institute of Workers' Education, University of Colombo) 4: 31–53.

Department of Census and Statistics. Various years. "Quarterly Report of the Sri Lanka Labor Force Survey." Colombo.

DTET (Department of Technical Education and Training). 2002. "Tracer Study of Technical College Graduates 1995–1996." Study conducted in collaboration with the Department of Census and Statistics and National Education Research and Evaluation Center, Faculty of Education, University of Colombo.

———. 2005a. "A Tracer Study on the First Batch of Students Who Followed National Certificate in Engineering Draftsmanship Course Introduced in Year 2000." Proceedings of the Research Convention, 2005. Ministry of Skills Development and Technical Education, Colombo.

———. 2005b. "A Study to Identify the Causes that Lead to Poor Participation of Students in Common Subject Components in Engineering Craft Courses." Proceedings of the Research Convention, 2005. Ministry of Skills Development and Technical Education, Colombo.

Ministry of Labour Relations and Manpower. 2007. *LMI Bulletin* 1 (3): 9–11.

NAITA (National Apprentice and Industrial Training Authority). 2001. "Report on Tracer Study Survey Results for Monitoring and Evaluation of Vocational Training." Planning and Information Division, NAITA, Colombo.

———. 2005a "An Investigation on the Efficiency of the Enterprise Based Craft Apprenticeship Training Program Offered by the NAITA." Proceedings of the Research Convention, 2005. Ministry of Skills Development and Technical Education, Colombo.

———. 2005b. "Factors Leading to Low Enrollment Rates and High Dropout Rates in Selected Courses Conducted by NAITA." Proceedings of the Research Convention, 2005. Ministry of Skills Development and Technical Education, Colombo.

———. 2005c. "A Study to Evaluate the Contribution of Government TEVT Institutions for Accomplishing the Training Requirements and Upgrading Occupational Areas in the Industrial Sector." Proceedings of the Research Convention, 2005. Ministry of Skills Development and Technical Education, Colombo.

NYSC (National Youth Services Council) 2005. "The Diploma in Computer Science Courses Conducted by the National Youth Services Council at the Maharagama Training Centre. Some Proposals for Improvement Based on the Experience of Students Who Have Completed the Course." Proceedings of the Research Convention, 2005. Ministry of Skills Development and Technical Education, Colombo.

Presidential Task Force on TEVT Reforms, Ministry of Vocational Training and Rural Industries. 1997. "Technical Education and Vocational Training Reforms, Policies, Strategies and Action Program." Colombo.

TVEC (Technical and Vocational Education Commission). 2004. *Labor Market Information Bulletin* 2 (December): 38.

———. 2005. *Labor Market Information Bulletin* 1 (June).

———. 2007. *Labor Market Information Bulletin* 1 (June): 36–37.

VTA (Vocational Training Authority). 2001. "Report on Tracer Study Survey Results for Monitoring and Evaluation of Vocational Training." Colombo.

———. 2005a. "Tracer Study on the Participants Who Had Undergone the Career Guidance Awareness Program Conducted by Vocational Training Authority in Moneragala District." Proceedings of the Research Convention, 2005. Ministry of Skills Development and Technical Education, Colombo.

———. 2005b. "A Study to Identify the Factors that Leads High Drop-out Rates in the Courses Conducted at the RVTC of the VTA, Sri Lanka." Proceedings of the Research Convention, 2005. Ministry of Skills Development and Technical Education, Colombo.

World Bank. 2005. "Training and Links to the Labor Market." In *Treasures of the Education System in Sri Lanka: Restoring Performance, Expanding Opportunities, and Enhancing Prospects,* pp. 93–118. Washington, DC: World Bank, Human Development Unit, South Asia Region.

CHAPTER 5

School-to-Work Transition of Sri Lankan University Graduates

Milan Vodopivec and Nimnath Withanachchi

Although the unemployment rate in Sri Lanka has dropped substantially during the past decade, the unemployment rate among young people has remained high. In 2006 the Labor Force Survey estimated the overall unemployment rate at 6.5 percent, while the jobless rate for young people (ages 15–29) stood at 17.1 percent (DCS 2007). The unemployment rate for the better educated is particularly high. It is therefore not surprising that Sri Lankan young people perceive Sri Lankan society as unjust and unequal (see chapter 8) and that they are frustrated by the failure of mainstream institutions to address existing inequalities in the distribution of both resources and gains generated by economic development.

Several hypotheses have been advanced to explain unemployment in Sri Lanka (see the introductory chapter). The skills mismatch hypothesis maintains that educated workers possess the wrong sets of skills, making them unmarketable (World Bank 1999). The queuing hypothesis argues that the unemployed wait for an opportunity to take a job in the civil service, which is known for offering stable jobs with generous fringe benefits (including pensions) and for requiring low work effort. Similarly, the institutional, or slow job creation, hypothesis maintains that unemployment arises because job creation in the "protected" private sector is hindered by high labor costs. Recent evidence (Heltberg and Vodopivec

2008; Rama 2003; World Bank 2007) supports the queuing and institutional hypotheses linked to labor market rigidities.

This chapter discusses additional evidence about the reasons for unemployment by evaluating factors that contribute to successful school-to-work transitions for social science university graduates. Using data from a retrospective survey of University of Colombo graduates, the study focuses on the relationships between unemployment and social status and availability of social networks, field of study, and active labor market programs (the Tharuna Aruna hiring subsidy program and government recruitment campaigns).

The study finds that in the first four years after university graduation, the proportion of unemployed graduates who found a job remained below 20 percent each year, so that by the end of the fourth year after leaving school, just over half of the graduates surveyed had found a job. Interestingly, jobs for all remaining unemployed graduates in our sample were provided through the government's 2005 recruitment campaign, which targeted unemployed graduates and provided jobs to 42,000 persons. Among factors that helped graduates to find jobs, the study confirms the impact of social status and networks (as proxied by mothers' education level), access to roads, and field of study. The study also finds that males and graduates of higher social status are more likely to be absorbed into the formal private sector than into the public sector. Perhaps surprisingly, reported job satisfaction was the highest in the public sector, even though the wages were the lowest, and among graduates who changed jobs, none moved out of public sector. Our results thus render direct or indirect support for all three hypotheses advanced to explain Sri Lankan unemployment.

Unemployment Trends and Institutional Background

To provide the necessary labor market context, we describe unemployment trends in Sri Lanka and compare the prevalence of unemployment by age, gender, and education. We also describe youth employment promotion and creation programs, including those targeted at university graduates. And we review key clauses of Sri Lanka's extremely rigid employment protection legislation, which is often cited as a possible deterrent of youth employment.

Sri Lanka's unemployment rate has declined by more than half since 1990, dropping from 14.5 percent in 1992 to 6.5 percent in 2006. But the unemployment rate varies widely across population groups, and it is particularly high among females, young people, and well-educated people. In 2006 the female unemployment rate (9.7 percent) was slightly more than twice the male rate (4.6 percent). By age group, the unemployment rate in 2006 was highest for those ages 15 through 19 followed by ages 20 through 24, at 23.1 percent and 21.0 percent, respectively. In contrast, the jobless rate for persons 30 years old and above was one-tenth as high, at 2 percent. The unemployment rate is particularly high for the well educated: in 2006 (in the middle of our sample period), 11.6 percent of those with A (advanced)-level qualifications and 9.9 percent of those with O (ordinary)-level qualifications were without a job. Unemployment among graduates was also above the average.

A majority of young people feel they are treated unfairly both by society and by the country's political institutions. According to the Presidential Commission on Youth (1990) and Hettige and Mayer (2002), these experiences are not just youthful complaints but are based on real experiences. A highly politicized society has resulted in people relying on political favors and influential social networks for employment opportunities rather than on a system of merit. Research on youth unrest both in the south and north indicate that it is caused largely by frustration and disappointment with policies and programs that are often perceived as discriminatory (Thangarajah 2002).

Because violent conflicts in Sri Lankan society have often been attributed to the lack of employment and education opportunities of young people (see chapter 10), the government has been particularly sensitive to the unemployment of graduates. In 1997 the government launched the Tharuna Aruna program, which provided a subsidy to employers for hiring graduates; among other things, this program was explicitly aimed at redirecting career aspirations of graduates toward the private sector. Additionally, the government has conducted large recruitment campaigns of unemployed graduates, despite government reports showing overstaffing of the civil service.

The Tharuna Aruna program provides a 12-month subsidy to employers for hiring a graduate and is carried out under the auspices of four leading chambers of commerce in Sri Lanka. The primary goal of the program is to encourage graduates to take private sector jobs, although eligible employers include national and international nongovernmental organizations and selected commercial public enterprises. During program participation, graduates receive a minimum salary of SL Rs 6,000 a month, of which Tharuna Aruna reimburses SL Rs 4,000. To put this number in perspective, the mean monthly wage of Sri Lankan wage earners in 2006 was

SL Rs 14,457 (DCS 2008). During the program, graduates also undergo job search, information technology, and English language training. When introduced in 1997, the program was aiming to provide placements to 10,000 graduates over a period of five years.

In their efforts to secure political support and fulfill election campaign promises, governments often offer civil sector appointments to graduates. The political motivation behind regular large-scale recruitments is evident from the fact that such recruitments often mirror electoral cycles. In 2005, for example, the government recruited 42,000 graduates, initially hiring many of them as temporary workers for a salary of SL Rs 10,000, and giving them training. The recruits have subsequently been absorbed into the permanent workforce. Before 2005 recruitment of public sector employees had been frozen for about three years.

Sri Lanka's severance pay system, embodied in the Termination of Employment of Workmen Act (TEWA) introduced in 1971, is one of the most restrictive severance pay systems in the world. The TEWA system not only calls for high compensation to the laid-off workers, but its discretionary nature and lengthy procedures further restrict the ability of employers to manage their employment needs. Compensation formulas introduced in 2005 reduced the nontransparency and arbitrariness of the firing process, but separation costs remain extremely high by international standards, the process of separation still involves "prior approval" by the labor commissioner, and arbitrariness and lack of transparency are still significant problems.[1] It has long been asserted that TEWA's opaque, discretionary, and costly regulations discourage employment growth.

There is growing evidence that TEWA regulations discourage employment growth in formal firms and have particularly adverse implications for access to formal jobs by young people. For example, chapter 2 points to the TEWA system as a likely source of Sri Lanka's depressed job flows. Moreover, using 1995–2003 panel data for all Sri Lankan private, formal sector firms, Babatunde, Orazem, and Vodopivec (2009; see also chapter 2) find that firms at or below the threshold of 14 workers (the employment level under which the TEWA system does not apply) are less likely to increase employment compared with firms above that threshold and that an exceptionally large productivity shock is required to cross the threshold. These findings suggest that the TEWA system, designed to preserve employment, has the opposite effect of slowing down employment growth—and because of their lack of experience, young workers are likely to be particularly affected.

Data and Methodology

The study described here uses data obtained from a retrospective survey of 517 University of Colombo graduates who obtained their degrees in 2000 or 2001, covering five years of work history immediately following their graduation (the survey was administered in early 2006). Duration models are used to examine determinants of exit from unemployment, and a selectivity-corrected earnings function is estimated to analyze determinants of earnings.

Data

The survey included questions on personal, family, and community characteristics and (retrospectively) on the respondents' labor market history after finishing school. In addition, the survey gathered qualitative information on the respondents' health status, job satisfaction, attitudes, and perspectives. Two clusters were selected, 527 "odd-number" enrollees at the Faculty of Management, University of Colombo, in 1997 (who graduated in 2000), and a randomly selected 426 Colombo University graduates who graduated in 2001. The field survey began toward the end of January 2006 and was completed by the mid-March 2006. Because of tracing difficulties, the study team was able to interview only 517 members of the selected clusters. Therefore, a selection bias stemming from the inability to trace a significant proportion of the respondents cannot be excluded.

Basic statistics on the 517 respondents are as follow: 44 percent were male. Seventy-seven percent were Sinhala, 11 percent Sri Lankan Tamil, 11 percent Moor, and 2 percent Indian Tamil. The most common degree was a bachelor of commerce, which 33 percent of the graduates received. Over half of the respondents had mothers who had not received their O-level qualifications—our proxy for social background. Further descriptive statistics are available in the annex tables.

Methodology

We define unemployment duration as a function of a set of individual and community characteristics. Since information about unemployment duration is available only in years, we use a complementary log-log (cloglog) model as a discrete time representation of a proportional hazard model:

$$\log[-\log(1-h_i(t))] = z_i(t), \tag{5.1}$$

where $h_i(t)$ is the discrete time hazard function, $z_i(t) = c(t) + X_i\beta$ for a representative i person in the year t, and $c(t)$ is the difference between the baseline hazard evaluated at the end and the beginning of the interval, X_i is a set of individual and household socioeconomic and demographic characteristics, and β is the set of regression parameters to be estimated.

We also use a logistic hazard model, which provides a discrete-time method:

$$\log[h_i(t)/(1-h_i(t))] = z_i(t),\qquad(5.2)$$

where $h_i(t)$ is the discrete time hazard function, $z_i(t) = c(t) + X_i\beta$ for a representative i person in the year t, and $c(t)$ is the baseline logistic hazard function, X_i represents a set of individual and household socioeconomic and demographic characteristics, and β is the set of regression parameters to be estimated.

The choice of employment type for the first job—public, private-formal, and private-informal sector—is treated as an unordered categorical variable and is estimated by a multinomial logit model. That is,

$$\log\left[\frac{P(H_i = j)}{P(H_i = 1)}\right] = X_i\beta_j,\qquad(5.3)$$

where the log of the odds that individual i will choose employment-type j ($j = 2,3$), relative to type 1 is estimated, where type 1 is public sector employment, 2 is formal private-sector, and 3 is informal private-sector, X_i is a set of individual and household socioeconomic and demographic characteristics, and β_j is the set of regression parameters to be estimated.

Corrected for selection bias from equation 5.3 by a variant of the Dubin-McFadden (1984) correction method suggested in Bourguignon, Fournier, and Gurgand (2007), we specify a modified Mincer function, in which the logarithm of income of the first job is taken as a function of education type, and individual socioeconomic characteristics:

$$w_{i,j} = X_i\beta_j + e_j,\qquad(5.4)$$

where $w_{i,j}$ is the log of wage of the individual i in the employment category j, X_i is a set of individual and household socioeconomic and demographic characteristics, and β_j is the set of regression parameters to be estimated.

Results

The results are detailed under four subheadings: importance of social status, gender, and location; value of the field of study; impact of labor market programs; and choice of sector of work and job satisfaction.

A large percentage of university graduates remain unemployed for long periods after completing studies. The hazard rate of exit from unemployment remained below 20 percent in the first three years after graduation (figures 5.1 and 5.2). At the beginning of 2005 (three or four years

Figure 5.1   Hazard Rate of Exit from Unemployment for 2000 Graduates

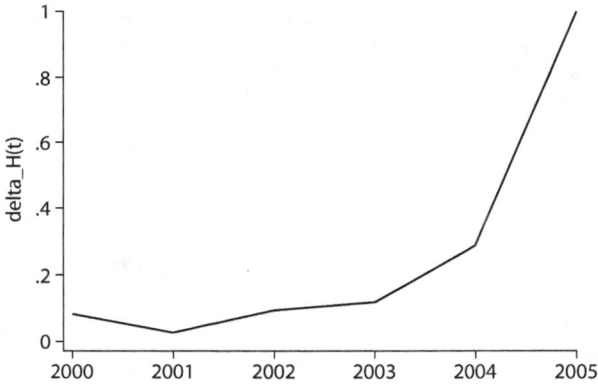

Source: Authors' calculations.

Figure 5.2   Hazard Rate of Exit from Unemployment for 2001 Graduates

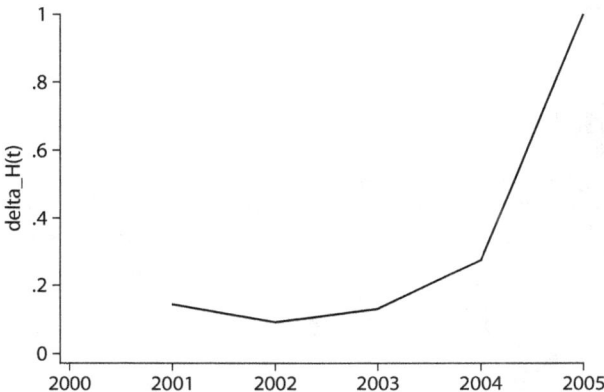

Source: Authors' calculations.

after graduation), about half of the sample graduates were still unemployed, but by the end of 2005 all had found a job, because all of those still searching were absorbed into the public sector through a government recruitment campaign. Reflecting this, the average number of jobs per graduate at the end of year 2005 jumped to 1.14, from 0.59 at the beginning of 2005.

Importance of Social Status, Gender, and Location

Graduates from low socioeconomic strata face a significant disadvantage in securing a job (tables 5.1 and 5.2), and female and rural graduates have

Table 5.1   Association of Socioeconomic Variables with Unemployment Duration (Cloglog Proportional Hazard Model)

Variable	Coefficient	Standard error	Hazard ratio	Standard error	P > z
Gender–Male	0.01	0.12	1.01	0.12	0.90
Ethnicity					
Sri Lankan Tamil	0.56	0.19	1.76	0.33	0.00
Moor	−0.21	0.19	0.81	0.15	0.25
Indian Tamil	−0.01	0.45	0.99	0.45	0.99
Type of degree					
Bachelor of Commerce	−0.03	0.17	0.98	0.17	0.89
BA (Economics)	0.19	0.27	1.21	0.33	0.48
BA (History)	0.09	0.30	1.10	0.33	0.76
BA (Sinhala)	−0.26	0.33	0.77	0.26	0.44
BA (Geography)	−0.15	0.26	0.86	0.23	0.57
BA (English)	0.03	0.76	1.03	0.78	0.97
BA (Demography)	−0.63	0.31	0.53	0.16	0.04
BA (Political Science)	−0.61	0.29	0.54	0.16	0.04
BA (Journalism)	−0.50	0.32	0.61	0.20	0.12
BA (General)	−0.13	0.45	0.88	0.39	0.78
Mother's education					
Passed year 6 /grade 5	0.72	0.38	2.05	0.78	0.06
Passed year 13 / GCE (A-level), HNCE	0.97	0.29	2.63	0.77	0.00
Passed GAQ/GSQ and above	0.50	0.25	1.65	0.41	0.04
Marital status					
Married	−0.20	0.12	0.81	0.10	0.09
Widowed	0.24	0.96	1.27	1.22	0.80
Divorced	0.44	0.79	1.55	1.23	0.58
Separated	−0.61	0.78	0.54	0.42	0.43

(continued)

Table 5.1   Association of Socioeconomic Variables with Unemployment Duration (Cloglog Proportional Hazard Model) *(Continued)*

Variable	Coefficient	Standard error	Hazard ratio	Standard error	P > z
Minutes from home to a main road	−0.03	0.01	0.98	0.01	0.00
Self-assessed health status					
Very good health	0.08	0.25	1.08	0.27	0.75
Good health	0.11	0.24	1.11	0.27	0.66
Fair health	−0.23	0.29	0.79	0.23	0.43
Cluster variable–Graduates of year 2000	−1.21	0.42	0.30	0.13	0.00
Jobsnet registered[a]	−0.10	0.15	0.90	0.14	0.50
Year 2002	−0.48	0.17	0.62	0.11	0.01
Year 2003	0.40	0.14	1.50	0.21	0.01
Year 2004	3.12	0.18	22.67	4.19	0.00
Constant	−1.49	0.38			0.00
Number of observations: 1,545					
Prob > chi^2					
Log likelihood ratio					−638.31

Source: Authors' calculations.
Note: dF/dx is for discrete change of dummy variable from 0 to 1; education type, base = bachelor of business administration; mother's education, base = passed year 3 /grade 2; marital status, base = never married; self-assessed health, base = excellent health; base year = 2001. GCE = General Certificate of Examination; HNCE = Higher National Certificate of Education; GAQ = General Arts Qualifying Exam; GSQ = General Science Qualifying Exam.
a. Jobsnet is an Internet- and town-center-based national job-matching service.

Table 5.2   Association of Socioeconomic Variables with Unemployment Duration (Logistic Hazard Model)

Variable	Coefficient	Standard error	Odds ratio	Standard error	P > z
Gender–Male	0.04	0.15	1.04	0.16	0.80
Ethnicity					
Sri Lankan Tamil	0.68	0.24	1.98	0.46	0.00
Moor	−0.29	0.24	0.75	0.18	0.22
Indian Tamil	−0.11	0.57	0.89	0.51	0.84
Type of degree					
Bachelor of Commerce	0.01	0.21	1.01	0.21	0.97
BA (Economics)	0.26	0.33	1.30	0.43	0.43
BA (History)	0.15	0.36	1.16	0.42	0.68
BA (Sinhala)	−0.30	0.41	0.74	0.30	0.47
BA (Geography)	−0.17	0.32	0.84	0.27	0.59

(continued)

Table 5.2   Association of Socioeconomic Variables with Unemployment Duration (Logistic Hazard Model) *(Continued)*

Variable	Coefficient	Standard error	Odds ratio	Standard error	P > z
BA (English)	0.15	0.97	1.16	1.12	0.88
BA (Demography)	−0.81	0.39	0.45	0.17	0.04
BA (Political Science)	−0.80	0.37	0.45	0.17	0.03
BA (Journalism)	−0.63	0.41	0.53	0.22	0.13
BA (General)	−0.09	0.61	0.92	0.56	0.89
Mother's education					
Passed year 6 /grade 5	1.00	0.50	2.71	1.34	0.05
Passed year 13 / GCE (A-levels) HNCE	1.24	0.38	3.44	1.30	0.00
Passed GAQ/GSQ and above	0.70	0.33	2.01	0.66	0.04
Marital status					
Married	−0.20	0.15	0.82	0.12	0.18
Widowed	0.29	1.09	1.34	1.46	0.79
Divorced	0.24	1.05	1.27	1.33	0.82
Separated	−0.77	0.99	0.46	0.46	0.44
Minutes from home to a main road	−0.03	0.01	0.97	0.01	0.00
Self-assessed health status					
Very good health	0.04	0.31	1.05	0.32	0.88
Good health	0.07	0.30	1.08	0.32	0.81
Fair health	−0.40	0.38	0.67	0.25	0.29
Cluster variable– Graduates of year 2000	−1.20	0.58	0.30	0.17	0.04
Jobsnet registered	−0.08	0.19	0.93	0.18	0.69
Year 2002	−0.54	0.19	0.58	0.11	0.00
Year 2003	0.48	0.17	1.62	0.28	0.01
Year 2004	4.37	0.28	79.19	21.93	0.00
Constant	−1.47	0.49			0.00
Number of observations: 1,545					
Prob > chi²					0.00
Log likelihood ratio					−649.66

Source: Authors' calculations.
Note: See table 5.1 for definition of terms.

a lower relative likelihood of being employed in the formal private sector compared with the public sector (table 5.3). Seventy-one percent of the graduates obtained their first job either after applying for an advertised vacancy or after registering with Jobsnet, 24 percent were told about the job by someone they knew, and 5 percent were offered a job by someone

Table 5.3 Association of Socioeconomic Variables with Employment Sector (Multinomial Logit Regression)

	Dependent variable = Employment sector (Base = Public sector)				
	Coefficient	Standard error	Relative risk ratio	Standard error	P > z
Private sector with unions					
Gender–Male	0.90	0.26	2.47	0.64	0.00
Ethnicity					
Sri Lankan Tamil	0.82	0.36	2.28	0.81	0.02
Moor	-0.30	0.40	0.74	0.30	0.46
Indian Tamil	-0.26	1.21	0.77	0.93	0.83
Type of degree					
Bachelor of Commerce	0.02	0.36	1.02	0.37	0.95
BA (Economics)	0.51	0.56	1.66	0.94	0.37
BA (History)	-0.47	0.75	0.62	0.46	0.53
BA (Sinhala)	0.05	0.69	1.05	0.72	0.94
BA (Geography)	-0.37	0.61	0.69	0.43	0.55
BA (English)	1.80	1.30	6.06	7.87	0.17
BA (Demography)	-0.41	0.72	0.66	0.48	0.57
BA (Political Science)	-0.56	0.66	0.57	0.37	0.39
BA (Journalism)	-0.26	0.73	0.77	0.57	0.72
BA (General)	-2.45	1.10	0.09	0.10	0.03
Mother's education					
Passed year 6 /grade 5	0.98	0.81	2.66	2.16	0.23
Passed year 13 / GCE (A-levels) HNCE	0.90	0.63	2.46	1.54	0.15
Passed GAQ/GSQ and above	0.10	0.56	1.11	0.62	0.85
Marital status					
Married	-0.36	0.26	0.69	0.18	0.16
Widowed	0.89	1.59	2.44	3.86	0.58

(continued)

Table 5.3 Association of Socioeconomic Variables with Employment Sector (Multinomial Logit Regression) *(Continued)*

	Dependent variable = Employment sector (Base = Public sector)				
	Coefficient	Standard error	Relative risk ratio	Standard error	P > z
Divorced	−32.00	$1.58*10^7$	0.00	0.00	1.00
Separated	0.42	1.42	1.53	2.17	0.77
Minutes from home to a main road	−0.05	0.02	0.95	0.02	0.00
Self-assessed health status					
Very good health	0.24	0.56	1.27	0.71	0.67
Good health	0.99	0.55	2.68	1.46	0.07
Fair health	−0.80	0.81	0.45	0.36	0.32
Cluster variable—Graduates of year 2000	2.46	1.02	11.65	11.93	0.02
Jobsnet registered	−0.08	0.34	0.92	0.31	0.82
Constant	−1.67	0.82			0.04
Private sector without unions					
Gender—Male	0.26	0.27	1.29	0.35	0.33
Ethnicity					
Sri Lankan Tamil	−0.37	0.47	0.69	0.33	0.44
Moor	−1.04	0.51	0.35	0.18	0.04
Indian Tamil	−0.36	1.18	0.69	0.82	0.76
Type of degree					
Bachelor of Commerce	0.19	0.38	1.22	0.46	0.61
BA (Economics)	0.11	0.63	1.11	0.70	0.87

BA (History)	0.45	0.58	1.57	0.91	0.43
BA (Sinhala)	−0.59	0.84	0.56	0.47	0.48
BA (Geography)	0.51	0.53	1.67	0.88	0.33
BA (English)	−32.07	$1.88*10^7$	0.00	0.00	1.00
BA (Demography)	−0.47	0.72	0.62	0.45	0.51
BA (Political Science)	−1.85	1.08	0.16	0.17	0.09
BA (Journalism)	−0.33	0.72	0.72	0.52	0.65
BA (General)	−0.43	1.25	0.65	0.81	0.73
Mother's education					
Passed year 6 /grade 5	0.37	0.79	1.45	1.15	0.64
Passed year 13 / GCE (A-levels) HNCE	−0.17	0.65	0.84	0.54	0.79
Passed GAQ/GSQ and above	−0.28	0.53	0.76	0.40	0.60
Marital status					
Married	−0.13	0.26	0.88	0.23	0.63
Widowed	−32.03	$1.82*10^7$	0.00	0.00	1.00
Divorced	−32.82	$1.79*10^7$	0.00	0.00	1.00
Separated	−32.42	$1.41*10^7$	0.00	0.00	1.00
Minutes from home to a main road	−0.02	0.01	0.98	0.01	0.16
Self-assessed health status					
Very good health	0.45	0.61	1.56	0.95	0.46
Good health	0.75	0.60	2.11	1.26	0.21
Fair health	1.08	0.67	2.95	1.97	0.11

(continued)

Table 5.3 Association of Socioeconomic Variables with Employment Sector (Multinomial Logit Regression) *(Continued)*

	Dependent variable = Employment sector (Base = Public sector)				
	Coefficient	Standard error	Relative risk ratio	Standard error	P > z
Cluster variable–Graduates					
of year 2000	−0.31	1.21	0.74	0.89	0.80
Jobsnet registered	−0.69	0.32	0.50	0.16	0.03
Constant	−0.77	0.85			0.37
Number of observations: 515					
Prob > chi²					0.00
Log likelihood ratio					−423.78

Source: Authors' calculations.

Note: Hausman test of IIA assumption: Odds are independent of other alternatives (P > chi² = 1.00); ethnicity, base = Sinhala; education type, base = bachelor of business administration; mother's education, base = passed year 4 /grade 3; marital status, base = Never married; self-assessed health, base = excellent health.

they knew. Before 2005, that is, before the government recruitment drive, 8 percent were given the job, and 38 percent were told about the job, by someone they knew.

Female graduates had a 60 percent lower likelihood of being employed in the formal private sector than they did in the public sector, although Blinder-Oaxaca decomposition failed to reject equal gender-wage status at the 10 percent level. Moreover, graduates residing in remote locations were shown to be at a disadvantage: each additional minute to a main road increased the hazard of unemployment by 3 percent. Graduates from lower socioeconomic groups were also unemployed for longer periods of time than those who were more socially connected. The result was robust, that is, statistically significant in both duration models.

Value of the Field of Study

Our results also show that the field of study significantly affects employability and earning capacity (tables 5.3 and 5.4). A graduate holding a demography or political science degree had longer unemployment duration. A graduate with a specialization in history was likely to obtain a monthly salary that was 62 percent less than that of a graduate with a business administration degree in the formal private sector ($p = 0.01$). The comparative differences were markedly reduced in the public sector.

Impact of Labor Market Programs

Ninety-six percent of the graduates were aware of Tharuna Aruna, 62 percent contemplated applying to the program, and only 16 percent of them participated. Among the participants, the vast majority—79 of them—obtained placement in government organizations; only 3 were hired by private sector organizations. This is contradictory to Tharuna Aruna's primary objective of promoting employment in the private sector for the unemployed. However, all participants were able to keep their jobs with the same employers beyond the period subsidized by the program.

The government recruitment drive primarily attracted the unemployed, especially the ones who were in "long-term" unemployment (log-rank test for survival estimates: $p > chi^2 = 0.00$). Of the graduates who were recruited through this campaign, 85 percent were jobless before the campaign. Around 10 percent shifted from jobs in the private sector without unions, 3 percent from the private sector with unions, and 2 percent from the public sector.

Table 5.4 Association of Socioeconomic Variables with Gross Salary of the First Job (Selectivity Corrected Regression)

	Public sector			Private sector with trade unions			Private sector without unions		
	Coefficient	Standard error	$P > z$	Coefficient	Standard error	$P > z$	Coefficient	Standard error	$P > z$
Gender–Male	0.04	0.02	0.03	-0.01	0.12	0.95	0.06	0.20	0.75
Type of degree									
Bachelor of commerce	-0.05	0.03	0.05	-0.25	0.13	0.06	0.17	0.20	0.40
BA (Economics)	-0.06	0.05	0.27	-0.18	0.21	0.37	-0.14	0.42	0.75
BA (History)	-0.10	0.06	0.10	-0.97	0.34	0.00	-0.06	0.35	0.87
BA (Sinhala)	-0.09	0.05	0.09	-0.70	0.41	0.09	-0.06	0.33	0.86
BA (Geography)	-0.07	0.04	0.12	-0.50	0.30	0.10	-0.19	0.36	0.60
BA (English)	0.00	0.04	1.00	-0.12	0.17	0.48			—
BA (Demography)	-0.12	0.06	0.04	-0.21	0.28	0.46	-0.51	0.42	0.22
BA (Political Science)	-0.07	0.05	0.15	-0.12	0.32	0.72	0.59	0.60	0.32
BA (Journalism)	-0.10	0.06	0.08	0.38	0.35	0.28	0.87	0.62	0.16
BA (General)	-0.05	0.03	0.08	-0.05	0.16	0.78	-0.08	0.27	0.78
Ethnicity									
Sri Lankan Tamil	0.02	0.03	0.61	0.05	0.13	0.71	-0.15	0.38	0.70
Moor	0.05	0.07	0.48	-0.13	0.19	0.52	-1.07	0.67	0.11
Indian Tamil	0.01	0.04	0.87	0.01	0.25	0.96	-0.09	0.41	0.83

Control variables—Year of recruitment

Year 2000	0.24	0.13	0.06	−0.39	0.42	0.35	−0.37	0.30	0.22
Year 2001	0.20	0.14	0.14	0.05	0.40	0.89	−1.03	0.46	0.02
Year 2002	0.00	0.13	1.00	0.00	0.40	1.00	−1.13	0.41	0.01
Year 2003	0.11	0.13	0.43	−0.29	0.39	0.46	−0.81	0.49	0.10
Year 2004	0.14	0.13	0.28	−0.13	0.39	0.75	−0.64	0.45	0.16
Year 2005	0.10	0.13	0.46	−0.23	0.40	0.56	−0.34	0.44	0.44
Constant	9.43	0.15	0.00	10.29	0.58	0.00	11.42	1.56	0.00
Number of observations:		317			110			86	
Prob > F		0.00			0.00			0.00	
R^2		0.21			0.33			0.47	

Source: Authors' calculations.

Note: Ethnicity, base = Sinhala; education type, base = bachelor of business administration; control variables—year of recruitment, base = 1999.

Choice of Sector of Work and Job Satisfaction

Job satisfaction was higher in the public sector, even though the wages were the lowest among the three categories (see table 5.5). Because our survey was conducted within a year after the government recruitment drive, the result that the public sector has the highest job satisfaction rate should be interpreted with caution—the newly recruited graduates may not yet have been fully exposed to the organization's culture. The public sector offered lower working hours (a weekly average of 35 hours compared with 46 hours in private firms) and greater stability in the form of a higher share of permanent employment contracts and contributions to old-age saving schemes (tables 5.6 and 5.7). Only 8 percent of graduates taking jobs in the public sector were unhappy with their job, compared

Table 5.5   Gross Salary by Employment Sector (First Job)
Sri Lankan rupees

Sector	Number of observations	Mean	Standard deviation	Min	Max
Public	318	11,577	1,693	7,000	17,500
Private, with unions	111	18,098	8,590	5,000	50,000
Private, without unions	86	14,445	8,632	4,500	41,000

Source: Authors' calculations.

Table 5.6   Type of Contract by Employment Sector (First Job)

Sector	Permanent	Temporary	Casual	Total
Public	316	2	0	318
Private, with unions	101	9	0	110
Private, without unions	51	35	1	87
Total	468	46	1	1515

Source: Authors' calculations.

Table 5.7   Contribution Status of the Employer to Employees Provident Fund/ Employees Trust Fund by Employment Sector (First Job)

Sector	Yes	No	Not relevant	Do not know	Total
Public	290	23	2	3	318
Private, with unions	97	13	0	1	111
Private, without unions	44	40	1	2	87
Total	431	76	3	6	516

Source: Authors' calculations.

with 18 percent and 43 percent of those taking jobs in the private formal and informal sector, respectively. The mean gross salary for the first job in the private formal sector was 56 percent higher than in the public sector and 25 percent higher than in the informal sector, but working hours were also longer. Wage per hour in the formal private sector was thus 17 percent higher, and in the informal sector 7 percent lower, than in the public sector.

Of the graduates who changed jobs, none moved out of the public sector. Forty-one percent of the moves were from the informal sector to the public sector, 20 percent from the informal to formal private sector, and 14 percent from the formal private sector to the public sector, with the balance consisting of job changes within a particular sector. Graduates changed jobs primarily to increase income (61 percent) and reduce work hours (21 percent). Thirteen percent said their new job required less effort and provided more vacation. Ninety-six percent of the changes were associated with an increment of income, with a mean increment being SL Rs 4,687 per month. Sixty-nine percent of the changes were associated with a reduction in the number of work hours, with a mean reduction of 14 hours per week. Of the graduates who shifted from the private to the public sector, only 5 percent experienced a wage reduction, and this 5 percent shifted from the private informal sector.

Conclusions and Policy Implications

This chapter presents evidence showing that Sri Lankan graduates of state universities encounter severe difficulties in finding employment, with a significant proportion experiencing long unemployment spells following their graduation. Other findings can be summarized as follows:

- Social status affects the ability of graduates to secure employment, with rural young people lacking such contacts being particularly affected. This result can be interpreted in two ways. First, formal private sector employers may prefer graduates from urban areas because these graduates have a better command of English (we could not test this argument because information about the language skills of graduates was not available). Alternatively it may be correct, as some young Sri Lankans claim, that privileged, elite families with access and control over resources use their social and political networks to promote employment of their children. In this case, students of lower social status also face weaker incentives to participate in higher levels of education, because their reduced chance of obtaining adequate employment lowers the expected returns from schooling.

- Women face more difficulties than men in finding employment in the formal private sector. Because our model could not control for unobservable heterogeneity pertaining to motivation and other factors affecting productivity, this finding cannot be taken as a proof of discrimination against women.

- The choice of the field of study matters, with graduates of certain fields facing fewer employment opportunities and lower earnings.

- Government labor market programs strongly affect behavior and employment outcomes of graduates. The public sector recruitment campaign in 2005 proved extremely effective in providing jobs to unemployed graduates—in fact, it provided jobs to all graduates included in our sample who were still unemployed three years after their graduation. But this recruitment campaign absorbed a significant proportion of potential clients of the government's Tharuna Aruna hiring program, thus undermining that program's objective of increasing the placement of graduates in the private sector. In any event, almost all Tharuna Aruna participants were placed in the public sector, contrary to the program's stipulated objective.

- Sri Lankan graduates seem to prefer working in the public sector over the private sector, receiving lower pay but enjoying higher job security and nonwage benefits. However, because the average salary of the graduates included in our sample in the private sector was higher than in the public sector, our results may be driven by a selection process in which graduates with low productivity sought jobs in and were absorbed by the government sector.

These results render direct or indirect support to all three hypotheses maintained about the Sri Lankan unemployment. The skills mismatch hypothesis is confirmed by the finding that graduates of certain fields experienced longer unemployment durations and were paid lower wages. The effectiveness of the government recruitment campaign confirmed that waiting for public sector jobs makes good sense and thus must affect employment decisions of jobseekers. And the institutional hypothesis is given an indirect confirmation, if one is willing to accept the proposition that employers use social networks to overcome costs imposed by rigid employment protection legislation.

These findings lead to three key policy implications. First, in view of the low employability of graduates in certain fields, it would be advisable for universities to review and adjust their enrollment quotas based on observed labor market success of graduates.

Second, the government needs to standardize its recruitment and should avoid haphazard recruitment drives that undermine other labor market support programs, reduce incentives for youth to take nongovernmental jobs, and contribute to queuing for government jobs. Recruitment of graduates through competitive examinations and setting long-term hiring schedules based on human resource needs of the government—thus refraining from mass recruitments—will facilitate smooth functioning of the labor market support program; reorient young job seekers to search for jobs outside the public sector, thus increasing the pool of talents available to private employers; and ultimately improve productivity of the public sector as well as overall capacity of the economy.

Finally, these findings also provide support, albeit weak, to the recommendation to reduce excessive employment protection legislation embodied in the TEWA system. This support hinges on accepting the hypothesis that social and political networks are important to securing private sector employment.[2] The logic of the argument is as follows: if employment protection legislation is restrictive, formal private sector employers are reluctant to hire young, inexperienced workers because there is no information about their job performance. To hedge against the risk of hiring bad workers, these employers rely on their social networks when hiring young workers.

Annex A Characteristics of Respondents

Table A5.1   Distribution of Gender

Gender	Frequency	Percent
Male	227	43.91
Female	290	56.09
Total	517	100.00

Source: Authors' calculations.

Table A5.2   Distribution of Ethnicity

Ethnicity	Frequency	Percent
Sinhala	396	76.74
Sri Lankan Tamil	55	10.66
Indian Tamil	8	1.55
Moor	57	11.05
Total	516	100.00

Source: Authors' calculations.

Table A5.3   Distribution of Marital Status

Marital status	Frequency	Percent
Married	210	40.62
Never married	300	58.03
Widowed	2	0.39
Divorced	2	0.39
Separated	3	0.58
Total	517	100.00

Source: Authors' calculations.

Table A5.4   Distribution of Type of Education

Degree type	Frequency	Percent
Bachelor of business administration	79	15.28
Bachelor of commerce	169	32.69
BA (Economics)	29	5.61
BA (History)	26	5.03
BA (Sinhala)	20	3.87
BA (Geography)	36	6.96
BA (English)	3	0.58
BA (Demography)	24	4.64
BA (Political Science)	30	5.8
BA (Journalism)	21	4.06
BA (General)	80	15.47
Total	517	100.00

Source: Authors' calculations.

Table A5.5   Distribution of Mother's Education

Mother's education	Frequency	Percent
Passed year 3 /grade 2	7	1.35
Passed year 4 /grade 3	5	0.97
Passed year 5 /grade 4	30	5.8
Passed year 6 /grade 5	30	5.8
Passed year 7 /grade 6	10	1.93
Passed year 8 /grade 7	38	7.35
Passed year 9 /grade 8	72	13.93
Passed year 10 /grade 9	67	12.96
Passed year 11 / GCE (O-levels) NCGE	145	28.05
Passed year 12 /grade 11	16	3.09
Passed year 13 / GCE (A-levels) HNCE	61	11.8
Passed GAQ/GSQ	12	2.32
Degree	14	2.71
Postgraduate degree /diploma	4	0.77
No schooling	6	1.16
Total	517	100.00

Source: Authors' calculations.
Note: National Certificate of General Education.

Notes

1. For example, a Sri Lankan worker with 20 years of experience is awarded severance pay equal to 39 months of wages, in contrast to the average severance pay of 16.3 months in other Asian countries, 11.9 months in Latin America, 7.1 months in Africa, 6.4 months in developed countries, and 4.4 months in transition countries (World Bank 2007).

2. This argument is strengthened by the finding of Hettige, Mayer, and Salih (2005, p. 61) that 64 percent of young workers reported that they were recruited through social and family networks, and connections were particularly important for employment in the formal private sector, where the correct social connections and a shared cultural ideology were seen as basic requirements.

References

Babatunde, A., P. Orazem, and M. Vodopivec. 2009. "Firing Cost and Firm Size: A Study of Sri Lanka's Severance Pay System." Social Protection Discussion Paper Series no. 0916. World Bank, Washington, DC.

Bourguignon, F., M. Fournier, and M. Gurgand. 2007. "Selection Bias Corrections Based on the Multinomial Logit Model: Monte Carlo Comparisons." *Journal of Economic Surveys* 21 (1): 174–205.

DCS (Department of Census and Statistics). 2007. *Sri Lanka Labour Force Survey Final Report: 2006.* Colombo. http://www.statistics.gov.lk/HIES/HIES2006 _07Website/Publications/HIES200607Final%20ReportWeb%20.pdf (December 22, 2008).

———. 2008. *Household Income and Expenditure Survey: 2006/07 Final Report.* Colombo. http://www.statistics.gov.lk/samplesurvey/2006-annual1% 20reduce%20file%20%20size.pdf (December 22, 2008).

Dubin, J. A., and D. L. McFadden. 1984. "An Econometric Analysis of Residential Electric Appliance Holdings and Consumption." *Econometrica* 52: 345–62.

Heltberg, R., and M. Vodopivec. 2008. "Sri Lanka: Unemployment, Job Security and Labor Market Reform." *Peradeniya Journal of Economics* 2 (1–2): 1–41.

Hettige, S. T., and M. Mayer. 2002. *Sri Lankan Youth: Challenges and Responses.* Colombo: Friedrich Ebert Stiftung.

Hettige, S. T., M. Mayer, and M. Salih. 2005. "School-to-Work-Transition of Youth in Sri Lanka." International Labour Organization, Employment Policies Unit, Geneva.

Presidential Commission on Youth. 1990. *Report of the Presidential Commission on Youth,* Colombo: Government Publication Bureau.

Rama, M. 2003. "The Sri Lankan Unemployment Problem Revisited." *Review of Development Economics* 7: 510–25.

Thangarajah, C. Y. 2002. "Youth, Conflict, and Social Transformation in Sri Lanka." In *Sri Lankan Youth: Challenges and Responses,* ed. S. T. Hettige and M. Mayer, pp. 177–215. Colombo: Friedrich Ebert Stiftung.

World Bank. 1999. "Sri Lanka: A Fresh Look at Unemployment." Report 19609-CE, Washington, DC.

———. 2007. "Sri Lanka: Strengthening Social Protection." Report 38197-LK, Washington, DC.

CHAPTER 6

Youth Mobility and Overseas Migration in Sri Lanka

Asha Abeyasekera

This study investigates youth mobility and migration in the overall context of Sri Lanka's international labor migratory patterns and trends for the specific purpose of exploring employment opportunities for youth.[1] Its main focus is on the availability of *productive* overseas employment opportunities for youth.[2] The chapter attempts to identify key characteristics of Sri Lankan migrants, the trends and patterns associated with migration from the country, and the impact of migration on individuals. It discusses policies that affect migration and provides recommendations based on key findings. For its data, the chapter relies primarily on a desk review of available literature on migration complemented by interviews with key informants.

Migration for employment at the macroeconomic level can no longer be considered a temporary phenomenon. In Asia internal migration is driven by the ever-expanding "megacity," which is the center of wealth accumulation and private consumption. As the agriculture sector contracts, people move continuously and inevitably from the "periphery" to the "center." With globalization and the liberalization of trade, international migration has become a permanent characteristic of the global labor force. In Sri Lanka, rural-to-urban migration has been marginal until recently because of the pro-rural policies of successive governments

(Hettige and Mayer 2002:3). The majority of Sri Lankans who migrate overseas do so for short periods of time to ease economic burdens but almost always with a hope of return (Kottegoda 2004). So while migration is a key feature of Sri Lanka's labor market, at the individual level migration is mostly a temporary phenomenon. Policy formulation, therefore, must also carefully balance *national* issues and trends with the needs and concerns of *individual* citizens.

Based on the key findings, I argue that temporary overseas migration can be promoted as a viable employment option for youth. However, youth labor migration must be a clearly articulated strategy of Sri Lanka's employment policy and should not be an ad hoc, stopgap solution to youth unemployment. The state's promotion of overseas employment must be complemented by developments in the local labor market. If young people have to return to a state of indefinite unemployment, then promoting migration may be counterproductive because it would not address youth concerns but would instead result in further frustration and sense of isolation.

Definitions

Youth

The standard United Nations definition of youth is people ages 15 through 24. The International Labour Organization (ILO) follows the UN definition. Both organizations, however, recognize that the operational definition of youth varies widely from country to country depending on cultural, institutional, and political factors (Higgins 2007). In Sri Lanka the National Youth Survey defines youth as those ages 15 through 29 years. As in most industrial countries, the lower age limit corresponds to the statutory minimum school-leaving age. The upper limit of 29 years reflects several factors. One has to do with the average age of a university student. Sri Lankan students are usually 19 when they complete their secondary school education. The results of the General Certificate of Education Advance-level, or A-level, examination are usually released in the following year and university entrance is exclusively contingent on these results. This long lag time combined with a history of youth unrest, student strikes, and political instability in the country, which have all led to temporary closures of the universities, mean that a student's actual entry to university is often delayed for at least one or two years. Moreover, students are allowed to retake the A-level exams twice if they are interested in improving their aggregate score to be eligible for university entrance. As a result, by the time university students graduate and enter the job market they are usually between the ages of 24 and 27.

Cultural factors also influence conventional definitions of youth in Sri Lanka. A key differentiation is between unmarried and married youth. In general, if a young person is married, then he or she is considered to be an adult. When young people take on the responsibilities of running a family and bringing up children they are not considered youth by their communities; neither do they self-identify as youth. Several studies indicate that marital status is intimately tied to the motivation to migrate, especially for women who seek temporary overseas employment mainly for family survival; it is usually married women who migrate with the hope of improving their family's economic situation (Kottegoda 2004; Gamburd 2005). In formulating a policy for youth employment, therefore, it would be important to examine the motivating factors of unmarried youth as a separate category because their reasons for migrating are, most probably, different from those of their married counterparts.

Overseas Migration

Migration studies in general are influenced by several different discourses. The feminist critique points out the feminization of the international migrant labor force and the casualization of labor, where more people are hired on short-term contracts or for a daily wage, as key features of globalization. It critically examines the impact of female-dominated migration on the social fabric of sending countries and notes that the benefits of migration to receiving countries go largely unnoticed. The feminist critique also argues that labor regulations are inadequate, largely because poor women with little political power or voice constitute a majority of the migrant labor force. The rights discourse describes overseas employment undertaken by the people of poorer countries in the South as "3D" jobs—"dirty, dangerous, and degrading." It stresses the importance of protecting the civil, political, and economic rights of people, especially given the disappearing "rights culture" as a consequence of globalization and, more recently, the international war on terrorism. The popular discourse tends to be paternalistic, with discussions of protecting women by restricting their movements. Mainstream economic analyses discuss migration in purely macroeconomic terms: international migration provides a safety valve for relieving unemployment in the sending country while at the same time providing a major source of foreign exchange earnings for the economy through a regular flow of remittances. While benefits to the receiving countries are acknowledged, there is very little discussion in Sri Lanka on the impact of migrant workers on the receiving economies.

Key Features of the Migrant Labor Market

Internal Migration

In Sri Lanka a majority of the workers who migrate internally from rural areas to urban centers are employed in the informal sector in low-status, casual jobs mainly in the construction industry and in the free-trade zones (Hettige and Mayer 2002:3). The informal sector is characterized by low job security, low wages, poor working environment, little internal structure with arbitrary rules, and few benefits. Work in the free trade zones is predominantly female. Various forms of gender subordination characterize what is considered a "footloose" sector: the suppression of creativity stemming from assembly production and fragmentation; deskilling with no upgrades; low wages and long working hours; occupational health hazards with little or no compensation; the lack of trade unions; and job insecurity. Moreover, a lack of diversity characterizes the export sector in Sri Lanka; the three main sectors are food and beverages, tobacco, and textiles and garments, with the apparel industry accounting for 87.5 percent of the total export industry (Jayaweera 2001a, 2001b).

Overseas Migration

There are several types of international migration: seasonal, project-tied, contract, temporary, and highly skilled or professional (ILO 2005:24). The contract labor migrants to the Middle East since the early 1980s differ from the economic migrants of the preceding decades. Before economic liberalization in the late 1970s, overseas migration was undertaken by highly skilled professionals whose migration tended to be long-term or permanent (Kottegoda 2004:179). In the decade following World War II professionals such as doctors, accountants, and university professors began to leave Sri Lanka in search of better economic opportunities. New political policies in the early 1970s forced English-speaking middle-class businessmen as well as middle-class professionals to migrate to Australia, the United Kingdom, the United States, and Canada (Waxler-Morrison 2004). Today, overseas migration from Sri Lanka is dominated by low-skilled workers on fixed-term contracts, usually of two to five years in length, mainly to oil-rich Middle East countries (SLBFE 2007).

Local studies on international migration for employment focus on three main characteristics: the preponderance of low-skilled female migrants, who account for 65 percent of the total stock of overseas contract workers; the significant contribution overseas migrants make to the economy through remittances; and exploitative practices that typify all stages of the migratory process. From a macroeconomic perspective, the main beneficiary of migration is seen as the sending countries' economy, which gains valuable foreign exchange for its balance of payments. Migrant workers' contributions have been estimated to be as much as one-third of Sri Lanka's national savings (Rodrigo and Jayatissa 1989). Benefits to the receiving countries' labor market, whose labor shortages are filled by migrants, are also discussed in these studies, but to a lesser degree. From the perspective of individuals, migration is mainly undertaken as a means of family survival and a way out of poverty. While some migrants achieve a certain level of socioeconomic security through savings, many others find themselves in a cycle of remigration where they return home only to migrate within a couple of years (Kottegoda 2004).

A Statistical Overview of Overseas Migration in Sri Lanka

Foreign employment is the second largest earner of foreign exchange in Sri Lanka. Private remittances for 2006 amounted to 241,816 million rupees (SL Rs), of which 57.1 percent were from migrant workers in the Middle East. In fact, 95 percent of employees working abroad are in the Middle East, where Saudi Arabia, Kuwait, the United Arab Emirates (UAE), Qatar, and Lebanon are the major labor-receiving countries, capturing 83 percent of Sri Lanka's export labor market. The number of departures for employment abroad steadily increased until 2006, when there was a 12 percent decrease. Fifty-two percent of the departures in 2006 were women, 89.3 percent of whom worked as housemaids.

It is estimated that about 1.5 million Sri Lankans are currently overseas for employment (table 6.1). Approximately half of those are housemaids. The skilled and unskilled categories combined account for another 600,000, or 42.3 percent, of the estimated stock of overseas contract workers. Professional, mid-level, and clerical workers account for only 8.7 percent of the total jobs filled.[3] Engineers, medical professionals, accountants, administrative staff, and teachers make up the majority of professional-level staff, and the mid-level workers are dominated by clerical and technically qualified subordinate staff. Construction workers, cooks, drivers, and mechanics form the majority of the skilled workers (SLBFE 2007).

In 2005 a total of 231,290 workers left for overseas employment, of whom 85,251, or 36.9 percent, were between the ages of 20 and 29.

Table 6.1   Estimated Stock of Sri Lankan Overseas Contract Workers by Manpower Levels, 2006

Category	Male	Female	Total	Percentage of total
Professional	10,750	2,536	13,286	0.9
Middle-level	33,250	9,500	42,750	3.0
Clerical and related	57,600	11,200	68,800	4.8
Skilled	222,750	101,225	323,975	22.4
Unskilled	210,640	76,810	287,450	19.9
Housemaid	0	711,446	711,446	49.1
Total	534,990	912,717	1,447,707	100

Source: SLBFE 2007.

Despite the significant numbers of youth migration, no specific analysis has yet been done on the youth component of the migrant labor force in Sri Lanka. The percentage of departures in the age 19 and below category is extremely small. The age category of 15–19 is a problematic one. Although this age group forms part of the legitimate workforce, a majority of them (those 15 to 18) are also classified as children under the UN Child Rights Convention. An assumption has been made in this chapter that this group may not have all the necessary coping skills to survive the migratory experience and benefit from it and, therefore, for them migration should not be actively promoted as an option.

As table 6.2 shows, women constitute more than half of the total numbers in each age group. Waxler-Morrison (2004) estimated that 80 percent of female migrants are married. An ILO study published in 1989 estimated that 66–72 percent of Sri Lankan female migrants were married and that 60 percent of those married had at least one child (Rodrigo and Jayatissa 1989:256). As mentioned in the introduction, many women seek overseas employment as a family survival strategy. Therefore any analysis of the youth category would require a comparison between married and unmarried youth.

In 2005 almost 42,000 Sri Lankans left to do unskilled work overseas. Of this number, more than half of the jobs were filled by migrants in the 20–29 age group. While the overall percentage of migration in the professional and mid-level categories is low, the percentage of young people seeking employment in these categories is even lower. The lack of qualifications and experience may be one of the more obvious reasons. It would be important, however, to investigate this phenomenon before migration is actively promoted among youth. A migrant labor

Table 6.2   Departure for Foreign Employment by Age Group and Sex, 2005

Age groups	Total departures	Share of total (%)	Male	Share of age group (%)	Female	Share of age group (%)
19 and below	1,311	0.6	416	31.7	895	68.3
20–29	85,251	36.9	38,843	45.6	46,408	54.4
30–39	74,548	32.2	22,638	30.4	51,910	69.6
40–49	49,843	21.6	14,516	29.1	35,327	70.9
50 and above	8,511	3.7	3,943	46.3	4,568	53.7
Not identified	11,826	5.1	7,757	65.6	4,069	34.4
Total	231,290	100.0	88,113	38.1	143,177	61.9

Source: SLBFE 2007.

market driven by employment agencies and the lack of a clear state strategy to promote employment abroad seem to have resulted in sparse information available to the general public regarding available job opportunities abroad. All migrant laborers are compelled to go through a private agency that coordinates their travel, work visas, and other logistical arrangements. It is these agencies that most hopeful migrants approach in search of overseas employment. The SLBFE is only a regulatory body, but it does not regulate or monitor agency fees, resulting in widespread irregularities.

Most female migrants in the 20–29 age group (86 percent) go to work as housemaids (table 6.3). The number of female migrants in the other job categories is significantly lower. Moreover, female who migrate to do housework make up nearly 32 percent of total departures in this age group. Women account for 25 percent of the skilled workers in this age group leaving for overseas employment, but only 5 percent of female migrants in this age group fall into this category.

Study Limitations and Research Gaps

Because the objective of this study is to investigate youth mobility and migration for the specific purpose of exploring employment opportunities for youth, it is important to point out some of the main limitations of the desk review of existing literature.

First, although the key features, trends, and patterns of overseas migration for employment have been studied in depth, youth as an analytical category do not feature in any of the existing studies in Sri Lanka. It is important, therefore, to develop a profile of the young people who migrate

Table 6.3 Departure for Foreign Employment of 20–29 Age Group by Job Category and Sex, 2005

| | | | | Departures of 20–29 year old age group | | | | |
| | | Total | | Male | | Female | | |
Job category	Total departures	Number	Percent	Number	Percent	Number	Percent
Professional	1,421	227	16.0	193	85.0	34	15.0
Middle Level	8,042	2,542	31.6	2,308	90.8	234	9.2
Clerical and Related	7,742	3,430	44.3	3,104	90.5	326	9.5
Skilled	46,688	17,848	38.2	13,423	75.2	4,425	24.8
Unskilled	41,904	21,580	51.5	20,215	93.7	1,365	6.3
Housemaid	125,493	40,045	31.9	0	0.0	40,045	100.0

Source: SLBFE 2007.

for overseas employment to gain a better understanding of current trends and patterns of youth mobility. Even in the numerous studies about female migrants, especially housemaids, no differentiation is made between the married and unmarried groups for the purpose of analysis. Therefore there is little information about the motivations and aspirations of young, unmarried women. Although some inferences are possible, broad generalizations cannot be made because one's marital status, family obligations, and social standing all play a key role in influencing the motivation to migrate and the impact of migration.

Because overseas migration in Sri Lanka is predominantly female, studies usually highlight the significant role gender plays in the way migration is experienced. The experiences of men, however, have not been researched in depth either by feminist researchers or labor studies in Sri Lanka. Although men outnumber women in all job categories except housemaid (see table 6.1), there is very little information available on what types of jobs men take and the working conditions and regulations affecting their employment. In the popular discourse on migration in Sri Lanka, including media coverage, male migrant figures are virtually invisible. Political and media discussions on migration always focus on women, whether it be highlighting the return of an abused worker or the recent discussion on banning married women with children under five years of age from migrating in order to ensure child protection. Language plays a powerful role in the perpetuation of patriarchal ideology, where "ideas circulate in the social world as utterances, as expressions, as words which are spoken or inscribed" (Thompson 1984:2). Therefore, policy makers must be aware of social discrimination and take care not to perpetuate it through a paternalistic discourse about protecting women, and perhaps even young people, from the snares of migration, while simultaneously promoting migration as being economically beneficial for the individual and the economy.

Second, gender plays a primary role in determining how men and women experience discrimination. For example, there are many news reports of abused migrant women and women returned in body bags but few, if any, reports of abuse or sexual exploitation of male migrant workers. While housemaids are especially vulnerable because they are confined within homes and at the mercy of household members, there seems to be an unacknowledged bias regarding the vulnerability of men. Because the work men undertake is considered to be of a slightly higher status than that of housemaids, they are perceived to have fewer problems than women both in their workplace and at home, where there is more social acceptance of jobs such as drivers, car wash attendants, agriculture work in orchards, and assembly line work in electronic factories. However, men too are severely exploited by recruitment agencies (Gamburd 2005). Men are often deceived or misled by agencies and friends regarding work permits and find themselves facing visa issues once they arrive in a country. Many remain illegally, hoping to sort out their visa issues, and are forced to "live underground, like vermin." For example, one of the people interviewed for this study reported that many groups of men lived "underground" in Italy and the Republic of Korea and emerged to work only when state surveillance was low.

Third, the significant role Sri Lankan migrant labor plays in sustaining the economies of receiving countries must be studied in depth to highlight the consequences both of labor shortages and of work withdrawals, which can result when sending countries impose regulations to stymie certain groups from migrating or when better employment opportunities become available in the home country. This information can be used by the Sri Lankan government to develop more equitable bilateral agreements with receiving countries.

Key Findings

Coping Skills

A rhetoric of victimhood seems to pervade the discourse on Middle East migrants, especially women. One sees an equally negative lens used in youth studies. In addition to being perceived as rebels, young people are perceived as lacking in motivation and drive and reluctant to take up challenges, especially in the employment sphere, where they are seen as shying away from private sector and self-employment opportunities. "According to employers, graduates lacked the following skills which were expected of them: communication skills, inter-personal skills and general transferable skills such as adaptability, decision making and organization skills" (Gunawardena and others, as quoted in Perera 2005:9–10). Studies undertaken on migration have neglected to focus on the coping skills required to actually embark on the migratory process and work overseas. Young women and men leave their homes to work in a foreign country, where they have to adapt to a totally different culture. Housemaids work in the isolation of homes and have little contact with the outside world. Many workers have little access to social networks and leisure time. Some do find it difficult to cope. In retrospect, however, many view the experience as having a positive impact on their lives. People working overseas have to learn to communicate in a foreign language with their supervisors, follow instructions, and maintain relations with colleagues while coping with isolation, loneliness, and being away from family and friends. They also learn to manage money, make financial decisions regarding expenditures and savings, and find ways to remit the money they earn toward meeting the needs of their families at home. These are skills that generally are not taught but must be learned.

Although the poor working conditions and exploitation of migrant labor have been exposed, men rarely lodge complaints with the Sri Lanka Bureau of Foreign Employment (SLBFE). In 2004 the SLBFE received a total of 8,108 complaints, only 1,169 of which were made by men. Four types of complaints accounted for nearly 80 percent of all complaints received: lack of communication (26 percent); physical and sexual harassment (21 percent); nonpayment of wages (19 percent); and breach of employment contract (14 percent). While women complained most about lack of communication and physical and sexual harassment, men complained about breach of contract and nonpayment of wages (SLBFE 2005). The huge disparity in the numbers are perhaps attributable to the dominance of female migrant workers. It is also reasonable to surmise that men are not aware of the complaints mechanism or are unwilling to complain—women have been the main focus of awareness-raising initiatives by the SLBFE and nongovernmental organizations working in this field.

It is important, then, to record the coping skills and strategies employed by women and men while working abroad to highlight how they affect character formation and contribute to empowerment. An understanding of coping mechanisms is also essential when formulating a strategy for youth employment so that training and orientation programs can use the information in preparing young people for migration.

Causes and Motives for Migration: Push and Pull Factors

At the macro level the impetus to migrate has resulted from the economic and financial crisis brought on by structural adjustment policies imposed in the 1980s and the transition to a market-driven economy. The crisis was then exacerbated by the political conflicts (ILO 2005:12). In Sri Lanka it is the population considered to be economically inactive that seeks jobs overseas, usually for a limited period of time. As many as two-fifths of migrants are from poor households, which helps explain the decision to migrate (Central Bank 2003).

The sparse research on youth mobility and migration makes it difficult to understand in depth the motivations for migration and whether overseas employment has met and can meet the aspirations of youth. However, some existing studies suggest that young people are willing to migrate mainly for economic gain for themselves and their families. The ILO Inception Report on Youth Employment states that parents encourage migration as a way for their children to improve their quality of life through access to a wider range of employment opportunities (2004:39). The National Youth Survey conducted in 2000 reported that almost half of those surveyed wanted to migrate because they felt the situation in the country was getting worse (Hettige 2002:37). According to one of our interviewees, a significant population of young Muslim women migrated to the Middle East to save money for their dowries. While loneliness, homesickness, and social isolation often characterize the on-site experience of migrant workers, for young people migration may allow a new sense of freedom. The absence of social inhibitors such as authority figures, peers, and relatives usually provides an opportunity for young people to experiment and create alternative lifestyles (Asian Migrant Centre 2004:2). But it can sometimes lead to high-risk behavior and make young people vulnerable to HIV-AIDS and other sexually transmitted diseases. Therefore, a promotional strategy should present overseas employment as an opportunity to explore while educating young people about potential risks. A media campaign can focus on the positive impact migration can have on the character formation of youth. The desire for freedom, economic independence, and the ability to help one's family may be motivating factors that can be used to promote migration.

In his concept paper "Youth: Addressing the Absences," Sasanka Perera reflects on key areas that existing research on youth in Sri Lanka has neglected. Perera notes that adolescence as "a period of wandering and exploration" is absent from the analyses (2004:3). It is important to consider to what extent the Western theoretical frameworks that Perera is referring to explain the behavior of youth in Sri Lanka and then to pay attention to the deviations. While the desire for independence is considered synonymous, even in Sri Lanka, with adolescence and youth, these desires must be analyzed within the context of cultural practices and norms. The National Youth Survey found that economic dependence was high among youth in Sri Lanka. Only 7 percent of women and 25 percent of men considered themselves economically independent; 85 percent of women and 61.7 percent of men relied on parents for basic material needs (Hettige 2002:18). Further investigations must be done to explore the cultural underpinnings of this trend, before an employment promotion strategy, especially one involving overseas employment, is developed. It is noteworthy that while young women seem to be more dependent than young men on family support, once they are married they shoulder the primary burden of the household survival (Kottegoda 2004).

Developing skills. Youth dependency may stem from the lack of viable employment opportunities both in the state and private sectors. The mismatch between what is taught in the current education system and the skills sought by employers has led to high unemployment rates among educated youth. The private sector is promoted as the "engine of growth," but it has failed to absorb even qualified university graduates, compelling the government to create jobs for nearly 40,000 unemployed graduates. The private sector actively rejects qualified university graduates who lack English language skills and favors English-speaking, and sometimes less-qualified, students over those from the national university system. Even special programs designed to encourage employment in the private sector, such as Tharuna Aruna, have had limited impact (Kelegama 2007:66).

Given the current institutional barriers facing youth, promoting temporary overseas migration must be undertaken with extreme caution. If Sri Lanka is to take advantage of knowledge and skills gained overseas, employment opportunities must be made available for returning youth. These opportunities should include the use of skills and experience gained to transition into careers in the public and private sectors along with self-employment and cooperative entrepreneur programs. In addition, in developing migration as a strategy for youth employment, mid- to long-term labor projections must be made of Sri Lanka's main receiving countries and those projections compared with a detailed profile of unemployed youth in Sri Lanka, taking into consideration sex, education levels, and location (urban, rural, or estate; home district). These projections should then be used to develop a strategy for skills training and development that matches likely employer demand. This training should become part of the curriculum in existing vocational training institutes and centers. A similar process could be used to develop training programs for Sri Lankan youth looking for employment within the country.

Female migrants. For a majority of female migrants, employment abroad is primarily a family survival strategy. Saving for the education of children, the building of a house, or starting a business are three of the main factors motivating women to seek work overseas (ILO 2005:11). Kottegoda's study of the urban poor reveals that while migration is undertaken as a means of social mobility, for most it remains a survival strategy. Reasons for migration include getting out of debt, buying land, and building a house (Kottegoda 2004). Gamburd's study indicates that saving money to educate their children and provide dowries for themselves or their daughters are two of the main motivating factors for overseas migration (Gamburd 2005:97). The decision-making process for women includes weighing financial necessity and household improvements against separation from family, taking out loans, and the availability of alternative arrangements for childcare (Gamburd 2005:97). While many women find it necessary to migrate to ensure better marriage prospects or a better standard of living, some also migrate to escape discrimination, domestic violence, and problematic relationships (Kottegoda 2003).

A majority of female migrants have not worked outside their home and so have little or no work experience when they migrate; upon their return they do not usually enter the labor force (Waxler-Morrison 2004:96). Female migrants, therefore, are said to belong to the "voluntary unemployed" category who take up overseas migration for a short period of time (Rodrigo and Jayatissa 1989). I would argue that such a classification fails to recognize the gender bias inherent in the local labor market, which, intertwined with a patriarchal and class-based social system, actively discriminates against women, preventing them from achieving economic empowerment or social mobility. Lower wages and poor working conditions coupled with lower-status jobs mean that women are reluctant to enter the labor force. Internal migration for domestic work is highly stigmatized by low pay and the perception that all domestic workers are sexually harassed. Higher salaries and greater distances mean that domestic work abroad carries less social stigma (Gamburd 2005:103).

Impact of Migration
Despite the victim rhetoric, some families do benefit from the migration experience and actually prosper economically. For individual female migrants, a certain level of economic empowerment is achieved through a stable income and individual control of money. However, the majority of women who work as housemaids and machine operators in garment factories do not acquire new skills or achieve upward mobility in occupation despite the hard work and long hours. Multiple periods of migration indicate that families are unable to pull themselves out of poverty. Gamburd's study of Sri Lankan migrants from a southern village also

revealed that migration did not often break the cycle of poverty. While household consumption levels rose, only some families were able to achieve their goal of building a house (Kottegoda 2004:204). Waxler-Morrison (2004:245) also found that some migrants have been able to build a house and establish a business.

A majority of overseas migrants from Sri Lanka take up fixed-term contractual employment, usually for two years. A key interviewee commented that two years is a grossly inadequate period of time for migrants to save a substantial sum of money. He pointed out that the majority of migrant Sri Lankans working in the semiskilled and housemaid categories earn between $100 to $150 a month, or approximately SL Rs 10,000–15,000, which is not worth the effort. SL Rs 120,000–180,000 would just about cover the debt incurred in agency fees and ticket expenses, which means that individual savings probably amount to less than $2,000 at the end of the two-year period. However, many migrants are willing to accept low wages because of the subsistence mentality promoted by the state, wherein people are made to feel that they should be satisfied if they have enough for survival and are able to build their own house.

Children of female migrants are said to be the worst affected by the absence of their mothers. The school dropout rate is high among children of migrants, with a number of them getting involved in illegal activities including drugs and child prostitution (Waxler-Morrison 2004:244–45). While feminist researchers acknowledge the repercussions of a mother's absence on children's well-being, they also point out that fathers must take equal responsibility for childcare and that women should not be blamed exclusively for child neglect. It is interesting that the impact of male migration on families and children has not been explored.

A parasite culture is also said to develop in families of female migrants, where men remain unemployed and waste their wives' earnings on alcohol and other addictions (Dias and Jayasundere 2004:176). In this culture, the migrant's remittances are consumed rather than saved. Voluntary unemployment is a common response by the male head of household. In her study of an urban slum, Kottegoda (2004:205) found that the principle income earners of the household (husbands, brother, fathers) "often stop or lessen whatever income-earning activities they were engaged in once the woman's earnings reach their household." Waxler-Morrison (2004:244) argues that women's higher earnings undermine men's position as head of household and make men feel threatened. They often resort to drinking, gambling, and loaning funds to family and friends as a way of enhancing their status.

Finally, as noted earlier, migrant workers are also vulnerable to health problems, especially exposure to sexually transmitted diseases. A new sense of freedom and the absence of social inhibitors may compel some, especially young men, to get involved in relationships that make them vulnerable to HIV/AIDS or other illnesses.

An Agency-Driven Labor Market for Migration

The Sri Lanka Bureau of Foreign Employment was established in 1985 within the Ministry of Labor. Its main objectives are the promotion, development, and standardization of migrant labor rules, as well as providing protection for employees and their families. While the SLBFE has played an important role in implementing policies that protect migrant workers, especially housemaids, it has done little to explore and diversify overseas employment opportunities. Neither the ministry nor the bureau have formally studied the international labor market with the intention of determining what categories of available jobs could be filled by Sri Lanka's export labor force. A senior staff member of Migrant Services Center describes Sri Lanka's export labor market as being entirely at the mercy of employment agencies. Most of these agencies are interested only in profits that come from supplying workers for easy-to-fill vacancies such as housemaid positions. Moreover, poor uneducated men and women are willing to pay high fees to obtain employment and are easily exploited.

Many women use local networks, namely, neighbors and friends who have migrated, to explore their migration options through direct contacts. For those without such direct contacts, local agencies, although known to be untrustworthy, are the only channel for finding overseas jobs. Overseas recruitment agencies advertise vacancies in two main ways. Job orders are sent directly to the SLBFE, which then distributes these vacancies among selected agencies that are registered with it. For example, if an overseas construction company is looking to hire 30 drivers from Sri Lanka, the job order would be sent to the bureau. The bureau in turn would, say, distribute 10 vacancies each to three recruitment agencies, which would take on the responsibility of filling these vacancies. A percentage of the commission the agency receives from the employer is shared with the bureau. Overseas companies or recruitment agencies often have direct links with agencies in Sri Lanka and send job orders directly to them. Many activists working in this sector complain that the recruitment process is highly political and that favoritism and nepotism are rife both in the way job orders are distributed and in the ways in which workers are recruited. Many vacancies are said to be filled by politicians who have to return favors to their supporters.

Nearly two-thirds of Sri Lanka's overseas employment agencies are based in the Colombo district (SLBFE 2007). Private agencies do not seem to be interested in setting up offices in the rural and estate sectors and instead use agents to recruit from these areas. Nor do agencies seem motivated to diversify the overseas job market by expanding the range of jobs available to migrant hopefuls. Perhaps the lack of capacity to sort applications and conduct interviews is one of the main reasons that a majority of agencies avoid recruitment in categories other than semi-skilled and housemaid.

Agencies also do not have the motivation to carry out studies and projections of the international labor market. Tables 6.4–6.8 show vacancies and the number of departures for various job categories, illustrating the significant gap that exists between vacancies made available for Sri Lankan workers and actual numbers filled.

Table 6.4   Job Vacancies and Departures: Professional Level, 2004 (est.)

Profession	Vacancies	Departures	Percent vacancies filled
Accountants	535	55	10.3
Engineers, all categories	1,531	111	7.3
Managers, general	526	67	12.7

Source: SLBFE.
Note: This table is only a sampler and does not include all vacancies.

Table 6.5   Job Vacancies and Departures: Mid-Level Positions, 2004 (est.)

Profession	Vacancies	Departures	Percent vacancies filled
Artist	78	4	5.1
Assistant accountant	54	24	44.4
Industry designer	62	5	8.1
Foreman, general	1,169	81	6.9
Nurse, general	497	20	4.0
Nurse, professional	180	17	9.4
Teacher, general	368	48	13.0
Technician, air cooling and refrigeration	1,102	257	23.3
Technician, general	1,898	435	22.9

Source: SLBFE.
Note: This table is only a sampler and does not include all vacancies.

Table 6.6   Job Vacancies and Departures: Clerical and Related Jobs, 2004 (est.)

Profession	Vacancies	Departures	Percent vacancies filled
Accountant, assistant	112	26	23.2
Ward attendant	246	64	26.0
Beautician	429	32	7.5
Cashier, general	262	59	22.5
Checker, final	809	109	13.5
Clerk, general	729	146	20.0
Quality controller	710	67	9.4
Cook, continental	235	14	6.0
Lifeguard	117	10	8.5
Officer, security	710	153	21.5
Computer operator	445	19	4.3
Sales work	2,476	427	17.2
Supervisor, general	1,061	142	13.4
Storekeeper	677	177	26.1
Room boy	287	55	19.2
Waiter	2,064	317	15.4

Source: SLBFE.
Note: This table is only a sampler and does not include all vacancies.

Table 6.7   Job Vacancies and Departures: Skilled Positions, 2004 (est.)

Profession	Vacancies	Departures	Percent vacancies filled
Baker	1,397	445	31.9
Carpenter	6,618	1,370	20.7
Electrician	4,308	1,045	24.3
Plumber	3,640	597	16.4
Mason	5,719	1,368	23.9
Driver, heavy vehicles	4,944	2,002	40.5
Driver, house	15,361	2,971	19.3
Driver, light vehicles	12,705	3,886	30.6
Office boy	1,917	182	9.5
Tailor, female	2,078	294	14.1
Design maker	75	21	28.0
Embroiderer	9	1	11

Source: SLBFE.
Note: This table is only a sampler and does not include all vacancies.

While the percentage of young people ages 20–29 leaving for employment in the professional category is low, migration of young professionals could be encouraged by disseminating vacancy announcements in universities and other tertiary-level educational institutes.

Table 6.8   Job Vacancies and Departures: Unskilled Positions, 2004 (est.)

Profession	Vacancies	Departures	Percent vacancies filled
Cleaner	15,104	8,489	56.2
Houseboy	10,168	965	9.5
Helper, garment	964	198	20.5
Female janitor	50	—	0

Source: SLBFE.
Note: This table is only a sampler and does not include all vacancies.

Once again, although the percentage of youth migrating to take mid-level jobs is low, the number of unfilled vacancies indicates, perhaps, a lack of information on available vacancies. English language requirements are probably another main reason for vacancies remaining unfilled. Further research must be done to find out whether employers are looking for high language competency and for experienced applicants to fill these positions, or whether young people could use overseas migration to gain valuable employment experience and develop skills they could then bring into the Sri Lankan job market, especially in the private sector. However, the state will have to take responsibility for developing young people's English language skills and for providing some initial training in "soft" skills such as interpersonal relations to give young Sri Lankans a comparative advantage over those from other countries.

Even in the clerical and related jobs category, many vacancies go unfilled. Even if one were to assume that young people do not have the necessary skills to work as lifeguards, cooks, and cashiers, these jobs do not require long-term training for the acquisition of necessary skills. Many young people take courses in computers, bookkeeping, and beauty culture, but these vacancies too remain unfilled. It is also noteworthy that jobs as room boys, waiters, and beauticians go unfilled. A study should be done to find out if young men and women who have higher aspirations consider these jobs too demeaning and whether social class plays a role in the decision to migrate.

Many jobs go unfilled in the skilled category as well. Here it is obvious that the poor dissemination of information has been instrumental for unfilled vacancies in jobs like drivers, bakers, and office boys because male migrants account for 75 percent of the total stock of skilled overseas contract workers. More skilled male Sri Lankans might consider migrating for work if they knew these vacancies existed.

Even within the female migrant category, very little research has been done into employment opportunities for women other than domestic work. For example, the number of vacancies in the unskilled category include helpers in garment factories and janitorial work. In the skilled category, jobs as tailors, patternmakers, and embroiderers mostly remain unfilled. Even within the housemaid category, it is the "general housemaid" position that is filled, while only 94 of the 2,199 vacancies for babysitter/nanny are filled.

The filling of overseas jobs vacancies is not only at the mercy of agencies but also affected by political patronage. One of the interviewees pointed out that "MP Lists" that exist in most sectors also exist in migration, where vacancy announcements received by the Ministry of Foreign Affairs are first exclusively circulated to members of parliament of the ruling party, who then fill the vacancies with relatives and supporters desiring to migrate. Many of the more well-paid jobs in Japan, Korea, and Singapore are filled exclusively through political patronage, and none of these jobs are made available to the general workforce. That young people feel systems and structures in Sri Lanka are inherently unjust is then not a baseless perception or a characteristic of youth angst, but an opinion based on fact. In the National Youth Survey, 37.1 percent of young people said that people with political connections are the ones who benefit from development (Hettige 2002:35). Therefore, it is imperative that any overseas employment promotion interventions strive to earn a reputation of fairness by recruiting on merit rather than on political favoritism.

Saving
The propensity to save is higher among skilled and semiskilled workers in contrast to professionals and higher-income earners (Amjad 1989). To encourage savings and assist in the transfer of remittances, state banks have set up branches in key receiving countries. Many migrants, however, continue to use informal channels (Dias and Jayasundere 2004:172). The semiskilled categories also contain youth and people who are part of the economically inactive labor force in Sri Lanka. To better promote saving among this disparate group, the propensity of members of this group to save should be analyzed in conjunction with their *motivation* to save.

Reintegration of Migrant Returnees
Interviews with a group women revealed that reintegration is not a significant problem for them (Gamburd 2005:106). For young women

and men, however, reintegration may be more difficult. Time away from home coupled with new experiences may affect the way they relate to family and friends. Time may be also needed to adjust to the home environment, where parental control may curtail the independence experienced abroad. The inability to relate easily to peers may change the nature of relationships, especially those with significant others left behind.

The government and some nongovernmental organizations have set up self-employment and entrepreneurship programs for returning migrants. The Bank of Ceylon, for example, has two credit programs for self-employment projects. Such programs are not complemented by a skills development program, nor do they have a monitoring arm to at least record the challenges faced by loan recipients. Since migrants may not have entrepreneurial skills, a loan scheme without an accompanying program to develop those skills may not be useful to a large segment of the migrant returnee population.

Entrepreneurship is perceived by young people as a lonely and isolating experience (ILO 2004:37). One study found that women were reluctant to risk their savings by investing in a business (Gamburd 2005:106). When migrants, including young people, return after several years of having had little contact with family and friends, pushing them toward yet another isolating experience may not be the best solution. In fact, it cannot be assumed that migrant returnees have either the desire or the ability to develop entrepreneurial skills. However, group saving schemes and entrepreneurship programs maybe a viable alternative.

The "Migrant Savings and Alternative Investments" program initiated by Migrant Forum Asia (MFA) is a pioneering strategy to promote migrant savings, social entrepreneurship, and reintegration for migrants, along with community economic development. Its objectives are to help migrants prepare economically for their return and reintegration; to develop the capacity of migrants and their families to build their savings and use them wisely; and to assist them in making alternative investments in social enterprises in their home countries. The basic operational strategy is the mobilization of migrant savings in host countries, especially group savings to build social enterprises in the home countries, such as jointly owned farms. The program is supported by governmental, intergovernmental, private, and development agencies on technical, infrastructure, logistical, and legal needs (Asian Migrant Centre 2004).

Reintegration initiatives have to include alternative livelihoods to encourage young people to use their experiences and new skills gained for the benefit of the local labor market. Employment opportunities in addition to self-employment schemes must be offered to young return-ing migrants to enable them to continue to be productive citizens.

Policy Environment

The Sri Lanka Foreign Employment Bureau Act is driven by a vision of Sri Lanka as "a provider of a globally employable competitive human capital" (Dias and Jayasundere 2004:153). The act promotes migration, but the protection of rights does not feature in its main text. Moreover, migration is seen as a safety valve for unemployment in a country where the government does not seem to be taking responsibility for employment creation. In contrast, the Philippines, despite its huge migrant labor force, still promotes *national* employment as a first option. The protection of migrants is the main focus of the Filipino act on foreign employment; its objective is to "institute policies of overseas employment and establish a higher standard of protection of the welfare of migrant workers, their families, and overseas Filipinos in distress," and it makes a commitment to providing "adequate and timely social, economic, and legal services" (Maznavi 2003:2).

The SLBFE has a compulsory registration scheme that includes an insurance scheme that covers contingencies like medical or other emergencies that may compel a worker to return home; 70 percent of all migrants register before departure. Workers who migrate without registering are not eligible for protection under the act (Dias and Jayasundere 2004:162). The amount of insurance paid to migrant workers in 2004 was SL Rs 52,562,832. The SLBFE also provides self-employment loans, scholarship schemes for migrant workers' children, and distribution of school equipment (SLBFE 2005). Other interventions include the establishment of safe houses in certain Middle Eastern countries and loan schemes by state banks to prevent exploitation by money lenders. However, the government does not regulate or monitor the fees levied by employment agencies on migrant hopefuls, who spend close to SL Rs 100,000 to obtain a job.

Training facilities for migrants are available almost exclusively to women, demonstrating the protectionist and paternalistic stance of both the state and the NGO sectors, which have promoted opportunities for women without giving much consideration to the vulnerability of men. Predeparture training and certification is compulsory for women migrants seeking employment as housemaids. There are currently 29 training centers, 22 of which are run by the SLBFE; the other 7 are run by private organizations. Of the training centers offering training for sewing machine operators, only one is open to men (Dias and Jayasundere 2004:162).

Countries of origin are often in a weak economic and political position and therefore find it difficult to exert diplomatic pressure on receiving countries. However, there is a strong network of regional NGOs and activist groups that the Sri Lankan government could partner with to exert international pressure, especially through shaming tactics and also through bodies of the United Nations. The weakness of the UN system is keenly felt here because, unlike the World Trade Organization, the UN has no power to impose sanctions on noncomplying countries. Sri Lanka has ratified the UN convention on migrant rights, but has not ratified the ILO conventions on labor standards. Because overseas migrants are vulnerable to exploitation, international legal instruments should be used in a regional collective to lobby receiving countries to meet international standards.

Memorandums of understanding have been signed with employment agents and governments in the Middle East, Singapore, and Hong Kong that require a contract to be endorsed by the Sri Lankan Embassy before soliciting migrant workers for housemaid positions. Contracts that are authenticated by the embassy bind sponsors and agents to fulfilling their obligations, help monitor activities, and hasten grievance procedures and settlements (Dias and Jayasundere 2004:162). Model contracts, operative in 10 countries, set out information on the monthly wage, leave, duties, hours of work, medical care, and procedures for terminating the contract (Dias and Jayasundere 2004:165). However, because the forms are printed in English and the onus of filing is on the employer, migrant workers have limited access and little control over the document. Moreover, these documents are not legally binding and depend on the goodwill of the signatories.

In a survey conducted on state responsibility, housemaids said they wished that, instead of new schemes, the government would enforce basic aspects of the labor migration process by "policing bogus agencies, ensuring the timely and full payment of wages, [and providing] more support at embassies during crises" (Gamburd 2005:93). Because embassies are understaffed or staffed by political appointees, they usually do not have the necessary experience to intervene nor the power to act assertively (Gamburd 2005:102).

Conclusion

Despite the problematic nature of overseas migration, especially with regard to the exploitative practices of recruitment agencies and employers and the often negligible response of the state, overseas employment provides job opportunities for people and has helped some families improve their economic conditions. Overseas migration for employment can be a valuable opportunity for young people to gain experience in a particular field and acquire transferable skills. A short-term assignment abroad can act as a stepping-stone to greater access to employment opportunities, and savings accumulated while working abroad can provide opportunities for employment creation at home. However, before overseas migration is promoted, research gaps must be addressed to gain an in-depth understanding of young people's motivations and aspirations. Furthermore, as stressed at the outset, migration must be a clearly articulated strategy of Sri Lanka's employment policy. It is also imperative that the local labor market be prepared to absorb youth migrant returnees and use their experience and skills gained for the development of the country. Therefore, promotion of youth migration must be complemented by developments in the local labor market.

A study by the Chamber of Commerce of Sri Lanka found that care for the elderly will be a new service area for migrant workers. With an increasing aging population in European and other developed countries, the study suggests that Sri Lanka should provide training in relevant skills and obtain contracts directly from insurance companies. This information was corroborated by interviews with key actors, who stressed the importance not only of adequate training, but also of an awareness about the demands of such employment where high physical exertion may be needed in carrying and bathing older people. Sri Lanka too will be faced with an aging population in the near future, and preliminary surveys have indicated that care for the elderly within the country is lacking both in quality and quantity (Hewage 2005). Therefore, becoming a care provider for the elderly in other countries may on the one hand create employment opportunities, but on the hand create a dearth of caregivers for the elderly in Sri Lanka as young people who traditionally take care of the elderly parents leave for overseas employment. In developing an employment policy, policy makers must strive to codify the values and principles that govern national policy so that the well-being of individuals, families, and communities in Sri Lanka are not compromised for the sake of "solving" national issues like unemployment and balance of payments.

There are indications that a significant number of young people who go to the United States, Australia, and Canada to pursue higher studies do not return after completing their degrees but instead seek employment in those countries. Many who have gained experience in the software and information technology (IT) field and in the consulting and market research field and have reached management or partner levels in the United States are now returning to Sri Lanka to form their own companies. Local companies like Stats and Virtusa undertake work exclusively for overseas companies. While many of their upper management are overseas returnees, other job opportunities are created within these companies. Other companies like Millennium IT have set up offices in the United States and provide opportunities for IT-educated young people to work overseas. Further research in this area should be conducted with the objective of encouraging people to return and invest in the country.

In sum, migration should be integrated into Sri Lanka's overall development planning. Sri Lanka must develop a long-term policy on migration that includes both the promotion of migration for employment and the protection of migrant workers and their families. The policy must take into consideration all stages of the migratory process: recruitment, departure, the journey, arrival and placement, work, termination, and reintegration.

Notes

1. The original version of this chapter was written as a background paper to inform the National Action Plan for Youth Employment in Sri Lanka. The paper was commissioned by the International Labour Organization (ILO) and the Youth Employment Network, Sri Lanka.

2. It must be noted, however, that international labor migration cannot easily be extricated from human trafficking and illegal migration, and the state must therefore take into consideration the characteristics of transnational and internal migration when designing its interventions.

3. "Clerical and related" refer to clerks and other office-related jobs.

References

Amjad, Rashid, ed. 1989. *To the Gulf and Back. Studies on the Impact of Asian Labour Migration*. Geneva: International Labour Organization.

Asian Migrant Center. 2004. *Harnessing "Migrant Savings for Alternative Investment (MSAI)" as a Community Development and HIV Resiliency Strategy*. Migrant Forum Asia.

Dias, Malsiri, and Ramani Jayasundere. 2004. "Sri Lanka. The Anxieties and Opportunities of Out-Migration." In *Migrant Workers and Human Rights.*

Out-Migration from South Asia, ed. Pong-Sul Ahn. Geneva: International Labour Organization.

Gamburd, Michelle Ruth. 2005. "'Lentils There, Lentils Here!' Sri Lankan Domestic Labour in the Middle East." In *Asian Women as Trans-national Domestic Workers,* ed. Shirlene Huang, Bredna S. A. Yeoh, and Noor Abdul Rahman.

Hettige, S. T. "Sri Lanka's Youth: Profiles and Perspectives." 2002. In *Sri Lankan Youth: Challenges and Responses,* ed. S. T. Hettige and Markus Mayer. Colombo: Friedrich Ebert Stiftung.

Hettige, S. T., and Markus Mayer, eds. 2002. *Sri Lankan Youth. Challenges and Responses.* Colombo: Friedrich Ebert Stiftung.

Hewage, Kalum. 2005. "The Elderly in Sri Lanka." Master's thesis in Women's Studies, University of Colombo.

ILO (International Labour Organization). 2004. *The National Employment Policy and Young People: The Youth Employment Challenge in Sri Lanka.* Colombo.

———. 2005. *Preventing Discrimination, Exploitation and Abuse of Women Migrant Workers. An Information Guide.* Geneva.

Jayaweera, Swarna. 2001a. *Impact of Macroeconomic Reforms on Women in Sri Lanka: Garment and Textile Industries.* Study Series 20. Colombo: Centre for Women's Research.

———. 2001b. *Women in Garment and Textile Industries in Sri Lanka. Gender Roles and Relations.* Study Series 21. Colombo: Centre for Women's Research.

Kelegama, Saman. 2007. "Global Integration and National Interests: Managing Change in Sri Lanka." *OPA Journal* 22 (May).

Kottegoda, Sepali. 2003. "Interventions in Poverty Alleviation: Women Recovering from Poverty or Women Recovering the Family from Poverty?" In *Poverty Issues in Sri Lanka: Towards New Empirical Insights.* Colombo: Centre for Poverty Analysis.

———. 2004. *Negotiating Household Politics. Women's Strategies in Urban Sri Lanka.* Colombo: Social Scientists Association.

Maznavi, Nuzra. 2003 "Reforming the Sri Lanka Bureau of Foreign Employment Act."

Perera, Sasanka. 2005. "Youth: Addressing the Absences." Concept Paper for Youth Conference. German Cultural Institute, Colombo Sri Lanka. August.

Rodrigo, Chandra, and R. A. Jayatissa. 1989. "Maximizing Benefits from Labour Migration: Sri Lanka." In *To the Gulf and Back. Studies on the Impact of Asian Labour Migration,* ed. Rashid Amjad. Geneva: International Labour Organization.

SLBFE (Sri Lanka Bureau of Foreign Employment). 2005. *Annual Statistical Report of Foreign Employment – 2004.* Colombo: SLBFE Research Division.

————. 2007. *Annual Statistical Report of Foreign Employment – 2006*. Colombo: SLBFE Research Division.

Thompson, John B. 1984. *Studies in the Theory of Ideology*. University of California Press

Waxler-Morrison, Nancy. 2004. "Who Will Care for Those Left at Home? The Effect of New Opportunities for Work on Families in Sri Lanka." In *Sri Lankan Society in an Era of Globalization: Struggling to Create a New Social Order*, ed. S. H. Hasbullah and Barrie H. Morrison. New Delhi: Sage Publications.

CHAPTER 7

Developing Youth Entrepreneurs: A Viable Youth Employment Strategy in Sri Lanka?

Nireka Weeratunge

Entrepreneurship training that leads to increased business creation and expansion is considered a viable employment strategy for youth globally. Advocates for youth entrepreneurship training see a multitude of benefits, although others have been more cautious.[1] Many organizations in Sri Lanka have provided entrepreneurship training for more than two decades, and while some established programs attract large proportions of youth, training directed specifically at young people is limited. With no central agency coordinating entrepreneurship training and related data collection, the overall numbers of youth who have received this type of training remain unknown. Current estimates indicate that relatively few youth in the country take advantage of the training and financial resources available for enterprise development; even smaller numbers start or expand enterprises after being trained.

The emerging international literature on youth entrepreneurship highlights several key issues involving youth participation in training and its impact on business creation or expansion. These include youth attitudes toward business and business people and the factors that motivate youth to go into business, as well as the paucity of rigorous frameworks and data to evaluate the impact of youth entrepreneurship programs globally.

This chapter argues that sociocultural aspects of youth entrepreneurship are as critical as technical and regulatory interventions and economic incentives in encouraging more youth to consider starting their own business. A comprehensive policy toward increasing youth entrepreneurship in Sri Lanka needs to focus on enhancing the enterprise culture by addressing underlying values and norms that could lead to more open attitudes toward enterprise as a desirable livelihood.[2] This "underdeveloped strategic area" is linked to motivating more youth to take entrepreneurship training and improving the quality of the training, as well as to creating an enabling regulatory environment.[3] The need to differentiate training programs that aim at inculcating entrepreneurial attitudes for employability from those aimed at increasing business start-ups is emphasized. Although constrained by a lack of rigorous impact assessment data for most entrepreneurship training programs in Sri Lanka, this analysis attempts to identify strategic areas for intervention as building blocks of an integrated entrepreneurship policy focused on youth.

Conceptual Issues

Entrepreneurship training programs have been offered in Sri Lanka for at least 20 years, and although not all are targeted at youth, youth have constituted a large share of the trainees. For example, in the International Labour Organization (ILO)–supported Start and Improve Your Business (SIYB) program, around 68 percent of trainees were estimated to be between 16 and 35 years old (SIYBSLA 2004), while around 52 percent of trainees in the German Development Cooperation–supported Competency-based Economies for the Formation of Entrepreneurs (CEFE) program were between 18 and 33 (Over 2004). Moreover, entrepreneurship training modules within vocational training courses also reach mostly youth. With no central government institution responsible for entrepreneurship training nationally, unlike in the case of vocational training, the overall number of youth receiving this type of training in the last 25 years is unknown. Furthermore, the literature on entrepreneurship training in Sri Lanka in general is limited to five main works: Ranasinghe (1996); Moonesinghe (2000); Weeratunge (2001); Over (2004); and Abeysuriya, Vithanage, and van Lieshout (2005). Apart from a few policy papers (Young 2004), the literature on entrepreneurship training targeted at youth is virtually nonexistent.

Youth entrepreneurship policy at the global level identifies two main goals for the promotion of training: to encourage young people to start entrepreneurial ventures or their own businesses; and to increase their general employability. Employability addresses the necessity for youth to acquire entrepreneurial attitudes and skills so that they can move away from an expectation of "job for life" careers to a more flexible notion of a "portfolio" of careers (Schoof 2006), as required by the current structural conditions of the labor market. While the goal of encouraging youth to start businesses has been pursued in Sri Lanka over a long period, the goal of encouraging employability has received attention only relatively recently. However, most programs focused on youth currently appear to pursue both goals simultaneously. The efficiency and cost effectiveness of inculcating enterprising attitudes among (potentially) all school leavers while concurrently providing basic entrepreneurship training for those who have the interest and aptitude to engage in self-employment need to be carefully considered.

Lundstrom and Stevenson (2002) emphasize that a multitude of factors account for entrepreneurship in different societies and that "context" is important in developing entrepreneurship policies. By context, they mean economic, social, cultural, attitudinal, and structural factors, and they caution against transferring isolated cases of "best practices" from one country to another without understanding these contextual differences.[4] Ray (1992) critically argues that most entrepreneurship development programs are based on an ethnocentric Anglo-American paradigm and questions its replicability in other countries. He critiques the weak empirical basis of knowledge on entrepreneurship outside the North Atlantic region and questions the lack of criteria for recognizing a best practice.

In Sri Lanka the National Employment Policy and the White Paper on Small and Medium Enterprises (SME) express the government's commitment to promote entrepreneurship in general. Entrepreneurship also has been added to a more elaborated SME policy, and creation of an entrepreneurial culture is part of the mandate of the new, state-supported SME Bank, established in 2004.[5] However, this policy orientation has not been translated into a well-articulated framework of focused activities. A holistic assessment of youth entrepreneurship issues conducted in Sri Lanka as a part of the ILO Roadmap initiatives for a National Action Plan for Youth Employment produced a set of core recommendations in this underresearched area (Young 2004). These related to attitudes of youth, links to the education system and career guidance, and the identification and coordination of special needs of youth. Specific programs for youth included business development services, mentoring programs, and an integrated program that links business support with financial credit.

Because of the paucity of data, however, the recommendations were not based on impact assessments of current entrepreneurship training programs used by youth in the country.

Young (2004) emphasized that entrepreneurship is both a set of skills, knowledge, attitudes, and values that can increase the employability of youth and a driver of social and economic innovation and value creation. He noted that entrepreneurship in Sri Lanka was generally associated with self-employment or owning a small business and that an expanded, more dynamic concept of entrepreneurship needed to be promoted. This orientation has been incorporated into the new National Action Plan for Youth Employment (YEN 2006).

A number of international studies (Goel and others 2006; Veciana, Aponte, and Urbano 2005; Lee and Wong 2004; Krueger 1993) have looked at youth attitudes toward entrepreneurship and entrepreneurs as a factor that can influence youth to participate in training programs. The consensus is that the majority of youth from developing economies such as China (including Hong Kong and Taiwan), India, and Singapore have positive attitudes. Those who have had more exposure to business because of family background, self-employed parents, or social networks are more open to entrepreneurship as well as to business as a career option. In a comparative study of India and China, Goel and others (2006) find youth in India to be more positive overall toward entrepreneurship but somewhat less inclined than Chinese youth to favor business as a career choice. The study only partially confirmed the hypothesis that youth from regions with higher entrepreneurial activity would be more favorable toward entrepreneurship.

Youth surveys in Sri Lanka have consistently shown a clear preference for government sector employment relative to private sector or self-employment (Hettige, Mayer, and Salih 2004; Ibarguen 2005). This finding has been confirmed by qualitative studies (Reinprecht and Weeratunge 2006). Although quantitative attitudinal surveys of youth toward entrepreneurship and entrepreneurs are still lacking in Sri Lanka, the single large-scale survey of attitudes of the general population (International Alert 2005) corroborates, with regional variations, earlier studies (Moore 1997; Southwold-Llewellyn 1994) that found an antipathy of Sri Lankans toward business as an activity and occupation.

In addition to attitudes, the global literature has also discussed the factors that motivate youth to engage in enterprise (Schoof 2006; Llisteri and others 2006; Kantis 2005). A distinction is made between youth who start businesses out of necessity and those who are looking for an opportunity. In the Latin American study (Llisteri and others 2006), youth who start businesses out of necessity are generally low income with no other livelihood options, few resources, and little education. Youth who are motivated by opportunity come from middle-class backgrounds, with self-employed, professional, or entrepreneurial parents, higher education levels, and access to resources. Such opportunity-driven youth make up an exceedingly large segment (49 percent) of dynamic entrepreneurs running fast-growing enterprises in Latin America. In Latin America these two youth categories are targeted separately: necessity-driven youth are absorbed into training programs aimed at improving employability and income, while opportunity-driven youth are provided training aimed at growth, innovation, and competitiveness.[6]

While opportunity-driven youth from business family backgrounds have been identified among successful starters in Sri Lanka (Weeratunge 2001), there have been few attempts to distinguish the opportunity-driven from the necessity-driven. Entrepreneurship training directed at starting a micro- or small enterprise has been primarily targeted toward low- and middle-income rural and small town youth, whether they are driven by necessity or opportunity. In 2003 ILO/SIYB introduced an Expand Your Business package aimed at growth-oriented entrepreneurs, but youth participation rates are not available.

Lack of systematic studies, evaluations, and assessments of the impact of youth entrepreneurship programs and the need to develop more rigorous frameworks are constantly emphasized in most of the available literature for both developed countries, where such programs have been implemented for decades, and developing countries (Ray 1992; Bronte-Tinkew and Redd 2001; Lundstrom and Stevenson 2005; Schoof 2006; Llisteri and others 2006; Aspen Institute 2008).[7] In Sri Lanka only two international programs have conducted a systematic impact assessment of entrepreneurship training (Over 2004; Abeysuriya, Vithanage, and van Lieshout 2005). These assessed the relevance and quality of the training, business start-up and expansion rates, changes in business practices, business indicators, and employment generation. They did not cover changes in enterprise culture, such as attitudes toward business in those who did not start businesses. They also did not investigate reasons for trainees' perceptions; for example, particular modules of the training are indicated as more useful than others, but in-depth data on why clients thought so are unavailable. A qualitative study on the impact of entrepreneurship training in Sri Lanka (Weeratunge 2001)[8] emphasized that the ways local entrepreneurs used their entrepreneurship training to change their business practices did not necessarily correspond with intended outcomes of globally designed packages.

Apart from generally negative attitudes among youth toward self-employment and business, recurring issues in the Sri Lankan literature (Young 2004, Reinprecht and Weeratunge 2006) are the quality of entrepreneurship training programs (lack of practice orientation and cultural grounding), the absence of a dynamic enterprise culture, and the lack of a regulatory and governance framework supporting entrepreneurship in the country. So far attempts that have focused on short-term technical interventions and economic incentives to increase entrepreneurship, such as training and institutional support to access finance, marketing links, and advice, have met with only limited success. The main reasons are shortcomings in the programs themselves and the problem of practical access to financial and marketing support, although in theory, there is sufficient institutional support available after training. However, the failure to pursue long-term strategies to create an enabling sociocultural and regulatory environment to support entrepreneurship has been a serious gap in Sri Lanka. This especially affects youth, because their perceptions of, and decision making about, training and careers are largely influenced by their families and peers (Hettige, Mayer, and Salih 2004; Ibarguen 2005; Reinprecht and Weeratunge 2006).

Factors that generate entrepreneurship in a society are complex (Ray 1992). A policy promoting youth entrepreneurship needs to be formulated based on experience and evidence from existing entrepreneurship programs and with a good understanding of the sociocultural, political, and historical context of Sri Lanka, in addition to its economic conditions. A patchwork of "best practices" transplanted from different parts of the globe will not amount to a viable framework for enabling youth entrepreneurship.

Methods

The following analysis of entrepreneurship training in Sri Lanka is based on a review of the literature, mainly relevant impact and tracer studies available from the two key training programs, ILO-SIYB and GTZ-CEFE, as well as on youth perceptions from two national youth surveys. It incorporates primary qualitative research by the author in both these areas for a nuanced analysis. It also includes information provided by key players in several nongovernmental, governmental, and private organizations involved in entrepreneurship development.[9] The discussion draws on an indicative sample of four types of training programs specifically targeted at youth or with significant numbers of youth trainees. A rigorous comparison among programs is precluded because the data available are too disparate; even the two available impact studies used different methods and criteria of evaluation.

Background on the Training Programs

Sri Lanka has a wide network of training provided by the state, the private sector, and nongovernmental organizations (NGOs) with a range of entrepreneurship training products. While many trainers are specialized in packages of one agency, a network of trainers extends across different agencies and programs as well. Most training programs are subsidized by the state or by NGOs and are provided free of cost to participants. A few organizations encourage participants to contribute at least a part of the cost. The structure of many of the courses is similar. The typical provider offers a short workshop on motivation, selection, and business idea generation (1–3 days), together with longer programs on starting up and expanding a business (5–21 days), which end with the preparation of a business plan that can be taken to banks. Many providers supplement these course with short business management, bookkeeping, marketing, and business plan preparation courses.[10]

Four types of entrepreneurship training programs accessed by youth can be identified, based on the institutional sector of their origin. State programs include the Small Enterprise Development Division (SEDD) of the Ministry of Youth Affairs and Sports, the Industrial Development Board (IDB), provincial Industrial Development Authorities (IDA), the Vocational Training Authority (VTA), and the National Apprentice Training and Industrial Authority (NAITA). Programs offered by microfinance institutions (MFI) and nongovernmental organizations include SEEDS and Agromart. International programs (ILO-SIYB and GTZ-CEFE) are supported by multilateral and bilateral organizations and are implemented through state, NGO, and private providers. The private sector also offers its own programs, such as Young Entrepreneurs Sri Lanka (YESL), Shell LiveWIRE, and Hambantota Youth Business Trust (HYBT). Many state and MFI-NGO institutions conduct their own entrepreneurship courses, while adding SIYB and CEFE packages to their portfolio of products. In some cases, SIYB packages have replaced previous CEFE packages, but the original core courses of these organizations continue to be offered. Table 7.1 provides an overview of the entrepreneurship training programs accessed by youth in Sri Lanka.

Table 7.1 Overview of Entrepreneurship Training Programs Targeted at and Accessed by Youth in Sri Lanka

Program (Year of origin)	Focus on youth (%)	Gender equity (% female)	Number trained (est.)	Number of trainers (est.)	Geographical spread	Types of packages	Subsidy (%)	Success rate (%)
State								
SEDD (1989)	±100	50 (S), 40 (E)	143,357 (1994–2004)	100	17 districts	Selection Workshop (2 days), Motivation/Achievement Workshop (4 days), Entrepreneurship Development Program (21 days)	100	30 (short packages) 40 (core package)[a]
VTA (2000)	±100	—	—	145	22 districts (including districts in Northern and Eastern provinces)	Awareness Training in Entrepreneurship (1 day), CEFE (10 days), Know About Business (95 hours)	100	—
Local NGO								
SEEDS (1986)	± 60[b] (20–35 years)	±60[c]	7,000–8,800 annually (2001–2005)	—	18 districts (including districts in Eastern Province)	Self-Employment Training (1 day), Small Business Development Training, Women and Enterprise Development Training (2 days), CEFE/SIYB programs	100	—
Agromart (1990)	—	±75	6,000–7,500 annually	—	7 districts	Enterprise Development Training/ Sector-Specific Skills (3 days), Economic Literacy Training/ Business Skills Training (2 days), Training for Everyone/Rural Polytechnic (1 day), SIYB programs	100[d]	—

International								
SIYB (2000)	68 (16–35 years)	57	9,255 (2000–04)	212	23 districts (including districts in Northern and Eastern provinces)	Generate Your Business (2 days), Start Your Business, Improve Your Business, Expand Your Business (5 days)	70	39 (S:1–3 years later) 46 (E: 1–3 years later)[e]
CEFE (1995)	54 (18–33 years)	42	7,987 (1995–2000)		21 districts (including districts in Northern and Eastern provinces)	New Business Creation, Small and Medium Business Management and Expansion, Combined Business Creation and Expansion, Agricultural Marketing and Diversification (10 days), Entrepreneurial Competencies, Finance and Marketing Module (2 days)	91	25 (S: 1year later); 49 (S: 1–8 years later) 41 (E: 1 year later); 81 (E: 1–8 years later)[f]
Private sector								
Shell LiveWIRE[g] (1999)	100 (16–32 years)	—	12,500 (1999–2006)	—	21 districts (including districts in Northern and Eastern provinces)	Bright Ideas Workshop (half day)	100	28[h]
YESL/JA[i] (1998)	100 (6–19 years)	55	55,000 (1998–2008)	40	—	Primary school age: economic, entrepreneurial, financial education; middle school age: personal economics, enterprise skills; high school age: enterprise and business skills	100	—

(continued)

Table 7.1 Overview of Entrepreneurship Training Programs Targeted at and Accessed by Youth in Sri Lanka (Continued)

Program (Year of origin)	Focus on youth (%)	Gender equity (% female)	Number trained (est.)	Number of trainers (est.)	Geographical spread	Types of packages	Subsidy (%)	Success rate (%)
HYBT (1997)	100 (18–35)	—	250 (1997–2007)	—	Hambantota district	Enterprise development training, Business mentoring (continuous)	—	70; 60 (3 years later)[j]

Source: Interviews, and published impact assessment statements.

Note: S = start-up programs. E = Expansion programs. — = Not available.

a. Based on key informant interviews; the 21-day Enterprise Development Program is considered the core package.

b. According to a qualitative study of the impact of the SEEDS credit plus program on poverty reduction (Weeratunge, Silva, and Renganathan 2002), around 59 percent of clients who received microcredit fell into this age range, and around one-third of the total accessed the in-house training packages.

c. Fifty-nine percent of the borrowers in 2008 were women.

d. Fee charged for the Rural Polytechnic program.

e. Based on impact assessment.

f. Based on impact assessment.

g. Shell Live WIRE is part of the corporate social responsibility program of the Shell Corporation of Sri Lanka.

h. Based on key informant interview.

i. Youth Entrepreneurs of Sri Lanka is part of Junior Achievement Worldwide, funded by global private corporations; YESL also receives funds from the U.S. Agency for International Development.

j. Based on website information.

Strengths and Weaknesses of the Entrepreneurship Training Programs

A main constraint in assessing entrepreneurship training programs is the lack of comparative data, making it difficult to use a uniform set of criteria. Thus tentative criteria used here for assessing effectiveness are youth focus, gender equity, success rates, sustainability, quality and client satisfaction, after-training services, geographical spread, availability in local languages, ease of access, and sociocultural grounding. Not all programs can be evaluated on all criteria. The two international programs, SIYB and CEFE, are the only ones with systematic impact assessment data. For the youth-focused programs, outcome evaluations relating to employability, civic engagement attitudes, interpersonal skills, academic attitudes, and life skills are nonexistent.[11]

Youth Focus

Of the five programs specifically targeted at youth, SEDD, YESL, Shell LiveWIRE, and HYBT are based on concepts of motivation, creation of enterprising attitudes, and an orientation toward achievement. The enterprise training modules within the VTA are only beginning to implement this approach with the ILO-KAB (Know About Business) package. YESL exposes primary and secondary school students to business with a practical, hands-on approach, while providing English language skills as a by-product. The Ministry of Education, with technical support from the ILO Enterprise for Pro-Poor Growth, introduced an entrepreneurial studies course to the school curriculum as an elective at the senior secondary level in 2007 and developed modules on entrepreneurship for the existing curriculum at primary and junior secondary levels. It is still too early to assess the outcomes.

SEDD, Shell LiveWIRE, and HYBT have the specific goal of creating youth entrepreneurs. HYBT is unique among these three programs in using mentoring and a practical hands-on approach. Shell LiveWIRE gets youth to think about business ideas within a very short time. SEDD has the longest experience in working with rural youth. Other programs such as SEEDS, Agromart, SIYB, and CEFE have not been designed with a youth focus. However, large proportions of youth access these programs, which emphasize motivation and achievement, in addition to providing business skills training. Data on how the assessment of the training might differ by age of clients are currently not available. A greater effort could be made to profile different age categories and address youth needs. Currently most youth-focused programs are supply driven.

Gender Equity and Sensitivity

Of youth-focused programs, around half of SEDD participants are reported to be female, although 60 percent of participants in the business expansion courses are male. YESL reports that 55 percent of its participants are girls. The slight gender disparity in favor of girls is consistent with junior and senior secondary-level enrollment in Sri Lankan schools. Data on gender are unavailable for Shell LiveWIRE.

Formal vocational training is mostly accessed by male youth, so the majority of participants in entrepreneurship modules can be assumed to be male. Of the other programs accessed by youth, Agromart is specifically targeted at women (about 75 percent women; the organization does not refuse men). It motivates rural women to consider business as a livelihood option, to become aware of resources available to them, and to engage in systematic planning and investment. In addition to business-related training and microcredit, it provides training in leadership, empowerment, and women's economic and legal rights to leaders of commodity production associations. It responds to sociocultural obstacles faced by women, such as mobility after dark and reluctance to participate in residential training, by providing training close to home within villages. The gender breakdown for SEEDS trainees is not available, although around 60 percent of its microfinance clients are women. The SIYB program emphasizes a gender balance in targeting, and the majority (57 percent) of its participants are women. Its higher business start-up rate of 34 percent for women, compared with 28 percent for men, is unique among mixed training programs in Sri Lanka (Abeysuriya, Vithanage, and van Lieshout 2005). Of all training programs with available data, CEFE shows the lowest female participation rate (42 percent) and its female start-up rate is also 6 percent lower than that of men (Over 2004). However, even where there is equal or higher participation by women in starter programs, female participation is lower in business expansion programs for which data are available, such as SEDD, SIYB, and CEFE.

Weeratunge (2001) revealed that among CEFE trainees, unmarried female youth (relative to older married women) generally have lower business start-up rates and tend to give up their business at marriage. Apart from Agromart, SIYB, and YESL, all other programs need to increase gender sensitivity and achieve gender parity in training.

Success Rates

Rigorous data on start-up and expansion rates are available only for SIYB and CEFE. The overall business start-up rate of the SIYB program is around 31 percent one to three years after training—15 percent for the Generate Your Business program, 39 percent for Start Your Business, and 46 percent for Improve Your Business (Abeysuriya, Vithanage, and van Lieshout 2005).[12] Of those participants with existing businesses, 76 percent are estimated to have improved their business performance (increase in sales and profits, product portfolio, investment, markets, and employment creation) following SIYB training.

The start-up rate in the CEFE program one year after training was estimated at 25 percent and the business expansion rate of existing entrepreneurs in the same period at 41 percent (Over 2004). Over also found that for those participants who came to the CEFE program with the serious intention of starting or expanding a business (about 90 percent of total participants), success rates over the eight-year project period were much higher: an estimated 49 percent for new business creation and 81 percent for expansion. Around 90 percent of those who expanded their business are reported to have increased sales and profits, while 60 percent of new businesses starters and 70 percent of the expansions created new employment (Over 2004). This reveals the importance of paying attention to the medium- and long-term impact of training, as well as to the short-term impact.

Of programs specifically targeted at youth, the highest success rate is claimed by HYBT, at 70 percent after one year. The SEDD program claims an overall success rate (start-up and expansion) of 30 percent; 40 percent of the participants in the 21-day core program started or expanded a business. According to a follow-up survey conducted by Shell LiveWIRE, 28 percent of participants in its half-day workshops went on to start or expand their business. All these are considered favorable outcomes, compared with international rates.

A factor that influences success is targeting and selection. Political and social connections often outweigh aptitude for or interest in business in the selection of trainees in Sri Lanka (Weeratunge 2001). There is also mistargeting—for example, starters end up in expansion programs and vice versa. Mistargeting has been close to 30 percent in the ILO-SIYB program (Abeysuriya, Vithanage, and van Lieshout 2005).

Sustainability

Very little information is available about whether enterprises started by youth trainees have been sustained over the medium and long term.[13] SIYB is the only program on which enterprise sustainability data exist for at least two years. Other programs need to monitor sustainability at least to that extent but preferably longer. SIYB data reveal that 77 percent of the newly started businesses and 90 percent of improved businesses were functioning one year after start-up or training (Abeysuriya, Vithanage, and van Lieshout 2005). Around 84 percent of start-ups and 90 percent of improved businesses were functioning two years later. It appears that some of those who started and stopped a business in the first year restarted it in the second year, after better planning or accumulating more capital for investment. HYBT estimates that 60 percent of its trainees' business start-ups were still operating after the second year (HYBT 2008).

The actual business practices of entrepreneurs who received SIYB training do not vary much from those of control groups. Entrepreneurs without training appear to be better at financial planning, while trained entrepreneurs are better at marketing (Abeysuriya Vithanage, and van Lieshout 2005). In terms of overall performance, however, entrepreneurs who received SIYB or CEFE training appear to increase sales and profits and to hire more workers than untrained ones (Abeysuriya, Vithanage, and van Lieshout 2005; Over 2004). Around 69 percent of CEFE trainees said they had made a moderate profit, while 23 percent indicated a high profit after training (Over 2004). Trainees also expanded beyond local markets, increased the product portfolio, developed new business links, and increased incomes (Abeysuriya Vithanage, and van Lieshout 2005). These business practices and indicators need to be assessed for adoption by other training programs, as do the factors that influence the business practices that trainees adopt.

The trainees in most of the programs are subsidized, so it is important to look at the financial sustainability of the training programs themselves.[14] The subsidies are necessary because most youth are unable to pay for the courses themselves and parents might not consider the training a worthwhile investment. SIYB and CEFE are the only programs that attempt some cost recovery, although Agromart and SEEDs charge nominal fees for some training. All training offered by the state sector is free. SIYB itself does not subsidize training; 74 percent of its costs are covered by partner organizations, which mobilize funds through donor agencies, while the remaining 26 percent was recovered through fees charged to trainees (SIYBSL 2004). CEFE initially subsidized nearly two-fifths of the training costs but phased out these subsidies by 2002. It received funding from partner organizations, course participants, and other sources (Over 2004; Reichert, Lempelius, and Tomecko 2000). MFI-NGOs remain dependent on donors to support their core training programs. Corporate social responsibility initiatives offer YESL, HYBT, and Shell LiveWIRE the possibility of raising funds to scale up their youth programs, but these programs had not yet taken advantage of those opportunities. The private sector in Sri Lanka tends to invest in social welfare rather than livelihood activities.

Quality Orientation and Client Satisfaction

The SIYB and CEFE programs are the only ones designed to international standards, emphasizing quality control through training of trainers and monitoring. They collect demographic data on trainees, business start-up and expansion rates, client satisfaction with the training, and changes in business practices and outcomes as a result of the training. The vast majority of SIYB trainees—95 percent of those in business and 80 percent of those not in business—rate their training as "very relevant" or "somewhat relevant" (Abeysuriya, Vithanage, and van Lieshout 2005). Around 80 percent of CEFE trainees said their training was "excellent" or "very good." Forty percent of participants indicated that "most" expectations were met, and another 36 percent indicated that "all" expectations or "more" expectations than they hoped for were met (Over 2004). Weeratunge (2001) found that 70 percent of CEFE participants who started a business and 100 percent of those who expanded their businesses rated the training course as among the most significant factors enabling them to go forward with their plans.

This kind of monitoring and evaluation is absent in all programs targeted at youth in Sri Lanka. Internal annual reviews of programs and revisions of course material, for example by SEEDS, are not available in published form. State training programs such as SEDD and vocational-based entrepreneurship training programs are weakest in quality orientation, training of trainers, and monitoring. For example, in the VTA program, a lack of dedicated trainers means that the available staff attends to a multitude of other tasks. None of the youth-targeted training programs or those offered by MFI-NGOs have collected data on client satisfaction. A qualitative assessment of SEEDS (Weeratunge, Silva, and Renganathan 2001) found that trainees highly valued the technical sector–related training and the CEFE program offered but did not remember exactly what they had learned in the one-day self-employment training program.

After-training Services

After-training services are particularly important for youth new to business. Among training programs specifically targeted at youth, HYBT provides both loans and mentoring. SEDD provides sector-specific technical support and referrals for financial credit through its well-established network of links with banks and other government agencies with technical expertise, such as Sri Lanka's Industrial Development Board/Industrial Development Authority, Industrial Services Board, and Agriculture Extension and Small Industries Departments. SEDD's long-term commitment to trainees has made it the state institution that "does not go away." However, because SEDD is completely dependent on state funds, resources for adequate support and follow-up are limited. State-supported vocational training programs are also weak; their lack of resources means they are unable to provide trainees with sufficient avenues of further development, such as technical and entrepreneurial advice. The Sri Lankan central bank administers a loan program, Nipuna, for the self-employed, but loan sizes are considered too small to purchase the equipment necessary for most start-ups.

The MFI-NGOs are best at after-training services. All their trainees are assured of financial credit. Their in-house entrepreneurship training has been designed to be integrated with sector-specific technical training, business development services, and various other follow-up activities. The kinds of after-training services available to SIYB and CEFE trainees are dependent on partner organizations implementing the training. Around 43 percent of CEFE trainees received after-training services, mostly business counseling, with expanders being more apt to receive these services than start-ups. The training enabled around half of the trainees to access capital, 69 percent of which came from a bank or NGO fund (Over 2004). Around one-third of SIYB trainees received after-training services directly through the program, which were given a high quality rating by about 80 percent of the recipients (Abeysuriya, Vithanage, and Lieshout 2005). About 60 percent of trainees received banks loans, while about 40 percent received market information, skills and management training, and business counseling. The significance of after-training services is clearly revealed in the SIYB impact assessment, where the business start-up rate among those who had received such services was, at 56 percent, four times as high as the rate among those who did not receive the services.

Geographical Spread

Among the youth-targeted training programs, Shell LiveWIRE has the broadest geographical coverage, which includes the conflict-affected Northern and Eastern provinces of the country. However, this program reaches smaller numbers than most other programs. SEDD, although the biggest program in overall numbers with a wide coverage in the noncon-flict regions, does not have a presence in the north or east. HYBT is restricted to Hambantota District, but since 2007 the Ceylon Chamber of Commerce, headquartered in Colombo, has been replicating the pro-gram nationally. The government's vocational training program has a potentially wide geographical spread, including the north and east, because of its large network of training centers (250), including 12 Career Guidance units, if it can expand its entrepreneurship modules. YESL reaches only 1 percent of public schools in Sri Lanka. SEEDS, CEFE, and SIYB have a wide outreach, including many of the districts in the north and east. Although SEEDS provides training to more than three times as many people as the CEFE and SIYB programs reach, it is still unable to cover all its microfinance clients with the basic in-house training in self-employment. Agromart is currently working in only seven districts (including Ampara in the east), but its total number trained approaches that of SEEDS.

Availability in Local Languages

With one exception all of the entrepreneurship programs, including those specifically targeted at youth, conduct training in Sinhala and Tamil. YESL conducts its training in English because it uses course material pro-vided by Junior Achievement Worldwide. YESL does not consider this an obstacle but rather sees it as a means for trainees to obtain highly valued English language skills in addition to enterprise awareness. SEDD does not have an adequate number of Tamil language trainers, and thus partic-ipation in its programs of youth of minority ethnic groups (Tamil and Muslims) is low. Of all the youth-targeted programs, Shell LiveWIRE is the one that provides several attractive and comprehensive brochures, facilitating decision making on business start-up, in both Sinhala and Tamil languages. SIYB and CEFE provide training material in the two local languages. Because these are translated from English, however, there are issues of language dealing with cultural nuances that go beyond sim-ple direct translation. A fifth of participants in SIYB programs indicated that the training manuals were either too difficult to understand or irrel-evant to their needs. Only 40 percent of those who started or expanded a business consulted the manuals after training (Abeysuriya, Vithanage, and van Lieshout 2005). This finding was confirmed by interviews with key informants (in relation to SIYB) and trainees (in relation to CEFE), where trainees frequently complained about convoluted language and lack of materials in the local idiom. Local MFIs and NGOs develop their in-house material directly in the local languages and are thus more conversant with local idiom.

Ease of Access

The ease of access to training might be a factor for the relatively small proportion of youth who access enterprise training. Training is often provided in district capitals and centers. Many rural youth who live in villages far from these centers are not aware of the availability of the training, and if they are, they might not have the financial means to travel to the training centers. In the case of female youth, cultural restrictions relating to mobility are a significant issue; parents do not often give their daughters permission to stay in residential facilities. Thus, one- or two-day-long programs conducted in villages by organizations such as SEEDS, Agromart, and SEDD have a greater chance of reaching these youth. Shorter-term (or staggered) training closer to their homes makes training more accessible to youth in remote locations.

Sociocultural Grounding

The evidence given by youth, public perceptions gleaned from business surveys, and qualitative studies all indicate an antipathy toward business in Sri Lanka. In such a context, it is important that training courses are well grounded in local sociocultural realities. The likelihood of this happening is greater when training is designed (or co-designed in the case of global programs) within the country and when trainers have accumulated sufficient experience through long years of implementation.

Of the youth-targeted programs, SEDD has the longest experience in implementation and has a cadre of relatively well-trained trainers in the districts where it is active. SEDD trainers and extension officers tend to have a good grasp of local conditions and a "cultural orientation" that is conducive to understanding and addressing the needs of local youth entrepreneurs.[15] HYBT also has this local grounding because it is located within a district chamber of commerce and is based on mentoring by experienced business people. Of the other programs, core training packages by SEEDS and Agromart have been designed locally and implemented for 15 to 20 years. Their "cultural orientation" is based on local knowledge of grassroots conditions, and their range of packages is tailored to different needs.

YESL by contrast uses the concept and materials from Junior Achievement Worldwide with barely any modification in English. While

English language learning by rural students is a very useful by-product of the program that should be retained, a bilingual program more attuned to local sociocultural realities would have a larger impact. Similarly, even though Shell LiveWIRE, CEFE, and SIYB claim adaptation to local conditions, they are global in origin and relatively new in the training landscape of Sri Lanka. The local trainers have sufficient knowledge of the training context, but most do not have practical knowledge of running a business within this sociocultural context. There is insufficient use of existing entrepreneurs who could convey knowledge and lessons of practical experience through mentoring. Learning through games (virtual reality) or by filling out self-assessment forms often has little focus on real situations in Sri Lanka. Trainers need to be aware that in addition to "technical" business skills they are also imparting a particular value orientation. Moreover, if programs are also based on motivation and achievement concepts, trainers need to understand that what motivates or enables Sri Lankan youth to start or expand enterprises might differ from what is assumed in course concepts or content.

In addition, the content does not cover broad but relevant issues such as globalization and Sri Lanka's place in the global economy. Youth need to know that they live in a changing world and understand how to start and run an enterprise within increasingly globalized markets. Even though global awareness is an important ingredient of entrepreneurship education promoted by organizations such as the Aspen Institute (2008), it has been missing in most training programs in Sri Lanka. There also is a need to do more awareness raising among people who have influence over training youths' decisions, such as education officials, teachers, community leaders, and parents. For example, both YESL and the Entrepreneurial Studies course supported by the government have run into institutional obstacles within the education system. Thus, although recommendations such as incorporating entrepreneurship education into the school curriculum are theoretically easy to make, the difficulty in implementing these confirms the importance of generating the enabling sociocultural conditions for successful entrepreneurship education in Sri Lanka.

Differentiating the Two Goals of Entrepreneurship Training

This overview of entrepreneurship training programs indicates the need to differentiate between inculcating enterprising attitudes among school leavers in general and providing entrepreneurship training for those who have the interest and aptitude to engage in self-employment. Following Chigunta (2002), this would mean separating out "pre-entrepreneurs" (15–19 years, "formative stage") from "budding" (20–25 years, "growth stage") and "emergent" (26–29, "prime stage") entrepreneurs. YESL is more focused on the "pre-entrepreneur" phase of training, while all other programs targeted at youth combine the three phases. Programs accessed by youth also incorporate awareness creation and attitude-changing tactics with training in business start-ups.

Available impact studies show that youth who have no intention of engaging in self-employment or starting businesses are selected for entrepreneurship training programs, which are primarily designed for those who do wish to become entrepreneurs. While all youth need to have enterprising attitudes to find and pursue their livelihoods, training all of them in full-scale programs for entrepreneurship development is an inefficient use of both resources and time. Thus, what is needed is for all school leavers to go out into the world having been exposed to some basic values about being enterprising, preferably within the school system. Until such a concept is adequately implemented within the school system, there is a need to help those youth who have already left school to acquire the basic enterprising values and attitudes that will expand their livelihood options.

Creating an Enabling Sociocultural Environment for Promoting Youth Entrepreneurship

The antipathy toward businesses in Sri Lanka and the reluctance of youth to consider enterprise as a career option reveal the need for an enabling sociocultural environment. The first national survey of public perceptions on business confirmed what stakeholders in the enterprise development sector, as well as qualitative studies, had already found (International Alert 2005): significant majorities of people believe that businesses exploited consumers (69 percent) and destroyed cultural values (58 percent). While a large majority (76 percent) agreed that businesses helped society by providing employment, only a minority (46 percent) believed that they helped by providing goods and services to communities. In addition, a large majority (77 percent) believed that businesses need to be socially responsible and take into account the impact of their decisions on employees, local communities, and the country, in addition to making profits. Thus, the success of enterprise in Sri Lanka is judged as much by sociocultural as by economic expectations.

It is within this sociocultural milieu that youth make decisions on what training they will engage in and what career options they will consider. Ranasinghe's (1996) analysis of school curricula shows that there is very little reinforcement of entrepreneurial qualities or values in school textbooks. The new Entrepreneurial Studies course and modules introduced in 2007 have yet to make a dent within the education system. There is much evidence that the predominant culture in Sri Lanka emphasizes affiliation (social ties with family, community, and business associates) over achievement and planning values (Perera 1996; Nanayakkara 1997, 1999; Weeratunge 2001, Buddhadasa 2003; Reinprecht and Weeratunge 2006). Affiliation is essential for good customer relations and network-building and should be reinforced. In addition, however, enhancing achievement and planning values—especially opportunity-seeking, innovation, information-seeking, and planning—would increase the life chances of youth.

In assessing motivation among school leavers in four districts, Reinprecht and Weeratunge (2006) found that whereas the majority of school leavers with O-level (ordinary level) or less education perceived income and money as significant measures of success, the majority of those who had A-level (advanced level) or more education found education, achieving a goal, being a good human being, and not harming others to be more important. Both groups also valued good social relations and a good house. Interviews with entrepreneurs of varying age groups found that money and profit are not the primary motivating factors for the majority doing business in Sri Lanka.[16]

These qualitative findings are confirmed in the School-to-Work Transition for Youth Survey (Hettige, Mayer, and Salih 2004), where youth indicated that being successful in work, making a contribution to society, and having a good family life were more important than having a lot of money. Moreover, for the majority the major reason for accepting their current job was not financial but rather personal interest or the lack of other options (exceptions were youth in the conflict areas and the estate sector). Thus the entrepreneurship model for Sri Lanka should be grounded in family and community, rather than in the high-achieving, risk-taking individual that is often emphasized in global packages. Some planning and achievement values also need to be inculcated for youth to be successful in an employment market that is increasingly globalized.

All three available youth surveys (National Youth Survey 2000, School- to-Work Transition for Youth 2003, and Youth and Poverty Survey 2005) are consistent in showing that around 20–24 percent of youth cite self-employment as their employment preference; that percentage is about the same for both men and women and for youth both in and outside the conflict areas. However there is some difference between urban and rural youth, and great variation according to education level. What is noteworthy is that self-employment (this does not differentiate between business per se and skilled crafts, agriculture, or fishing) generally emerges as the second-most desired preference, next to state employment, which is preferred by 40–50 percent of survey respondents. More urban than rural youth are oriented toward business.

The Youth and Poverty Survey (Ibarguen 2005) found that 35 percent of school leavers with junior secondary education, 26 percent with O-levels, and 13 percent with A-levels cited self-employment as their first preference. However, asked about their ideal job, almost 30 percent overall mentioned self-employment. Thus, it appears that although more youth, given freedom to decide on their own, might opt for self-employment, family and social pressures orient them toward the government sector as their first preference. These results should be treated with caution because the question was related to self-employment in general rather than to business alone. Where the questions are related specifically to business, there is some consistency with the survey results. The findings on the decision-making process of school leavers in the qualitative study of four districts (Reinprecht and Weeratunge 2006) showed that while only a small minority was actually planning to engage in a business, 45 percent, when specifically asked, said they would consider business as an option. More school leavers with O-levels than with A-levels, and more non-Sinhalese Buddhist youth considered business as an option.

The results of the School-to-Work Transition survey (Hettige, Mayer, and Salih 2004) show that the preference for "starting my own business" increases progressively from those youth still in school to those actually engaged in some sort of self-employment. Thus while only 21 percent of youth in school considered starting a business to be an option, 23 percent of job seekers, 37 percent of those already employed, and 66 percent of self-employed youth wanted to start their own business. There was a noteworthy gender difference, with more men than women wanting to start their own business. There was no ethnic variation between Sinhalese and Tamils, but among those in school and job seekers, considerably more Muslim than Tamil youth wished to start a business. Among self-employed youth, more Sinhalese than Tamils wished to start their own business. Nearly two-thirds (63 percent) of all self-employed youth indicated independence as the primary reason for their choice. Inability to find salaried work (16 percent), flexible working hours (9 percent), and higher income (8 percent) were other reasons for selecting self-employment.

The youth surveys found that lack of social respect, stability, and security were the primary reasons youth did not prefer self-employment. Additionally, youth saw business as exploitative. In the qualitative study, reasons for shunning self-employment ranged from dislike of business, lack of knowledge or skills for business, and lack of social respect, to lack of markets and capital.

Overall, the results of the studies indicate that youth are pressured by family and society not to consider business as an option. Thus, changing attitudes of youth per se is insufficient. There needs to be a widespread, long-term effort to promote a positive attitude toward business among the Sri Lankan population in general. The need is greatest in the rural areas. Preliminary results from a social marketing campaign implemented by the ILO Enterprise for Pro-Poor Growth project reveal that more concerted awareness initiatives can lower the preference among youth and parents for government employment and increase openness toward business as a career option.[17]

Creating an Enabling Economic and Regulatory Environment for Youth Entrepreneurship

In making a strong case for creating an enabling sociocultural environment in which youth entrepreneurship can flourish, this chapter is by no means advocating the neglect of an enabling economic and regulatory environment. The disabling economic factors for promoting entrepreneurship among youth have been discussed comprehensively by Young (2004). Three main issues are highlighted here.

Access to Finance
Despite the availability of many loan schemes through banks and microfinance institutions, youth still face difficulties in accessing capital. The main obstacles are related to collateral in obtaining bank financing. In contrast to some other countries, "angel investors" are lacking.[18] Many youth are also unwilling to borrow for sociocultural reasons—a life free of debt is highly valued and brings social status. Few safety nets exist for young business starters, such as security funds existing in other countries. In addition, the loan sizes available though MFIs to youth are often too small to finance a start-up business.

Access to Business Support

Sri Lanka has no sizable market for business development services yet, because many entrepreneurs do not see their benefits. In any case, youth tend to use these only if they are made available free of cost. Information is lacking on chambers of commerce and other institutions that promote enterprise development among youth, and more business counseling is needed, especially in rural areas, to help young entrepreneurs identify markets, as well as to manage day-to-day business.

Policy and Regulatory Environment

Currently youth have few incentives to start a business and many reasons not to try. Sri Lanka's cumbersome registration, permit, and tax systems, as well as its labor laws, discourage youth from considering business as an option. These various systems need to be streamlined, and state officials made more aware of the need to provide adequate support to youth engaging in enterprise.

Recommendations

The following recommendations, based on assessing the strengths and weaknesses of current programs available to youth, encompass existing concepts and resources for the development of an integrated, two-pronged strategic approach to youth entrepreneurship in Sri Lanka. The first component would promote an enterprise culture among all youth within and outside the school system, focusing on sociocultural aspects. The second component would improve entrepreneurship training and the enabling environment for those youth who wish to become entrepreneurs, focusing on economic, regulatory, and sociocultural aspects. A more rigorous approach to monitoring, evaluation, and impact assessment needs to be the cornerstone of such a strategy.

Promotion of an Enterprise Culture

Four core value messages need to be conveyed to youth through the school and vocational training systems, as well as through a social marketing campaign: the value of being "enterprising" (opportunity and information seeking, creative and innovative, self-confident, and persistent); the value of business as a respectable option for a livelihood; the value of training and planning to run a successful enterprise; and the value of operating a socially responsible enterprise to help one's family, village, and region to develop. Initiatives to incorporate entrepreneurship into the school curriculum, as promoted by the ILO Enterprise Growth project, need to be monitored and strengthened. Extracurricular programs such as YESL need to be more localized and scaled up. These steps will accommodate different learning styles in both classroom and nonclassroom environments.

For school leavers, entrepreneurship modules in vocational training, as supported by the ILO project, need to be strengthened and scaled up. Shell LiveWIRE's "Bright Ideas" workshop is useful for creating awareness among youth who do not access the vocational training system. Career guidance within schools and brochures for youth outside the school system on decision-making related to livelihood choices could address the current information gaps on enterprise as a viable career option. Television and radio at the national level, as well as street and forum theater at the grassroots level, are media that can be used to provide information on entrepreneurial traditions and role models and to generate discussions on issues relating to enterprise. Youth entrepreneurship awards such as those promoted by YESL and Shell LiveWIRE need to be expanded to all the districts. In addition to donor and government support, more corporate social responsibility funds need to be mobilized for activities connected to generating an enterprise culture.

Promotion of Entrepreneurship Training

To promote entrepreneurship training, a "pathways to business" concept needs to be institutionalized within and outside the school system, so that school leavers at all levels, as well as graduates of vocational training institutions and universities, can access training at appropriate points in their lives. This system should be inclusive, providing access to young women following marriage, the disabled, and young offenders. Better information (such as attractive brochures) needs to be made available to youth to make them aware of and help them select appropriate entrepreneurship training options. Targeting and selecting youth with an interest and aptitude for business is essential. Promoting gender and ethnic equity in training should be a fundamental concern. The quality of courses needs to be enhanced by training sufficient trainers, and by improving the practice orientation and sociocultural grounding of courses. Training needs to be linked to mentoring and after-training services. The HYBT model, now expanded to the national level, needs to be monitored and strengthened. In addition, a youth entrepreneur forum to exchange experiences and promote a dialogue among youth engaged in the private, state, and nongovernmental sectors would improve the enabling sociocultural environment for entrepreneurship.

Promotion of an Enabling Economic and Regulatory Environment

Better access to business development services (training in marketing, business management, bookkeeping, and sector-relevant technical skills), as well as institutional financing without current collateral restrictions, are important aspects of an enabling economic environment. A social safety net for young entrepreneurs, such as a security fund, to reduce risk, has been initiated in other countries. To improve governance, introducing efficient registration, licensing, and permit procedures and exempting youth entrepreneurs from labor and tax regulations for a prescribed period during the start-up phase would be helpful. In addition, awareness-raising programs among state officials to change attitudes toward youth entrepreneurship can be promoted. Introducing a universal tax system, so that businesspeople are not the only visible citizens who have to pay taxes, would also be conducive to changing attitudes toward business. Developing a consistent policy approach toward youth entrepreneurs within an overall entrepreneurship policy for Sri Lanka is essential.

Monitoring, Evaluation, and Impact Assessment

Sound monitoring and rigorous impact assessment of entrepreneurship programs is a precondition for an entrepreneurship training strategy. There is a great need to maintain an integrated database with detailed statistics on youth entrepreneurship training. If such a database were available, identifying and promoting or supporting programs based on performance by looking at choices of youth and success rates would become easier. Disseminating best practices to increase the quality of programs and encouraging cross-agency learning would be an integral part of impact assessment.

This chapter has provided an assessment of the current approaches and implementation of entrepreneurship programs in Sri Lanka in relation to youth employment and has argued for a better incorporation of sociocultural issues in the design and delivery of future programs. Recommendations are made for a comprehensive integrated approach to youth entrepreneurship, focused both on generating an enterprise culture among youth, as well as providing an enabling economic and regulatory environment for start-up and expansion of youth-owned enterprise. Sound data on the impact of current entrepreneurship programs targeted at or accessed by youth are conspicuous by their absence. Thus, the need for a more consolidated approach to collection of statistics, monitoring, evaluation, impact assessment, dissemination of best practices, and cross-agency learning to understand what works and what does not, cannot be overemphasized.

Notes

I thank the editors of this volume, Ramani Gunatilaka, Milan Vodopivec, and Markus Mayer, for their continuous support, and the two anonymous reviewers for their invaluable comments. I express my deep appreciation to my colleagues at the ILO Entergrowth Project; Karin Reinprecht, who collaborated on some of the research on which this paper is based; as well as Roel Hakemulder for his continuous support of this work. I also thank Ralf Starkloff for his substantive and editorial feedback. I acknowledge the support of the WorldFish Center for providing me a conducive environment to complete this paper.

1. Harper (1988), White and Kenyon (2001), and Chiguta (2002) have outlined multiple benefits in addition to creating employment opportunities, such as incorporating alienated and marginalized youth into the economic mainstream, addressing delinquency and psychosocial issues arising from unemployment, developing new skills and experiences to be applied to general challenges in life, promoting innovation and resilience, revitalizing local communities, and using the dynamism of young entrepreneurs to respond to new economic trends. Curtain (2000), Chiguta (2002), and Schoof (2006) have cautioned against considering youth entrepreneurship as a panacea for youth unemployment, emphasizing the importance of specific economic conditions, market opportunities, and consumer spending power in developing countries for business start-up. Lundstrom and Stevenson (2002) have used a model incorporating motivation, opportunity, and skills to analyze incidence of business entry.

2. Gibb (1998:4) described an "enterprise or entrepreneurial culture" as "sets of values, beliefs and attitudes commonly shared in a society which underpin the notion of an entrepreneurial 'way of life' as being desirable and in turn support strongly the pursuit of 'effective' entrepreneurial behavior by individuals or groups." See also Kolshorn and Tomecko (1995) and Luczkiw (1998).

3. Lundstrom and Stevenson (2002:12) pointed out that promoting an entrepreneurial culture is "one of the more underdeveloped strategic areas of entrepreneurship development. It is not well articulated in policy terms and the area most subject to rhetoric." They further elaborated that while many policymakers talked about it, few formulated concrete action for implementation.

4. Lundstrom and Stevenson (2002:10–11) identified four policy orientations toward entrepreneurship in their 10-country study: SME policy extension; niche entrepreneurship policy; new firm creation policy; and holistic entrepreneurship policy

5. For example, the mission statement of the SME Bank specifies: "To develop small and medium enterprises through introduction of innovative financial products and development services, building a strong entrepreneur culture in Sri Lanka."

6. In another study, Lee and Wong (2004) have stressed the importance of recognition of opportunity, fear of failure, and self-efficacy, in addition to networks, in new venture creation by young people in Asia.

7. Some comprehensive studies looking at outcomes and impact of entrepreneurship training and education include Rasheed (2000) and Botham and Mason (2007).

8. This independent study of the CEFE program was done on behalf of the Center for Poverty Analysis, Colombo, and was used by CEFE Sri Lanka to address sociocultural gaps in its training program.

9. Sarvodaya Economic Enterprise Development Services (SEEDS), Agromart Foundation, Small Enterprise Development Division (SEDD) of the Ministry of Youth Affairs and Sports and the Vocational Training Authority (VTA), Shell LiveWIRE, Young Entrepreneurs of Sri Lanka (YESL), and Hambantota Youth Business Trust (HYBT).

10. The YESL programs directed at school children as an extracurricular activity after school throughout the school year, as well as modules within vocational training courses distributed during the course period (averaging around six months) differ from this pattern.

11. Outcome evaluations based on pre- and post-tests, as well as qualitative interviews are common practice in many youth entrepreneurship programs in the United States (see, for example, Bronte-Tinkew and Redd 2001).

12. Although the latter package is intended for those already in business, the course attracts starters as well.

13. Lundstrom and Stevenson (2002:5) have indicated 3.5 years (42 months) as the critical survival period of a fledgling enterprise.

14. Data on cost effectiveness and financial sustainability of programs are not readily available for most programs and difficult to compare because of the range of products, so the assessment here is tentative.

15. The author has interviewed several SEDD personnel and traveled in the field with them in Kurunegala and Puttalam districts during the course of several studies.

16. Criteria for success might reveal differences among countries, ethnic groups, and genders. For example, Kyro (2001), using narratives of 17 female entrepreneurs, argued that women might have different criteria for success, such as customer satisfaction and professional performance, and might be motivated to start an enterprise for self-fulfillment rather than for financial need.

17. The preliminary results of a qualitative impact assessment (Weeratunge 2008) on the social marketing campaign reveal very positive outcomes in increasing openness to business as well as improving perceptions toward business people.

18. Angel investors offer capital for start-ups (especially potentially high-growth ones) in return for an equity stake.

References

Abeysuriya, A., Vithanage, C. D. and S. van Lieshout. 2005. *Start and Improve Your Business Sri Lanka: Impact Assessment.* Colombo: International Labour Organization.

Aspen Institute. 2008. "Advancing Entrepreneurship Education: A Report of the Youth Entrepreneurship Strategy Group." Washington, DC.

Botham, R., and C. Mason. 2007. *Good Practice in Enterprise Development in U.K. Higher Education.* London: National Council for Graduate Entrepreneurship.

Bronte-Tinkew, J., and Z. Redd. 2001. *Logic Models and Outcomes for Youth Entrepreneurship Programs.* Washington, DC: Child Trends.

Buddhadasa, S. 2003. "Challenges, Issues, and Growth Orientation of Sri Lankan Entrepreneurship." *Economic Review* (People's Bank, Sri Lanka) 29: 1-2-3 (April/June).

CEFE (Competency-based Economies for the Formation of Entrepreneurs). 1995. *The CEFE Approach to Small Enterprise Development.* Colombo.

———. 2000. "Tracer Studies." Colombo.

Chigunta, F. 2002. "Youth Entrepreneurship: Meeting the Key Policy Challenges." Oxford University.

Curtain, R. 2000. "Towards a Youth Employment Strategy." Report to the United Nations on Youth Employment, New York.

Gibb, A. 1998. "Strategies to Implant an Entrepreneurial Culture in Key Actors Influencing SME Development." Paper presented at CEFE's Third International Conference, Belo Horizonte, September.

Goel, A., Vohra N., Zhang. L. and B Arora. 2006. "Attitudes of Youth towards Entrepreneurs and Entrepreneurship: A Cross-cultural Comparison of Indian and China." *Journal of Asia Entrepreneurship and Sustainability* 3 (1): 1–35.

HYBT (Hambantota Youth Business Trust). 2008. http://www.hdcc.lk/hybp.lk/hybt_Progress.htm.

Harper, M. 1998. "Can the Training of Enterprising Competencies Challenge the Menace for Micro and Small Enterprises (MSE) in a Globalizing World?" Paper presented at CEFE's Third International Conference, Belo Horizonte, September.

Hettige, S. T., and M. Mayer, eds. 2002. *Sri Lankan Youth: Challenges and Responses*. Colombo: Friedrich Ebert Stiftung.

Hettige, S. T., M. Mayer, and M. Salih, eds. 2004. *School-to-Work Transition of Youth in Sri Lanka*. Geneva: International Labour Organization.

Ibarguen, C. 2005. *Youth Perceptions: Exploring Results of the Poverty and Youth Survey*. Colombo: CEPA.

International Alert. 2005. "Peace through Profit: Sri Lankan Perspectives on Corporate Social Responsibility. Colombo.

ILO (International Labour Organization). 2004. *The National Employment Policy and Young People: The Youth Employment Challenge in Sri Lanka*. Colombo.

Kantis, H. (with P. Angelelli and V. Moori). 2005. *Developing Entrepreneurship: Latin America and Worldwide Experience*. Bogota: Inter-American Development Bank.

Kolshorn, R., and J. Tomecko. 1995. *Understanding Entrepreneurship and How to Promote It*. Eschborn, Ger.: CEFE International.

Krueger, N. F. 1993. "The Impact of Prior Entrepreneurial Exposure on Perceptions of New Venture Feasibility and Desirability." *Entrepreneurship Theory and Practice* 18: 5–21.

Kyro, P. 2001. "Women Entrepreneurs Question Men's Criteria for Success." Paper presented at the 21st Annual Entrepreneurship Research Conference. Babson College, Babson Park, MA.

Lee, L., and Wong, P. K. 2004. "Attitude towards Entrepreneurship Education and New Venture Creation." Working paper, Singapore National University, Singapore.

Llisteri, J. J., H, Kantis, P. Angelelli, and L. Tejerina. 2006. *Is Youth Entrepreneurship a Necessity or an Opportunity? A First Exploration of Household and New Enterprise Surveys in Latin America*. Washington, DC.: Inter-American Development Bank.

Luczkiw, E. 1998. *Global Enterprise: Instilling the Spirit; Learning Strategies for the New Millennium*. St. Catherine, Ont.: Institute for Enterprise Education.

Lundstrom, A, and L. Stevenson. 2002. *Entrepreneurship Policy for the Future*. Stockholm: Swedish Foundation for Small Business Research.

———. 2005. *Creating Opportunities for Youth Entrepreneurs: Nordic Examples and Experiences*. Stockholm: Swedish Foundation for Small Business Research.

Moonesinghe, B. 2000. "Enterprise Development and Leadership: Sri Lankan Experience—Agromart Foundation." Paper presented at the Seventh National Convention on Women's Studies, Centre for Women's Research, Colombo, March 23–26.

Moore, M. 1997. "The Identity of Capitalists and the Legitimacy of Capitalism: Sri Lanka since Independence." *Development and Change* 2 (2): 331–66.

Nanayakkara, G. 1997. "Some Reflections of Buddhism on Morality in Business and Management." *Sri Lankan Journal of Management* 2 (3): 217–32.

———. 1999. *Culture and Management in Sri Lanka*. Colombo: Post-graduate Institute of Management.

Over, A. 2004. *The Sri Lanka-German CEFE Program 1995–2002: An Evaluation.* Colombo: CEFE.

Perera, T. 1996. "The Need for Affiliation as a Moderator in the Behaviour of Entrepreneurs." *Sri Lankan Journal of Management* 1 (3): 252–61.

Perera, T., and S. Buddhadasa. 1992. "Characteristics of Sri Lankan Entrepreneurs: How Valid Is the Schumpeterian Model? Paper presented at the PIM Conference on "Management Studies" in Colombo, December 15–18.

Ranasinghe, S. 1996. "Entrepreneurship Education and Training in Sri Lanka." *Sri Lankan Journal of Management* 1 (3): 262–77.

Rasheed, H. S. 2000. "The Effects of Entrepreneurial Training and Venture Creation on Youth Entrepreneurial Attitudes and Academic Performance." University of South Florida, Tampa. http://www.coba.usf.edu/departments/management/faculty/rasheed/youth_entrepreneurship.htm.

Ray, D. M. 1992. "Assessing Entrepreneurship Training as a Strategy of Economic Development." *Asian Entrepreneur* 11 (no. 1).

Reichert, C. 1999. *Linking CEFE Entrepreneurship Training to Technical and Vocational Education in Sri Lanka: A Model*. Colombo: CEFE.

Reichert C., C. Lempelius, and J. Tomecko. 2000. "The Performance Measurement Framework (PMF) for Business Development Services (BDS) applied to CEFE projects in Laos, Thailand, and Sri Lanka." Paper presented at the Donor Committee on Small Enterprise Promotion Conference on Business Development Services in Hanoi, April 3–7.

Reinprecht, K., and N. Weeratunge. 2006. *ILO Enterprise for Pro-Poor Growth Project: Cultural Assessment*. Colombo: ILO.

Rideout, E. and D. Gray. 2007. "Evaluation of Entrepreneurship Education Programs: What Do We Really Know?" Presentation made at the National Science Foundation, Science and Technology Center, Washington D.C.

Schoof, U. 2006. *Stimulating Youth Entrepreneurship: Barriers and Incentives to Enterprise Start-ups by Young People*. Series on Youth and Entrepreneurship. Geneva: International Labour Organization.

SIYBSLA (Start and Improve Your Business, Sri Lanka Association). 2004. "Quarterly Report: Third Quarter 2004." International Labour Organization, Colombo.

Southwold-Llewellyn, S. 1994. "The Creation of an Outsider's Myth: The *mudalali* of Sri Lanka." In *The Moral Economy of Trade: Ethnicity and Developing Markets*, ed. H-D Evers and H. Schrader, pp. 175–97. London: Routledge.

Veciana, J. M., M. Aponte, and D. Urbano. 2005. "University Students' Attitude towards Entrepreneurship: A Two-Countries Comparison." *International Entrepreneurship and Management Journal* 1: 165–82.

Weeratunge, N. 2001. "Micro-entrepreneurs and Entrepreneurial Cultures in Sri Lanka: Implications for Poverty Reduction." Centre for Poverty Analysis, Colombo.

————. 2006. "Reviewing and Analyzing Projects and Programs on Youth Entrepreneurship." Background paper for the National Action Plan for Youth Employment in Sri Lanka. International Labour Organization, Colombo.

————. 2008. "Enterprise for Pro-Poor Growth Project: Impact Assessment of the Enterprise Culture Component." Draft report, ILO Entergrowth Project, Colombo.

Weeratunge, N., K. T. Silva, and V. Renganathan. 2002. "The Poverty Impact of the SEEDS "Credit Plus" Approach: An Independent Client-based Assessment. Centre for Poverty Analysis, Colombo.

White, S., and P. Kenyon. 2001. "Enterprise-based Youth Employment Policies, Strategies and Programs: Initiatives for the Development of Enterprise Action and Strategies." Working paper, InFocus Program on Skills, Knowledge and Employability, International Labour Organization, Geneva.

YEN (Youth Employment Network). 2006. *Strategic Assessment and Policy Recommendations for a National Action Plan for Youth Employment: Sri Lanka.* YEN Secretariat, Colombo.

Young, C. 2004. "Sri Lanka Youth Entrepreneurship Roadmap." International Labour Organization, Colombo.

CHAPTER 8

Discrimination and Social Exclusion of Youth in Sri Lanka

Harini Amarasuriya

In Sri Lanka politicians and development policymakers and practitioners perceive the need to focus on youth issues, especially the issue of youth unemployment, to be of the utmost importance. The history of violent antigovernment insurgencies in Sri Lanka that were led mainly by angry and frustrated youth means that a concerted response to the problems of youth is an important part of economic, political, and social development in Sri Lanka.

Youth unemployment is a serious issue in Sri Lanka. The country boasts of high achievements in education, including gender equality in primary and secondary school enrollments and more than 90 percent literacy rates among both women and men (Central Bank of Sri Lanka 2003/4; ADB 2004). Yet only about 2 percent of those who qualify for higher education are actually admitted to universities, and unemployment rates among such youth are roughly double the national unemployment rate. The jobless rate for young people with advanced-level education qualifications or better was 10.5 percent in 2007, compared with a national rate of 5.6 percent (DCS 2007). Although youth employment is discussed as a serious problem, how much of it is a consequence of the discrimination and social exclusion that exists in Sri Lankan society is less well understood.

This chapter looks at some of the ways in which Sri Lankan young people as a group experience discrimination and social exclusion, especially in employment. In particular it looks at the ways in which sociocultural values and practices have differentiated Sri Lankan society along class lines, which also parallel or are *perceived* (especially by youth) to parallel the distribution of power and privilege in society.

This chapter acknowledges the significance of factors such as gender and ethnicity in Sri Lankan society as the basis of discrimination and exclusion, but it focuses on other social and cultural factors that also lead to class and status inequalities and that cut across issues such as gender and ethnicity. Here, class is defined not only by economic factors but by other social and cultural factors such as language, social networks, and symbols of westernization that are considered to be markers of modernity and progress. The chapter's emphasis on class is not in any way meant to minimize the significance of gender and ethnicity as sources of discrimination but to draw attention to other, less obvious sources of discrimination at work in Sri Lanka.

The chapter discusses the concept and problems of youth as they have been constructed in Sri Lanka, and it briefly examines how the failure to understand the less obvious factors of discrimination and exclusion has resulted in ineffective policy responses that have sometimes reinforced (perhaps unconsciously) some of the sources of discrimination that they ostensibly seek to eliminate.

Analyzing and understanding the factors of discrimination and exclusion are important aspects of policy development. Unequal treatment of people within societies based on various factors such as ethnicity, class, caste, and gender are recognized, at least at a theoretical level, as significant determinants of people's ability to access the power and resources necessary for economic and social development. The increasing fascination of the humanitarian and development sector with the "rights-based approach" and the importance given to "mainstreaming gender in development" and "assessment of vulnerability" attest to the growing acceptance of the need to understand the sources of inequality in society. As a result, development and policy initiatives increasingly tend to focus on particular groups that are considered more vulnerable or marginalized.

The understanding that policy and development initiatives need to deal with the differential distribution of power and privilege is a significant shift within development discourse. With the linking of human rights to development, the definition of development has shifted from a sole focus on improving people's material conditions to a more human-rights oriented goal of eliminating constraints to human dignity and oppressive processes that deny people the right to develop their full potential (Marks 2005). However, the translation of these theoretical shifts into development policy and program interventions has sometimes been at the cost of isolating particular groups for interventions, while ignoring the complex systemic and historical sources of discrimination.

Youth "Problems"

In Sri Lanka the problems of youth are inextricably bound up in violent conflict, which has led to perceptions that youth are the problem. The Janatha Vimukthi Peramuna (JVP), a political movement that led the antistate insurgencies in the south in 1971 and 1989, and the militant groups—mainly the Liberation Tigers of Tamil Eelam (LTTE) in the north and east that have been fighting for a separate state—were mainly made up of young people. As a result, youth, especially educated but nonwesternized youth from poor families in rural areas, are perceived by politicians, policymakers, and development practitioners as being frustrated and angry at their inability to find work and fit into the larger society and thus as being "ripe" for violence. The identification of youth as a vulnerable group has taken on special significance because if an inherent characteristic of frustrated youth is the potential for violence or revolt, then neglecting the needs of youth can be seen as a possible danger for social cohesion and order.

Generally the government has responded to youth unrest in one of two somewhat contradictory ways: brutal state repression to quell actual violence (leading to the killing, torture, and "disappearance" of perhaps 100,000 or more youth, if both the JVP rebellions and the LTTE conflicts are taken into account); or policy attempts to manage youth anger and frustration by setting up special programs targeting young people, be it in the form of employment creation, cultural and sports activities, or poverty alleviation schemes. Very rarely have policies and development interventions actually acknowledged that the anger felt by youth may be legitimate, based on very real experiences of injustice and discrimination. Nor has there been much acknowledgment that many of the factors underlying the anger and frustration among youth stem from serious flaws in economic and social policies and programs, particularly those directed toward marginalized, outcast, and underprivileged groups.

One early recognition of these underlying problems came from the Presidential Commission on Youth, set up in 1990 by then-president

Ranasinghe Premadasa. The commission documented the sense of alienation from established political, social, labor, and community institutions felt by many young people and concluded that the "stark injustices [in the treatment of rural youth] apparent to all as a blemish on society, aggravated by the brazen arrogance with which they were perpetrated, provided a sympathetic rural background to the politics of violence" (Presidential Commission 1990). The commission found that youth did not have confidence that any existing institutions would help them meet their aspirations and so took a fundamentally antiestablishment stance. The commission also noted how removed the aspirations of these youth were from the priorities of national planners. The commission laid out a number of issues that it said should be dealt with, including the lack of public confidence in institutions; the abuse of political power, especially with regard to the public sector; inadequate education policy; discriminatory language policy; caste and ethnic issues; and rural-urban disparities. Nearly 20 years later, little progress has been made, an indication of how reluctant those in power have been to address the issues underlying youth violence.

Youth Perceptions of Discrimination

Many studies of youth in Sri Lanka indicate that the problems they say they experience are similar across both gender and ethnic divides. This is not to say that young people do not face gender or ethnic discrimination, and there are clearly many differences based on both gender and ethnicity, but these are not the only sources of discrimination. What is significant is that young women and men, across ethnic groups, tend to share similar opinions about many other issues that they perceive as sources of youth anger and frustration.

Instead of exploring these issues, however, most policy and development initiatives tend to interpret the anger and frustration youth express as something that needs to be managed rather than as a symptom of legitimate concerns. While youth violence is understood as mainly stemming from frustration, there is little recognition that the sources of much of this frustration result from huge disparities between individual aspirations and basic opportunities, as well as from unequal distribution of the benefits of development and economic growth (Mayer 2004).

The National Youth Survey, which was conducted in 1999–2000, provides some interesting insights into the ways that youth perceive and experience discrimination. According to this survey, social justice is an important value for Sri Lankan youth. However, a large majority

(71.2 percent) of youth felt that Sri Lanka was not a just society (Hettige 2002: 34). This sense of injustice was also identified 10 years earlier by the Presidential Commission on Youth, which said that a fundamental cause of youth unrest was the feeling of injustice, lack of equity, and denial of opportunities in society. The commission observed a profound sense of dissatisfaction with the inability of established institutions and mechanisms, such as the electoral system, the police, and the bureaucracy, to meet the aspirations of people. Young people said they felt that corrupt and opportunistic politicians in particular were responsible for the failure of the state to look after the needs of its citizens (Hettige 2002; Presidential Commission 1990; Thangarajah 2002). In addition, a significant percentage of youth surveyed by the presidential commission and the National Youth Survey said the failure of the establishment to respond to these problems justified violence as a means of achieving their ends (Presidential Commission 1990; Thangarajah 2002).

Youth also felt a class gap between those who have power and the common people. The concept of class in this context is not seen merely in terms of income but also in the kind of social connections and networks people are able to forge. Youth acknowledged that the correct political and social connections have a significant impact on the ability to access resources. But such connections are not available or accessible to the majority, and youth viewed the lack of these connections as a fundamental reason for their inability to obtain employment. According to a study on school-to-work transition in Sri Lanka, 64 percent of young jobholders were recruited through recommendations of their friends and relatives (Mayer and Salih 2003). The correct social connections and a shared cultural ideology were seen as essential for gaining jobs in the private sector. Job applicants who wanted work in the formal sector but who did not have the correct old-school or family ties found themselves at a great disadvantage. Many youth from less privileged backgrounds (those who did not go to prestigious schools or do not have influential family connections) find that the only kind of connection they may have is a political connection (to a village or district-level political leader, for example). That explains why youth tend to feel that political connections are important in finding employment.

The National Youth Survey also indicated that Sri Lankan youth were attracted more toward socialist, communist political ideologies (Hettige 2002:32). Given their strong sense of injustice, this is not surprising. It also explains why populist political parties such as the JVP are extremely successful in mobilizing youth and why, especially in the early years, many of the militant groups in the north and east had strong Marxist-Leninist orientations. Even the LTTE, especially in its early days, was seen as an anti-elite movement, especially in terms of its stands against caste discrimination (Thangarajah 2002; Uyangoda 2003). Perhaps youth universally tend to be more attracted to radical, revolutionary politics, but for many Sri Lankan youth, life experience seems to provide plenty of examples of the failure of established institutions to meet their aspirations and to fuel the justification of even violent means of challenging positions of power and privilege.

These feelings of injustice and dashed expectations at the hands of the state machinery need to be examined within the context of Sri Lankan politics, where political patronage has been an important means of accessing resources. The idea of the state as primarily responsible for social welfare as well as being the key source of resources was established quite early in the formation of the postcolonial Sri Lankan nation-state (Spencer 1990; Wickramasinghe 2006). The social and cultural elitism that existed in the early political leadership of Sri Lanka resulted in the institutionalization of a system of political patronage and favoritism in the distribution of the "spoils" of government. Thus, the public understands that despite the rhetoric, receiving protection and welfare from the state is not an entitlement but a privilege of social and political connections.

The introduction of neoliberal economic and social policies in the latter part of the 1970s, with its underlying principle of minimizing the role of the state, had little impact on this system of political patronage. In fact, in many instances, foreign aid flows to a new government seen as liberal and pro-Western made more resources available that enabled the state to extend its patronage (Moore 1990). Thus, it is important for policymakers and others to understand that what is described as the common people's "dependence" on the state for welfare, protection, and employment is not merely a question of negative, lethargic attitudes but is based on their exclusion from the economic and social means to advance on their own. Furthermore, while political patronage and favoritism within the government has received some attention, its existence in the private sector is less well recognized—even though the "right" connections are generally needed to obtain and advance in a job.

Given the social rigidities in the culture and the pervasiveness of the patronage system, parents and family have a significant investment in the education and employment of youth, since they may very well be the means of achieving social mobility for the older generation as well as the rest of the family. Thus the jobs choices youth make are shaped not only by their own interests and aspirations but also by those of significant adults in their lives.

Common Assumptions in Analyzing Issues of Youth

A particular characteristic of policy and developmental interventions is that they tend to isolate categories analytically in ways that do not reflect the realities of people's lives or experiences. For example, "youth problems" cannot be accurately analyzed as a category without taking account of the particular socioeconomic and political circumstances in which youth live. Neither can the problems youth are perceived to face be isolated from their broader context. A more important factor for developing effective policy interventions might be to analyze whether the fact of being young means that circumstances affect young people differently from adults or whether youth and adults experience things differently within a broader context. Seeing problems in isolation or in terms of particular sectors, categories, or target groups is a peculiarity of development policy—one that tends to serve the needs of development and policy structures rather than describing what actually exists. The danger in seeing things in these isolated categories is that complex social phenomena tend to be simplified and then responses are developed in equally simplistic and isolated ways (de Sardan 2005).

One common assumption when analyzing youth unemployment is the existence of a mismatch between education and employment, that is, the education system does not provide youth with the skills needed in the existing labor market. This mismatch is sometimes explained as "voluntary unemployment," where youth, especially educated youth, are said to be waiting for the "right" job that fits their educational qualifications. Another common assumption holds that labor is accorded no dignity in Sri Lankan society and hence manual work is undervalued, resulting in overreliance on white-collar jobs in the public sector to provide employment. Youth are also seen to prefer jobs in the public sector because they find work in the private sector to be too demanding (ILO 2004).

Thus the situation is described in ways that associate the unemployment problem with the unrealistic and high aspirations of educated youth, who view white-collar jobs (preferably in the public sector) as the only type of suitable employment, and also with the education system that does not teach the necessary skills required by the labor market. In this regard, unemployed graduates gain a lot of attention, and there is significant pressure on the education system, especially higher education institutions, to align curricula to the job market. Within this context, for example, academic qualifications in the humanities or liberal arts are seen as being particularly out of step with the current labor market. Several points here need to be considered carefully.

Disparities in Education

Research has shown that although Sri Lanka has provided free education, making access to education more equitable, there are inequalities when it comes to the *type* of education that is accessible. Economic constraints on resource allocation have resulted in a deterioration of the quality of education that has affected schools differentially. For instance, only 26.2 percent of schools provided science education facilities at senior secondary level, while many schools did not have qualified teachers or laboratory facilities (Ministry of Education 2006). At least one study (ADB 2004) has found clear links between socioeconomic background, resource allocation, and school performance, adversely affecting youth from low-income backgrounds who attend poorly resourced schools. Almost a quarter of schools had less than 100 students apiece; these schools are neglected in the allocation of resources and face the threat of closure. School closures in remote areas have especially affected school attendance by girls, who face problems of mobility in areas with poor transport and infrastructure facilities (ADB 2004).

As mentioned earlier, only about 2 percent of those eligible for higher education actually seek it. Studies further suggest clear socioeconomic disparities with regard to family and educational background, school attended, and income, as well as gender differences among students who do pursue higher education. A high number of students enroll for liberal arts degrees, not necessarily out of choice but because they lacked opportunities at the secondary level to qualify for entrance in scientific fields. The majority of students who enroll for liberal arts degrees come from low-income, rural, disadvantaged families, where parents are not engaged in professional work, whereas students who are enrolled in science degrees, especially medical, engineering, and veterinary science, come from more privileged backgrounds (Jayaweera and Shanmugam 2002).

The number of women entering university has been increasing in recent years, but they seem to be concentrated in particular types of degree courses, such as the arts, law, and biological sciences. For example, in 2002 more than half of the university population was women, who were concentrated in liberal arts and law (Gunawardena 2003). Women graduates also tend to come from slightly more advantaged economic and

social backgrounds, indicating that women from disadvantaged backgrounds have more constraints in accessing higher education (Jayaweera
and Shanmugam 2002). However, the largest numbers of unemployed
are among liberal arts and law graduates, and unemployment among
women with A-level qualifications and above is 16.5 percent, compared with 7.7 percent among men with a similar level of educational
attainment (Gunawardena 2003, DCS 2006).

Thus, the problem is far more complex than a simple mismatch
between education and employment. Disparities in the provision of
secondary education, resulting in disparities in the types of educational
skills that are being learned, appear to have an adverse effect on the
employability of youth, particularly rural women.

The disparities in educational attainment become all the more stark
when considering regional and sectoral educational attainment levels
rather than national averages. For instance, while the national literacy rates
are over 90 percent, female literacy in the estate sector is 74.7 percent and
male literacy is 88.3 percent. Literacy rates in Eastern, Uva, and Central
provinces are also below 90 percent; the highest rate is in Western
Province. Eastern Province is a conflict-affected area, while both Uva and
Central provinces consist of large estate sector populations. Western
Province is the most urbanized as well as the wealthiest province, accounting for almost half of the country's gross domestic product. Research
has also shown that interdistrict disparities are increasing in Sri Lanka,
while a recent study by the Asian Development Bank (2007) shows
rapid increases in income inequality over the past two or three decades.
Inequality can be measured not only in terms of income and expenditure
but also in terms of access to services and the quality of services that are
available to the population. Unequal educational opportunities obvi-
ously skew the employability of youth in favor of those who have access
to educational institutions and other facilities with better resources.

It is also clear that when policymakers and others talk of the aspirations of "highly" educated youth, they are talking primarily about youth
who are either O (ordinary)-level or A-level qualified. Considering that
these are youth who have completed between 11 and 13 years of school,
this level of schooling constitutes what many would consider a basic level
of education. While it is important to look at the quality of education, it
is also necessary to look at the kind of opportunities that exist in the labor
market that match the reasonable aspirations of youth with a basic secondary education and to examine ways to diversify the opportunities in
the labor market rather than to blame youth for having high aspirations.

In fact, the low number entering universities should be a cause of concern, because it suggests that many eligible youths are unable to pursue higher education and are left with unfulfilled aspirations.

Alienation in the Private Sector

Since 1977 the private sector has been considered the "engine of growth" in the country. However, young people have not been employed in significant numbers in the sector other than in low-paying and informal work such as the export garment industry or in foreign employment. Conventional wisdom holds that youth are not interested in jobs in the private sector, because it is too demanding and competitive, but this conclusion needs to be examined more closely. What kinds of jobs in the private sector are available to youth? What skills and cultural norms are required by the private sector? Why do young people appear to be reluctant to look for work in the private sector but line up to apply for job vacancies in the public sector?[1]

While the education system needs to take some responsibility for not providing the necessary skills, there are also social and cultural factors that exclude a majority of youth from gaining employment in most areas of the private sector. Social networks play a crucial role in gaining employment in the private sector, especially in the corporate sector. English proficiency is a necessity, and status, such as family background and type of school attended, is equally important. In surveys, young job applicants have revealed that in job interviews in the private sector, they have been humiliated by overt references to their lack of certain preferred personality traits that indicate a more cosmopolitan and urban lifestyle, self-confidence, and English skills (Jayaweera and Shanmugam 2002). It should not come as a surprise that young people who are not from privileged backgrounds would choose to avoid such humiliations.

This sense of cultural alienation is reinforced by employment policies and programs that do not recognize the humiliation and resentment young people feel toward the private sector. Instead these programs blame youth and their families for having bad attitudes and focus their efforts on changing these attitudes.

Similar recruiting patterns exist even in nongovernmental organizations and the development sector, which supposedly have values that promote justice and equality. Informal surveys of the staff within the nonprofit development and humanitarian sector, particularly in urban areas, find no significant difference in the social or cultural expectations between this sector and the private sector. While job applicants from all backgrounds may find work in low-paid jobs in the field offices and in so-called "volunteer" positions, when it comes to the more prestigious, better-paid, and high-skilled jobs, there is clearly a preference for personal characteristics that only people from a specific elite socioeconomic background would possess.

The Politics of Language

Lack of proficiency in English is something that youth have identified as a significant reason for not being able to get jobs, especially in the private sector. English literacy has also been identified by policymakers, politicians, and all others concerned with education reforms and youth unemployment as one of the most urgent issues that needs to be addressed. However, the ways in which English proficiency is understood and also the ways in which attempts to increase English proficiency are undertaken need to be analyzed within the context of the contentious issue of the politics of language in Sri Lanka.

Language has been and continues to be a source of social exclusion in Sri Lanka. During Sri Lanka's colonial history, English was the language of the elite and the upper classes, which controlled (and to a large extent continue to control) social, economic, and political power in the country. The Presidential Commission on Youth referred to the English language as a *kaduwa* (sword) that gave the English-speaking elite the class power to cut down the Sinhala- and Tamil-speaking majority (Presidential Commission 1990). Language discrimination affects all spheres of life, including employment; it also impedes the social mobility of youth who speak only Sinhala or Tamil. While English is taught in all schools as a second language, many schools suffer from lack of adequate or trained teachers.

For a small elite in Sri Lanka, English is not a second language or a link language, it is the home language. A distinction is made between people who learn English at home and those who learn it only in school. This distinction is one of status and privilege, with those who learn it at home believing that the English they speak is based on the "more correct" British English as opposed to the "not pot"[2] English of the masses (Gunasekera 2005).

In this context, it is not whether one can read, write, and speak English proficiently that is important, but whether one can write and speak British English with the proper British accent. Inability to speak English "correctly" is considered indicative of a person's rural, nonurbanized, socially inferior background. Thus proficiency in English is about more than learning a world language that allows access to resources and the ability to communicate across cultures; it is also a *cultural* marker that differentiates between the haves and the have-nots, the elites and the masses, tradition and modernization, and the capital and the periphery (Rampton 2003). For Sri Lankan youth who do not speak English or who speak it with something other than a British accent, language has become a form of discrimination and social exclusion.

It is therefore ironic (and another source of humiliation) that attempts to make youth more employable, including teaching them English as is done in many universities now, also sometimes incorporates training on personal grooming and etiquette, including the proper use of cutlery and the rules of fine dining.[3] Some "mentoring" programs conducted by the private sector for youth include similar etiquette lessons. Thus, English is very much linked to certain cultural practices, images, and skills valued by the elite and considered, implicitly if not explicitly, as requirements for employment.

In contrast, the public sector has been the traditional source of employment for those coming through the free education system. Here the cultural markers of modernization and privilege are less important. However, language issues are a factor, especially for those who are Tamil-speaking. Unless one has Sinhala language skills, opportunities to work are extremely limited outside the north and east, where the majority of Tamils live.

Social Mobility and Status in the Public Sector

For those who do not already belong to the cultural elite, the kind of employment obtained can be a crucial determinant not only of social mobility but of one's ability to tap into existing systems of patronage for accessing even basic facilities and resources. Thus, the choices that young people make with regard to employment must be seen in a broader context than simply whether youth lack an adequate work ethic. Uyangoda (2003:47) argues that the social mobility of the underprivileged and marginalized groups in Sri Lanka is limited by the "rigid and inflexible structures of social dominance."

One way youth seek to escape these rigidities is through employment in the public sector. Public jobs are desirable not only for their economic benefits—higher pay, better benefits, and greater job security—but also because the public sector provides an extremely important space where people are able to compete on comparatively equal terms. Public sector employment is often also a strategy for developing the connections that are necessary for those without the connections or the financial strength to gain access to services and resources. The importance of knowing someone in order to obtain good treatment at a hospital, to get through the red tape in a government department, or to ensure admission of a child to a school is well understood in Sri Lanka. Having a member of the family working in a hospital or holding a position in a government department is therefore an extremely valuable asset. The fact that these connections are necessary is an indication of the difficulties faced by people who are excluded from positions of power and privilege in negotiating their everyday lives.

For many years after independence, the public sector provided employment to the underprivileged. But as more and more young Sri Lankans obtained education, and as agrarian reforms provided the means of moving out of rural poverty, the public sector was no longer able to fulfill the demand for jobs. Economic liberalization and structural adjustment that began in the 1970s slowed the growth of the public sector even as demand for jobs grew greater. Politicization and corruption in the public sector also narrowed the opportunities for social mobility within this sector.

Still, as demonstrated by the agitation for employment in the public sector and by the movement of young people from higher-paying jobs in the private sector to the public sector if such opportunities arise, the demand for public sector employment continues to be high. A job in the public sector is the top preference among all ethnic groups and among both men and women (Mayer and Salih 2005).

Gender and Caste

Employment statistics show that females experience more unemployment and underemployment than males, but neither young women nor men identify gender as a primary factor of discrimination. This may indicate a lack of gender awareness among both women and men, but it is more likely that young people view other socioeconomic factors, such as class, as the basis of discrimination. Studies have also revealed that economic constraints rather than gender affect girls' education, although women, at least so far, have not been able to translate their educational achievements into employment opportunities (ADB 2004).

The fact that gender constraints have limited women's achievements in employment is evident when examining some of the cultural values that shape attitudes and behavior that in turn influence young women's employment choices. Respectability, honor, and dignity are important culturally and shape many norms and practices that govern social behavior and relationships. The concept of *lajja-baya*, which has at various times being glossed as shame or respectability, is very much a part of the socialization process for young women. Avoiding being labeled as lacking *lajja-baya* is of special importance to women, who strive to embody the concept in their demeanor, appearance, and behavior (de Alwis 1997).

Women working in certain types of employment (garment factories, migrant workers, tourist industry) are extremely vulnerable not only to the kinds of exploitation that are inherent in some of these sectors but also to being said to be without *lajja-baya*, a label that can jeopardize a young woman's personal, social, and economic future. These jobs require women to leave the protection of their homes and communities and give them a degree of independence and freedom, but the jobs also raise stereotypical notions of their behavior. Reports of widespread sexual harassment, pregnancies, abortions, and sexually transmitted diseases have resulted in female migrant workers, most of whom work as housemaids, as well as women working in the free trade zones being viewed as victims of their own loose moral behavior (Hewamanne 2003). While these women have their own strategies for coping with the stereotypes and moral standards that are imposed on them, these jobs do not carry with them the level of respectability and status that is usually sought in employment.

Nor are the returns from these jobs so attractive financially or in terms of career advancement that women would willingly risk the possibility of flouting social norms. Most young, educated Sri Lankan women would not choose to work in these sectors unless driven to it through lack of other choices and severe financial need. However, the casualization (increase of informal jobs) of labor stemming from macroeconomic reforms has restructured women's employment opportunities mainly to these sectors, where they are exposed to exploitation, abuse, and stigmatization. Thus, to understand reluctance to take these jobs merely as indicating young women's lack of awareness of the notion of dignity of labor is to simplify the manifold issues women have to consider when making employment decisions and also to underestimate the social pressures on women.

In seeking to explain the high prevalence of suicide in Sri Lanka among women ages 16–30, Jeanne Maracek (2004) suggests that young women, already low in the status hierarchy because of their gender and youth, have few acceptable ways of articulating their distress and grievances, particularly toward those who are closest to them. Maracek documented many cases of self-harm where young women expressed emotions of "hurt, humiliation, betrayal and a sense of maltreatment" and said they had attempted to "right the wrong, to reassert one's dignity, or *aathma gavurawaya.*" This shows the force of concepts such as honor, shame, and dignity on the lives of young women, especially among young Sinhalese women.

An issue that is rarely discussed is that of caste discrimination within each ethnic group. The common belief is that caste is not a serious issue of discrimination and social exclusion in Sri Lanka, particularly among the Sinhala community. However, the National Youth Survey revealed that caste is an unacknowledged but present factor. For instance, significant numbers of youth, especially in the north and east where there is a higher percentage of Tamils, acknowledged caste as a factor to be considered in marriage. The Presidential Commission on Youth also identified caste as an issue and recommended specific steps to address discrimination. Although many experts argued that there was no connection between caste and youth, a significant number of people told the commission that caste played a very significant role in youth unrest. They claimed that some of the most brutal violence aimed at quelling the JVP insurgency in the late 1980s had taken place in lower-caste JVP villages. In the north too, it has been noted that the first militant movements were mobilized to protest caste oppression. It appears that caste is an unacknowledged factor in Sri Lankan society and needs to be recognized and addressed (Presidential Commission 1990; Rampton 2001).

Ethnicity

In addition to the perceptions of discrimination expressed by ethnic youth, the long-lasting conflict in Sri Lanka has had a significant impact on the opportunities available to minority youth. Quite apart from the conflict, data indicate that while unemployment rates have declined in rural and urban areas, they have *risen* in the estate sector, where a significant percentage of the population is Tamil (Central Bank 2004). Educational attainment is also lower than the national average in the estate sector. Furthermore, it appears that Muslim youth in the east have the longest waiting period before obtaining their first job (Mayer and Salih 2003). Significant numbers of Muslims (also called Moors) live in Eastern and Central provinces, which are among the most poorly resourced in the country, and ethnic discrimination is considered by some analysts to play a significant factor in allocation of government resources and service provision.

It is interesting that while both Tamil and Sinhala youth have taken to armed struggles at various times, and have therefore drawn the attention of policy makers, the same has not happened with regard to Muslim youth or to Tamil youth in the estate sector. The political representatives for both of these groups have also tended to be less confrontational and more inclined to collaborate with the government in power. For example, the Ceylon Workers Congress, which represents primarily estate workers, a majority of whom are Tamil-speaking, while agitating for estate workers' rights did not openly align itself with the armed struggle of the Tamils in the north and east.

The militarization of the north and east and security concerns in the rest of the country also meant that young men and women from the ethnic minorities were subject to increased surveillance and monitoring. That severely affected the mobility of these groups, which also affected their job-seeking opportunities. As mentioned earlier, the public sector has been an important source of employment for the minorities, more so during heightened periods of security concerns, because it provided a degree of legitimacy and identity. Strategies for improving employment among youth should consider whether opportunities for minority youth in the public sector have been declining as a result of the recent conflict and how that decline might be linked to the issue of language.

Conclusion

Policymakers and development practitioners are struggling with ways to address Sri Lanka's youth problems, especially the issue of youth unemployment. The frustrated aspirations of youth are seen as leading them toward violence, and thus addressing youth grievances is seen as necessary for maintaining cohesion and stability in the larger community.

However, as this chapter suggests, the current links that are drawn between youth violence, youth frustration, unemployment, and education often overlook some broad, structural issues that perpetuate an unjust and discriminating system. The factors that give rise to discrimination are linked to particular sociocultural aspects of Sri Lankan society that need to be understood carefully. If they are not, attempts to respond to the "problems" youth face will be driven by superficial and cursory analysis that blames youth for their problems. Furthermore, there appears to be a gap between what national and development policies propose and what people represent as their needs and aspirations. The question whether interventions purporting to respond to people's problems are actually based on consideration of ground realities or are instead linked to the political and economic needs of those in power both locally and globally is something that needs to be carefully explored.

Notes

1. Statement made by Minister of Labor at the launch of the YEN Youth Unemployment Report, September, 2007.
2. "Not-pot" English is a disparaging reference to the "incorrect" use of the English language as exemplified by the pronunciation these two words.
3. Personal communication, Romola Rassool, Head, English Language Teaching Unit, Kelaniya University.

References

ADB (Asian Development Bank). 2004. *Country Gender Assessment, Sri Lanka.* Manila: South Asia Regional Department and Regional and Sustainable Development Department, Asian Development Bank, Manila

———. 2007. *Inequality in Asia, Key Indicators 2007, Special Chapter Highlights.* Manila: Asian Development Bank.

Central Bank of Sri Lanka. 2004. "Consumer Finances and Socio-Economic Surveys, 2003/04." Colombo.

DCS (Department of Census and Statistics). 2006. "Sri Lanka Labour Force Survey, 4th Quarter, 2006." Colombo.

———. 2007. "Sri Lanka Labour Force Survey, 4th Quarter, 2007." Colombo.

de Alwis, Malathi. 1997. "The Production and Embodiment of Respectability: Gendered Demeanors in Colonial Ceylon." In *Sri Lanka: Collective Identities Revisited: Vol. 1*, ed. Michael Roberts. Colombo: Marga Institute.

de Sardan, Jean-Pierre Olivier. 2005. *Anthropology and Development: Understanding Contemporary Social Change*, translated by Antoinette Tidjani Alou. London: Zed Books.

Gunasekera, Manique. 2005. *The Postcolonial Identity of Sri Lankan English.* Kelaniya, Sri Lanka: University of Kelaniya.

Gunawardena, Chandra. 2003. "Gender Equity in Higher Education in Sri Lanka: A Mismatch between Access and Outcomes." *McGill Journal of Education* 38 (3).

Hettige, S. T. 2002. "Sri Lankan Youth: Profiles and Perspectives." In *Sri Lankan Youth: Challenges and Responses*, ed. S. T. Hettige and Markus Mayer. Colombo: Friedrich Ebert Stiftung.

Hettige, S. T., Markus Mayer, and Maleeka Salih, eds. 2004. *School-to-Work Transition of Youth in Sri Lanka.* Geneva: International Labour Organization.

Hewamanne, Sandya. 2003. "Performing Disrespectability: New Tastes, Cultural Practices and Identity Performances by Sri Lanka's Free Trade Zone Garment Factory Workers." *Cultural Dynamics* 15: 71.

ILO (International Labour Organization). 2004. "The National Employment Policy and Young People: The Youth Employment Challenge in Sri Lanka." Inception report, ILO, Colombo.

Jayaweera, S., and T. Shanmugam. 2002. *Graduate Employment in Sri Lanka in the 1990s*. Colombo: Centre for Women's Research.

Marecek, Jeanne. 2004. "To Die For? Suicide and Self-harm in Rural Sri Lanka." Paper presented at the Seminar on Suicide in Sri Lanka sponsored by Sumithrayo Rural Programme, September.

Marks, Stephen. 2005. "The Human Rights Framework: Seven Approaches." In *Reflections on the Right to Development*, ed. Arjun Sengupta, Archna Negi, and Moushumi Basu. New Delhi: Sage Publications for the Centre for Development and Human Rights.

Mayer, Markus. 2004. "Reinterpreting Ethnic Tensions in Sri Lanka." In *Race: Identity, Caste and Conflict in the South Asian Context*, ed. Ameena Hussain. Colombo: International Centre for Ethnic Studies.

Mayer, M., and M. Salih. 2003. "Poverty Alleviation and Conflict Transformation." In *Building Local Capacities for Peace: Rethinking Conflict and Development in Sri Lanka*, ed. M Mayer and others. New Delhi: Macmillan.

Ministry of Education. 2006. *School Census of 2006*. Colombo.

Moore, Mick. 1990. "Economic Liberalisation vs Political Pluralism in Sri Lanka?" *Modern Asian Studies* 24 (2): 341–83.

Rampton, David. 2003. "Sri Lanka's 'Many-Headed Hydra': The JVP, Nationalism and Politics of Poverty." In *Poverty Issues in Sri Lanka: Towards New Empirical Insights*. Colombo: CEPA/IMCAP/SLAAS.

Presidential Commission on Youth. 1990. *Report of the Presidential Commission on Youth*, Colombo: Government Publication Bureau.

Spencer, Jonathan. 1990. "Introduction: The Power of the Past." In *Sri Lanka: History and Roots of Conflict*, ed. Jonathan Spencer. London: Routledge.

Thangarajah, C. Y. 2002. "Youth Conflict and Social Transformation in Sri Lanka." In *Sri Lankan Youth: Challenges and Responses*, ed. S. T. Hettige and Markus Mayer. Colombo: Friedrich Ebert Stiftung.

Uyangoda Jayadeva. 2003. "Social Conflict, Radical Resistance and Projects of State Power." In *Building Local Capacities for Peace: Re-thinking Conflict and Development in Sri Lanka*, ed. Markus Mayer, Dharini Rajasingham-Sennanayake, and Yuvi Thangarajah. New Delhi: Macmillan India Ltd.

Wickramasinghe, Nira. 2006. *Sri Lanka in the Modern Age: A History of Contested Identities*. London: Hurst and Company.

CHAPTER 9

An Analysis of Gender and Ethnic Wage Differentials among Youth in Sri Lanka

Dileni Gunewardena

Wage inequality by gender and ethnicity characterize labor markets all over the world. In a labor market free of discrimination, unequal wages are the result of unequal productivity. Productivity differences are ascribed to differences in human capital accumulation, typically captured in endowments of schooling and experience. Group discrimination (such as sex or race discrimination) is evident when the average wage of a group in the labor market is not proportional to its average productivity.

Women in Sri Lanka have similar endowments to men at most levels of schooling. Starting in the 1940s female employment opportunities expanded from predominantly agricultural wage work in the pre-independence era to include a narrow set of state-dominated occupations (teaching, nursing, clerical, and finance-related jobs); since the 1980s women have also taken manufacturing jobs in export industries and jobs as domestic workers overseas.

The increase in female accumulation of human capital and the expansion of the range of occupations open to females in Sri Lanka suggest that at the turn of the millennium, younger females might have higher wages and face a smaller gender wage gap than older cohorts. Existing evidence from several studies (Aturupane 1996; Ajwad and Kurukulasuriya 2002; Gunewardena 2002), though not strictly comparable, indicates that the unconditional mean wage gap has indeed declined over time for women of all ages but that the remaining gap is unexplained. That is, while women have (more than) caught up with men in terms of productive characteristics, they continue to be paid less than men having the same characteristics.

Labor market institutions and practices also influence wage inequality. Considerable evidence suggests that unions, wage-setting mechanisms, and job-protection legislation in Sri Lanka all drive a wedge between "good" jobs in the regulated sector and "bad" jobs outside this sector (Rama 2003; Heltberg and Vodopivec 2004). Unexplained wage gaps or discrimination may occur because subordinate groups (like women and minorities) are tracked into lower-paying jobs (or are excluded from "good" jobs).[1] Women in the poorer regions may also be excluded from good jobs if these are concentrated in the growing urban regions located close to the capital city and cultural norms and restrictions on travel prevent them from accessing jobs in these areas. Minorities with restrictions on mobility may face similar constraints. The influence of cultural or institutional factors may have an indirect effect on the gender wage gap among different ethnic groups in the way that they determine geographical location and mobility.[2] Finally, gender-specific policies may influence employers' decisions in hiring and promoting women, thus widening the wage gap through employment discrimination.[3]

The context in which ethnic inequality in wages among the youth of Sri Lanka is analyzed is a 25-year-long conflict between the Liberation Tigers of Tamil Eelam (LTTE), a separatist group claiming to represent Tamils in Sri Lanka, and successive, predominantly Sinhala-majority governments. The economic roots of this conflict are attributed to public policy measures that were perceived as detrimental to the Tamil community: the Official Language Act of 1956 and provision of public sector jobs through political patronage, which limited Tamil access to these jobs; the use of affirmative action, which amounted to preferential treatment for Sinhalese students in university admissions in the 1970s; and the state-funded settlements of Sinhalese peasants in areas considered to be traditional homelands of the Tamil community. Related to the latter is the contention that central governments have done little to develop the Tamil hinterland. Sources of inequality and discrimination along ethnic lines, especially among youth, might then be related to education endowments and sector and occupation of employment, as well as to the region of employment.

The existing literature on Sri Lanka does not examine ethnic wage gaps, nor does it differentiate by sector and occupation in the examination of wage gaps. This study extends the Sri Lankan empirical literature by examining wage gaps between individuals who are of the same gender but of different ethnic groups (ethnic wage gaps) as well as between individuals of the same ethnicity but of different gender (gender wage gaps). The analysis is further disaggregated by sector (public, private, and agricultural) of employment. The study also examines the effect of occupational structure on wage gaps and focuses on the youngest wage cohort in the labor force.

The Sri Lankan Labor Market and Wage Inequality

Data: Sample Selection and Variable Definitions

Unit data come from the quarterly Labor Force Surveys (QLFSs) for the period from July 1996 to May 2004, conducted by the Sri Lankan Department of Census and Statistics (DCS). Each survey typically covers 18 of the 25 administrative districts in the country.[4] The survey is administered to approximately 4,000 housing units each quarter. The sample is selected using a two-step stratified random sampling procedure with no rotation, and a new random sample is drawn each quarter.

The sample in this study is restricted to individuals between the ages of 18 and 29 in all sectors of the economy (urban, rural, and estate), who were employees in their main occupation of work, who were "usually employed,"[5] and who had worked at least one hour in the week before the survey was administered. Individuals currently attending a school or educational institution or whose experience in the current job exceeded their potential experience (age minus years of schooling minus age schooling began) or who claimed to usually work less than 20 hours a week were excluded. Households in the 2003 and 2004 samples from Northern and Eastern provinces were also excluded from the main analysis to maintain comparability. Finally, the sample contains only individuals for whom the data on the characteristics listed in table 9.1 were available. The sample is disaggregated into public (nonagricultural), private (nonagricultural), and agricultural sectors. The private sector includes both formal and informal employees, but sample separation is not possible.

The sample of pooled observations from all nine years totals 25,125 observations (65 percent male, 35 percent female). About two-thirds (67 percent of males, 63 percent of females) are private sector employees,

15 percent of males and females are public sector employees, and 18 percent of males and 21 percent of females are agricultural sector employees (see table 9.1)

As in most government surveys, the QLFS questionnaire distinguishes between Sri Lankan Tamils and Indian Tamils. The latter are descendents of indentured workers from South India who migrated in the 19th and 20th centuries to work in the coffee, tea, and rubber plantations in the central highlands. The Indian Tamils continue to work in and around the estates of Central and Sabaragamuwa provinces, making up half of the population of the Nuwara Eliya district and almost one-fifth of the population of the Badulla district (DCS 2001). Sri Lankan Tamils have a much longer history in the country and engage in a variety of occupations. However, the distinction has become less meaningful over time, partly because of assimilation of Indian Tamils into the Sri Lankan Tamil identity, but mainly because many so-called Indian Tamils who have Sri Lankan citizenship consider themselves to be Sri Lankan Tamils and report their ethnicity as such in the census. For this reason, the distinction is ignored in this study and a single Tamil category is considered. Seventy-six percent of the male sample is Sinhala, 16 percent is Tamil, and 6 percent is Moor, while 74 percent of the female sample is Sinhala, 24 percent is Tamil, and 2 percent is Moor.[6]

Thirty-two percent of the sample is from the Western Province. Among the other provinces, a significantly higher share of females is evident in Central and Uva provinces, where plantation agriculture is a main source of female employment, mainly among (Indian) Tamils.

The definition of earnings underlying the wage gaps used throughout this chapter is the log of hourly earnings from the main occupation, where hourly wages are calculated as earnings in the last month from the main occupation divided by the hours usually worked in a month calculated as 30/7 times hours usually worked in a given week. Nominal values are converted to real terms using the Sri Lanka Consumer Price Index (SLCPI) with a base period of 1995–97. A second measure, the occupation-adjusted log of hourly earnings, eliminates between-occupation inequality from the distribution of earnings.[7] The occupation-adjusted earnings variable is a mean-preserving transformation of the log of hourly earnings that eliminates between-occupation variation, leaving only within-occupation variation.

Schooling is defined as years of schooling distinguished by n levels, which allows the coefficients on schooling to vary by level of schooling (primary; junior secondary; senior secondary including advanced, or

Table 9.1 Descriptive Statistics by Sector, Sex, and Ethnicity

	Public				Private				Agriculture				All			
	Male		Female		Male		Female		Male		Female		Male		Female	
Variable	Mean	sd	Mean	sd	Mean	sd	Mean	sd	Mean	sd	Mean	sd	Mean	sd	Mean	sd
All ethnicities																
Log of hourly earnings	2.849	0.474	2.876	0.525	2.584	0.560	2.473	0.494	2.292	0.453	2.127	0.382	2.572	0.554	2.463	0.528
Years of primary education	5.885	0.684	5.948	0.463	5.640	1.115	5.756	0.996	4.772	1.862	3.874	2.285	5.523	1.284	5.392	1.54
Years of junior secondary education	4.106	1.366	4.788	0.783	3.159	1.814	3.749	1.576	1.332	1.660	0.772	1.395	2.979	1.917	3.27	1.972
Years of senior secondary education	0.520	0.832	1.395	0.853	0.245	0.628	0.410	0.777	0.017	0.171	0.009	0.123	0.246	0.629	0.478	0.823
Years of postsecondary education	0.078	0.476	0.313	0.911	0.027	0.280	0.036	0.323	0.000	0.000	0.000	0.000	0.03	0.296	0.071	0.453
Occupational experience	3.633	2.542	3.188	2.119	2.998	2.477	2.548	1.953	4.628	3.260	5.103	3.453	3.384	2.714	3.182	2.577
Years of no experience in current occupation	4.867	3.084	4.182	2.553	5.642	3.699	4.619	3.500	6.938	3.949	8.254	4.199	5.754	3.71	5.312	3.848
Age	25.193	2.878	25.922	2.521	24.00	3.169	23.252	3.134	23.945	3.287	24.236	3.310	24.172	3.177	23.87	3.232
Married	0.321	0.467	0.391	0.488	0.304	0.460	0.188	0.391	0.423	0.494	0.652	0.477	0.328	0.469	0.317	0.465
Part-time	0.043	0.204	0.205	0.404	0.046	0.210	0.034	0.181	0.153	0.360	0.090	0.286	0.065	0.246	0.072	0.259
Western province	0.259	0.438	0.300	0.459	0.395	0.489	0.428	0.495	0.095	0.293	0.043	0.203	0.321	0.467	0.328	0.469
Sample size	2,486		1,358		10,946		5,596		2,898		1,841		16,330		8,795	
Sinhala																
Log of hourly earnings	2.863	0.461	2.869	0.522	2.611	0.567	2.485	0.477	2.346	0.494	2.059	0.469	2.626	0.558	2.532	0.521
Years of primary education	5.928	0.522	5.984	0.231	5.724	0.96	5.862	0.731	5.028	1.667	4.524	2.185	5.679	1.043	5.807	0.891
Years of junior secondary education	4.194	1.254	4.840	0.606	3.334	1.731	3.934	1.385	1.746	1.815	1.658	1.824	3.302	1.791	3.972	1.471
Years of senior secondary education	0.522	0.832	1.406	0.848	0.27	0.654	0.425	0.786	0.03	0.224	0.039	0.264	0.287	0.671	0.587	0.876
Years of post-secondary education	0.078	0.476	0.315	0.915	0.031	0.303	0.038	0.334	0	0	0	0	0.036	0.325	0.088	0.504

(continued)

Table 9.1 Descriptive Statistics by Sector, Sex, and Ethnicity (Continued)

	Public				Private				Agriculture				All			
	Male		Female		Male		Female		Male		Female		Male		Female	
Variable	Mean	sd	Mean	sd	Mean	sd	Mean	sd	Mean	sd	Mean	sd	Mean	sd	Mean	sd
Occupational experience	3.628	2.511	3.178	2.109	2.952	2.43	2.537	1.93	4.286	3.13	4.271	3.309	3.236	2.580	2.759	2.118
Years of no experience in current occupation	4.763	3	4.058	2.381	5.491	3.589	4.413	3.308	6.46	3.992	7.952	4.846	5.473	3.570	4.552	3.378
Age	25.221	2.872	25.882	2.534	24.076	3.142	23.322	3.122	23.87	3.304	24.611	3.352	24.262	3.148	23.88	3.198
Married	0.321	0.467	0.381	0.486	0.306	0.461	0.19	0.393	0.392	0.488	0.6	0.491	0.319	0.466	0.250	0.433
Part-time	0.036	0.186	0.165	0.372	0.048	0.214	0.032	0.176	0.164	0.37	0.232	0.422	0.060	0.237	0.069	0.253
Western province	0.263	0.44	0.314	0.464	0.393	0.488	0.424	0.494	0.135	0.342	0.108	0.311	0.338	0.473	0.385	0.487
Sample size	2,289		1,227		8,689		4,909		1,491		380		12,469		6,516	
Tamil																
Log of hourly earnings	2.556	0.598	2.892	0.526	2.408	0.532	2.315	0.536	2.219	0.394	2.144	0.355	2.327	0.487	2.216	0.443
Years of primary education	5.071	1.878	5.423	1.509	5.131	1.702	4.861	2	4.414	2.048	3.698	2.283	4.793	1.912	4.072	2.260
Years of junior secondary education	2.583	2.091	3.887	1.961	2.246	1.978	2.185	2.084	0.825	1.309	0.535	1.147	1.598	1.852	1.096	1.739
Years of senior secondary education	0.323	0.711	1	0.941	0.132	0.475	0.219	0.609	0.005	0.088	0.001	0.026	0.081	0.378	0.094	0.411
Years of post-secondary education	0.071	0.457	0.099	0.511	0.009	0.164	0.021	0.252	0	0	0	0	0.008	0.151	0.009	0.163
Occupational experience	3.881	3.085	3.561	2.424	3.244	2.721	2.694	2.161	5.122	3.392	5.333	3.447	4.151	3.202	4.558	3.333
Years of no experience in current occupation	6.496	3.978	5.742	4.005	6.431	4.214	6.351	4.423	7.504	3.823	8.352	4.012	6.935	4.059	7.721	4.235
Age	24.449	2.997	25.803	2.465	23.589	3.239	22.633	3.16	24.057	3.271	24.157	3.285	23.847	3.253	23.801	3.316
Married	0.315	0.466	0.479	0.503	0.277	0.448	0.167	0.374	0.46	0.499	0.669	0.471	0.364	0.481	0.526	0.499
Part-time	0.118	0.324	0.493	0.504	0.034	0.182	0.03	0.171	0.14	0.347	0.053	0.223	0.088	0.283	0.062	0.241
Western province	0.173	0.38	0.211	0.411	0.382	0.486	0.429	0.495	0.039	0.193	0.025	0.156	0.212	0.409	0.141	0.348
Sample size	127		71		1,340		562		1,286		1,443		2,753		2,076	

Moor

Log of hourly earnings	2.937	0.479	3.02	0.571	2.574	0.482	2.556	0.697	2.388	0.375	2.216	0.361	2.577	0.484	2.680	0.679
Years of primary education	5.924	0.319	5.845	0.875	5.574	1.2	5.478	1.346	5.391	1.309	4.278	2.109	5.576	1.181	5.476	1.380
Years of junior secondary education	4.091	1.556	4.776	0.937	2.784	1.881	3.12	2.127	1.574	1.493	1.056	1.514	2.733	1.893	3.47	2.07
Years of senior secondary education	0.818	0.943	1.621	0.697	0.167	0.532	0.696	0.923	0	0	0	0	0.189	0.564	0.94	0.958
Years of postsecondary education	0.091	0.518	0.483	1.096	0.01	0.177	0	0	0	0	0	0	0.014	0.207	0.167	0.680
Occupational experience	3.391	2.538	2.999	1.937	3.053	2.51	2.359	1.906	3.61	2.576	4.194	4.215	3.136	2.523	2.776	2.324
Years of no experience in current occupation	5.168	2.896	4.889	3.104	5.968	3.783	5.457	4.351	6.909	3.997	6.759	3.731	6.021	3.773	5.400	3.913
Age	25.621	2.71	26.879	2.153	23.858	3.294	23.283	3.417	23.626	3.232	22.667	3.662	23.944	3.281	24.458	3.529
Married	0.348	0.48	0.483	0.504	0.316	0.465	0.185	0.39	0.409	0.494	0.389	0.502	0.328	0.470	0.310	0.464
Part-time	0.167	0.376	0.69	0.467	0.043	0.203	0.141	0.35	0.165	0.373	0.056	0.236	0.064	0.245	0.321	0.468
Western province	0.227	0.422	0.138	0.348	0.424	0.494	0.446	0.5	0.2	0.402	0.111	0.323	0.387	0.487	0.304	0.461
Sample size	66		58		864		92		115		18		1,045		168	

Source: Author's computations based on data from DCS 1996–2004.

A-Level; and postsecondary). Experience is the individual's stock of experience with the current employer or firm. Another measure of (lack of) experience is defined as potential experience minus experience in the current occupation and is intended to capture time out of the labor force or current occupation. Marital status is a dummy variable taking the value of one if currently married. Part-time work is a dummy variable taking the value of one if an individual works between 20 and 35 hours a week. A dummy was included for Western Province, which has a higher level of economic activity than other provinces. The time dimension is incorporated by using dummy variables for each of the years in the sample (with 1996 as the reference year).

Potential Sources of Wage Disparities

Investments by the state education infrastructure in Sri Lanka both before independence and soon afterward have ensured high levels of primary enrollment (97 percent) and completion for all school-age children (World Bank 2005). At the lower secondary level, grade 9 completion rates are somewhat higher for girls (84 percent) than for boys (81 percent). Ethnic minorities, however, may have lower educational attainment at this level.[8] Table 9.1 shows higher endowments for Sinhalese and Moor women than for their male counterparts. Education gaps between Sinhalese males (females) and Tamil males (females) are large and significant, while small but significant education gaps occur between Sinhalese and Moor males at all levels.[9]

Human capital is also accumulated through experience and on-the-job training. Typically, married women tend to have less of both (because of intermittent labor force participation, reflecting their absence from the labor force during childbearing years), which may result in lower wages (Polachek 1975). Sri Lankan age-specific labor force participation rates show a pattern consistent with intermittency during childbearing years. Fifty percent of all women between 20 and 24 years of age are in the labor force, compared with 43 percent of those between the ages of 30 and 34 years. In the sample, which includes only younger women, intermittency is not evident, but women have significantly lower experience with the same employer than do men (last column of table 9.1).

The labor market attachment of women is influenced by child-care infrastructure and maternity or parental leave arrangements. Compulsory schooling in Sri Lanka begins at age 5, and there is very little state provision of child care for children younger than 5, except in plantation agriculture. Private provision of preschools and crèches (nurseries) is high and growing; about 60 percent of children ages 3 to 5 were estimated to have participated in preschool education in 2001 (World Bank 2005).[10] However, no information is available on the hours of child care provided per day. Sri Lankan maternity leave benefits during the period under study fully covered 84 days, which was on the upper boundary of the international norm of 12 to 14 weeks (Rodgers 1999). Provision of coverage and compliance are required only in the public sector and regulated private sector. Because there is no state allowance, the burden of providing leave in the private sector falls on the employer, creating a disincentive for employers to hire married women. The employment of women in the regulated sector is also subject to night-time work prohibitions and overtime limits.

Table 9.1 indicates that a lower share of married women work in the largely unregulated private sector and a higher share in the public sector. These figures are consistent with higher labor force attachment of females where compliance with maternity benefits is mandatory and workers may not be terminated. However, they could also be consistent with employment discrimination, if private sector workers avoided hiring married women and used subtle means to encourage married women to leave their jobs voluntarily before they give birth.

The shares of married women in the Tamil and Moor samples in the public sector were not significantly different from each other, but both were significantly lower than the share of Sinhalese married women in the public sector.[11]

Greater attachment in the agriculture sector is consistent with lower child-care constraints, either because of employers' actions, as in the provision of crèches in the plantations, or because of the flexibility provided by the nature of the hours and location of work and child-care provision within the family. In the agriculture sector, shares of married Tamil women were significantly higher than either of the other two ethnic groups. This is consistent with better institutional provision of child care for Tamil women in the plantation sector than for Sinhalese and Moor women who work in the unregulated nonplantation agriculture sector.[12]

The main employment and wage protection institutions that influence sectoral and occupational choice (segregation) in Sri Lanka are severance pay provisions embodied in the Termination of Employed Workmen's Act (Special Provisions) Act of 1971 (TEWA), the wage-setting mechanism and collective bargaining, and civil service hiring practices (World Bank 2006). Broadly speaking, while protecting employment, TEWA favors older employees (insiders) and restricts firm growth. However it does not apply to firms with fewer than 15 employees, to individuals with less than one year with the same firm or to firms in the Board of Investment (BOI) and free-trade zone (FTZ) sectors. Trade unions in these two sectors are also relatively weak, partly because of legislative provisions and partly because of the use of third-party contract systems to recruit workers and the practice of subcontracting work to home-based workers in the manufacturing export sector. Women are more likely to be employed in smaller, informal firms and in BOI and FTZ sectors. Information on experience with the same employer (see table 9.1) indicates that, on average, women in the public and private sectors (but not in the agriculture sector) have shorter spells with the same employer than their male counterparts. However, in all three sectors, ethnic minorities had similar or longer spells with the same employer than did Sinhalese.

Wages in the private sector are determined by 37 Tripartite Wage Boards, which set minimum wages for each skill level by sector.[13] Delegates to these boards are chosen from among major sectoral trade unions and active sectoral guilds of private employers and government nominees. While this system protects equal pay for equal work in the same job, it does not necessarily protect equal pay for work of equal value (comparable worth). Equal pay legislation has little impact on women's and minorities' relative wages when women and minorities are segregated by occupation and sector. However, in the plantation agriculture sector, which is strongly unionized, daily wage rates are similar, although men and women may engage in different tasks.

Sri Lanka has a large state sector, with 3.9 civil servants per 100 population, compared with the average of 2.6 per 100 population in Asia (World Bank 1998). Sri Lankan public sector jobs, like those elsewhere, are characterized by better stability, higher benefits, lower effort, more prestige—and better pay—than their private sector counterparts (Rama 2003). As in many countries, females have benefited from the large state sector. Relative sample sizes indicate that 15 percent of both men and women work in the public sector.

The sector is overwhelmingly Sinhalese (91 percent compared with 75 percent in the overall sample). Ad hoc recruitment policies of the government, which include patronage-based appointments to the civil service, are likely to benefit the majority Sinhalese group disproportionately. The official language policy is another means by which Tamil-speaking minorities in the south of the country (that is, the geographical area covered in this sample) are excluded from public sector jobs.

Methodology

The Model

The literature on decomposing wage gaps has its roots in Mincerian wage equations (Mincer 1974), where earnings are dependent on productive, income-generating characteristics that individuals possess such as schooling and experience.

$$\ln Y_i = bX_i + u_i, \tag{9.1}$$

where Y is the wage variable and X is a vector including all productivity-related characteristics for the ith individual.

Blinder (1973) and Oaxaca (1973) showed that mean wage gaps between groups could be decomposed into the effects of differences in average endowments of observable human capital and other productive characteristics, termed the characteristics effect or explained component (first term on the right), and differing returns to those characteristics, termed the coefficients effect or unexplained component or discrimination (second term). The assumption behind the method used is that in the absence of discrimination, the estimated effects of individuals' observed characteristics are identical for each group.

$$\overline{lny}_m - \overline{lny}_f = b_m(\overline{X}_m - \overline{X}_f) + \overline{X}_f \Delta b. \tag{9.2}$$

The formulation in equation 9.2 assumes that in the absence of discrimination, the "true" wage structure is the male wage structure, b_m. In other words, females would be paid as if they were males. The alternative assumption that the "true" wage structure is the female wage structure is given by

$$\overline{lny}_m - \overline{lny}_f = b_f(\overline{X}_m - \overline{X}_f) + \overline{X}_m \Delta b. \tag{9.3}$$

In this study, the basic Blinder-Oaxaca decomposition is used to examine gender and ethnic wage differentials. The original contributions of this study to the Sri Lankan literature examining gender and ethnic wage gaps include the use of nine years of labor force data, which when pooled yield relatively large sample sizes of ethnic minority employees, even when disaggregated by sector; the use of actual experience (tenure or experience with the same employer or firm) instead of potential experience; the incorporation of occupational structure using a measure of earnings from which between-occupation inequality has been eliminated, and the use of four alternative formulations of the discrimination-free wage structures (male, female, equally weighted, and coefficients from the pooled sample).[14] The covariates used are those described in the section on data, above.[15]

Limitations

The study has several limitations. The amount of schooling an individual possesses is treated as exogenous, when it could in fact be influenced by wages. Similarly, the endogeneity of labor force participation, sector, and occupation are not explicitly modeled. The difficulty in finding sufficiently good instruments to represent a labor market participation decision in the data, and the trade-off in using potential instead of actual experience in the selectivity model, are the main reasons that a selectivity correction is not made.

The results of this study should therefore be interpreted as conditional on the selected sample, and, in the absence of selectivity correction, the coefficients in the regressions should be considered as potentially biased and applicable only to the current sample and not to the working-age population in general.

In addition, the study examines disparities only in *wage* gaps. Evidence from other data sources indicates that including nonwage compensation (pensions, living quarters) increases the public sector earnings premium significantly (Heltberg and Vodopivec 2004).[16] Living quarters are included in the compensation package of (mainly Tamil) employees in the plantation agriculture sector but are not included in the data. This omission of nonwage compensation in the earnings variable may thus bias estimates of gender and ethnic discrimination.

Empirical Results

Gender Wage Gaps

Table 9.2 presents unconditional mean gender wage gaps, mean gender wage gaps conditional only on occupation, mean gender wage gaps conditional on the set of covariates described earlier, and mean gender wage gaps conditional on these covariates plus occupation.[17] A positive gap indicates that on average, male wages are higher than female, and a negative gap indicates that on average, female wages are higher than male.

Economy-wide mean unconditional gender wage gaps are given in the first row, first four columns of the first panel in table 9.2 and are roughly of the magnitude of 10 percent of the male wage; that is, young Sinhala and Tamil men have hourly wages that are approximately 9 percent and 11 percent higher, respectively, than young Sinhala and Tamil women.

Table 9.2   Mean Unconditional and Conditional (Unexplained) Gender Wage Gaps, by Sector and Ethnicity

Sector and decomposition	Unadjusted				Occupation, adjusted			
	All	*Sinhalese*	*Tamil*	*Moor*	*All*	*Sinhalese*	*Tamil*	*Moor*
All sectors								
Mean wage gap (unconditional)	0.109	0.093	0.111	−0.103	0.092	0.101	0.039	0.199
Female reference (conditional)	0.163	0.179	0.069	*0.064*	0.080	0.096	0.030	*0.085*
Male reference (conditional)	0.158	0.168	0.077	0.120	0.088	0.095	0.038	0.217
Pooled (conditional)	0.152	0.159	0.068	0.089	0.078	0.086	0.031	0.133
Equally weighted (conditional)	0.161	0.174	0.073	0.092	0.084	0.095	0.034	0.151
Public sector								
Mean wage gap (unconditional)	*−0.027*	*−0.006*	−0.336	*−0.083*	0.142	0.141	*0.072*	0.232
Female reference (conditional)	0.193	0.211	*0.011*	[a]	0.178	0.178	0.156	[a]
Male reference (conditional)	0.096	0.095	*0.053*	[a]	0.131	0.132	*0.118*	[a]
Pooled (conditional)	0.095	0.099	*0.020*	[a]	0.112	0.114	0.088	[a]
Equally weighted (conditional)	0.144	0.153	*0.032*	[a]	0.155	0.155	0.137	[a]
Private sector								
Mean wage gap (unconditional)	0.111	0.126	0.093	*0.018*	0.057	0.059	0.049	0.151
Female reference (conditional)	0.153	0.166	0.084	[a]	0.061	0.064	*0.031*	[a]
Male reference (conditional)	0.136	0.146	0.092	[a]	0.042	0.042	*0.035*	[a]
Pooled (conditional)	0.132	0.143	0.081	[a]	0.044	0.045	*0.027*	[a]
Equally weighted (conditional)	0.144	0.156	0.088	[a]	0.052	0.053	*0.033*	[a]
Agriculture sector								
Mean wage gap (unconditional)	0.165	0.286	0.076	[b]	0.180	0.318	0.089	[b]
Female reference (conditional)	0.153	0.274	0.051	[a,b]	0.166	0.304	0.060	[a,b]

(continued)

Table 9.2   Mean Unconditional and Conditional (Unexplained) Gender Wage Gaps, by Sector and Ethnicity *(Continued)*

Sector and decomposition	Unadjusted				Occupation, adjusted			
	All	*Sinhalese*	*Tamil*	*Moor*	*All*	*Sinhalese*	*Tamil*	*Moor*
Male reference (conditional)	0.134	0.295	0.051	a,b	0.147	0.332	0.059	a,b
Pooled (conditional)	0.126	0.270	0.043	a,b	0.136	0.303	0.050	a,b
Equally weighted (conditional)	0.144	0.284	0.051	a,b	0.157	0.318	0.060	a,b

Source: Author's computations based on data from DCS 1996–2004.
Note: All gaps that are not in italics are statistically significant at the 10 percent or higher level of significance.
a. Decomposition is not possible because at least one of the regressions is incompletely identified.
b. Wage gaps are not computed because the female Moor mean wage in agriculture is based on an extremely small (18) sample size.

Young Moor women have hourly wages that are approximately 10 percent higher than those of young Moor men.

The last four columns of table 9.2 present occupation-adjusted uncon-ditional wage gaps, that is, gaps where inequality between occupations has been eliminated. How should differences between occupation-unadjusted and occupation-adjusted unconditional wage gaps be interpreted?[18] A pos-itive unadjusted unconditional wage gap that changes very little when the wage distribution is adjusted for between-occupation wage inequality (as, for example, the aggregate Sinhalese gender gap, and Sinhala and Tamil wage gaps in the agricultural sector) is consistent with the gender gap reflecting *only* inequality within occupations or with similar between-occupation inequality for males and females.[19] A zero unadjusted uncon-ditional wage gap that expands when the wage distribution is adjusted for between-occupation wage inequality (all the Moor wage gaps and the Sinhalese public sector wage gap) is consistent with females being at the highest and lowest ends of the wage distribution (the zero wage gap resulting from a composition effect) with more females than males in the higher-paying occupations. A negative unadjusted unconditional wage gap that becomes a smaller negative, or zero, or positive, when the wage distribution is adjusted for between-occupation wage inequality (Tamil public sector wage gap) is consistent with females earning more than males on average, where some part of female higher earnings comes from females being in higher-paying occupations. On the other hand, a positive unadjusted unconditional wage gap that shrinks when the wage distribu-tion is adjusted for between-occupation wage inequality (the aggregate Tamil gender gap, and both Sinhalese and Tamil private sector gender gaps, for example) is consistent with a wage distribution where gender-based occupational wage stratification is stronger than gender-related wage inequality *within* occupations.

Next, wage gaps conditional on all the covariates described above based on Oaxaca decompositions are presented in the second to fifth rows of each section of table 9.2. The conditional wage gap is the *unexplained* component of the decomposition; it should, in the absence of discrimination, be zero or insignificant. Four references are presented for each conditional wage gap in terms of four references. First, the female reference decomposition is based on the assumption that in the absence of discrimination, the "true" wage structure is the female wage structure; thus, any unexplained portion of the wage gap that is larger than zero indicates that men are *overpaid*. Second, the male reference likewise presents any positive unexplained portion of the gap as the amount by which women are *underpaid*. Third, the equally weighted reference assumes a wage structure that is the (equally weighted) mean of the male and female wage (coefficients) structures (following Reimers 1983), while the pooled reference assumes the "true" wage structure to be that from the coefficients from a pooled model for both groups (Neumark 1988).

The decomposition of these gaps reveals that regardless of whether women are paid more or less than men, they are paid less than they should be given their productive endowments. For example, Sinhalese men are *overpaid* by approximately 18 percent (female reference); alternatively Sinhalese women are *underpaid* by 17 percent (male reference). That is, given the better productive characteristics (such as schooling) of Sinhalese women relative to Sinhalese men in the sample, they should actually be paid 7–9 percent more than the male wage; instead they are paid 9 percent less. At roughly 16–18 percent of the male wage, the magnitude of the underpayment is almost double the actual wage gap.

Similarly, given their endowments, Tamil women should be paid only 4 percent less than are Tamil men, but they are actually paid 11 percent less, indicating they are underpaid by 7–8 percent of the male wage.

On average, Moor men in the sample are paid 10 percent less than Moor women. If Moor women were paid like Moor men (that is, based on the male wage structure, row 3 of table 9.2), they would be paid 22 percent more than Moor men, indicating that Moor women are actually underpaid by approximately 12 percent of the male hourly wage. Moor male and female wage structures are different from each other: if the female structure was considered to be the discrimination-free structure, then Moor men are overpaid by only 17 percent (row 2 of table 9.2).

The first row of the second panel in table 9.2 indicates that on average men and women are paid similar wages in the public sector, except in the case of Tamils, where women are paid approximately 34 percent more. However, when otherwise identical men and women are compared, Sinhalese men are overpaid by 21 percent (female reference), or Sinhalese women are underpaid by 10 percent (male reference) of the wage structure.[20] The 34 percent higher wage that Tamil women are paid in the public sector is entirely explained by the better characteristics that Tamil women in this sector have compared with Tamil men.[21]

The male-favoring wage gap in the private sector is 13 percent among Sinhalese, 9 percent among Tamils, and zero among Moors. Sinhalese men are overpaid (Sinhalese women are underpaid) by approximately 15–16 percent of the hourly male wage. In the case of Tamils, men are overpaid (women underpaid) by the exact amount of the wage gap.

In the agriculture sector, the unconditional wage gap between Sinhalese is large, at almost 30 percent, while among Tamils, it is only marginally smaller than the private sector wage gap. The entire wage gap among Sinhalese is unexplained by productive characteristics—that is, women are underpaid (men are overpaid) by 27–30 percent of the male hourly wage. For Tamils in the agriculture sector, most of the (relatively small) wage gap is unexplained—women are underpaid by approximately 5 percent of the male hourly wage.

The second to fifth rows of the last four columns of table 9.2 present conditional wage gaps for distributions from which between-occupation inequality has been eliminated, and which include controls for the covariates described above. A positive unexplained component of the wage gap that diminishes in magnitude when occupational controls are included (as for example, with Sinhalese and Tamil aggregate and private sector gender wage gaps) is consistent with an occupational segregation explanation. The results suggest that part of the unexplained gender wage gap in the private sector is the result of Sinhalese and Tamil women being in lower-paying occupations relative to Sinhalese and Tamil men. The opposite is true for the aggregate Moor wage gap (table 9.2, first panel, last column, male, pooled and equally weighted reference) and Sinhalese and Tamil public sector gender wage gaps (second panel, sixth and seventh columns), where including occupational controls increases the size of the unexplained component of the wage gap. This is consistent with Moor women in general, and Sinhalese and Tamil women in the public sector being in higher-paying occupations relative to their male counterparts.

Ethnic Wage Gaps

Ethnic Wage Gaps among Males

Unconditional wage gaps between Sinhalese and Tamil males favor Sinhalese and are statistically significant in all sectors, ranging from 30 percent of the Sinhalese male wage in the public sector to 20 percent in the private sector and 13 percent in the agriculture sector (first panel, table 9.3). At least part of the gap is explained by poorer productive characteristics of Tamil males, but a large proportion of the gap is unexplained. In the public sector, Tamils are underpaid by 28 percent (Sinhalese are overpaid by 21 percent), while in the private and agriculture sectors, Tamils are underpaid by approximately 9—14 percent of the Sinhala male wage.

The use of different references for the discrimination-free wage structures has an impact on results for the male Sinhala-Tamil wage gap in the public and agriculture sectors, though not in the private sector.

Adjusting for occupation shrinks the Sinhala-Tamil unconditional wage gap (fifth to eighth columns in table 9.3) in all but the agriculture sector, where it remains the same. This suggests that wage gaps between Sinhalese and Tamil men in the public and private sectors owe more to occupational stratification along ethnic lines than to within-occupation inequality. Controlling for occupation reduces the unexplained component of the wage gap by almost half in the public sector, and by one-third in the private sector. This is consistent with Tamil men being in lower-paying occupations relative to Sinhalese men with identical characteristics.

In the public sector, occupational segregation by ethnicity may be influenced by the official language policy. Sinhala is the main official language in the districts included in this sample, but the districts in which Tamil is the official language are excluded from this sample. In addition, where political patronage and links with unions influence public sector hiring, Tamils are at a disadvantage. It is not clear how occupational segregation of minorities occurs in the private and largely informal sector. If hiring in the informal sector relies largely on private social networks, minorities who do not have their own economically strong social networks may be disadvantaged in accessing jobs in better-paying occupations.

The Sinhala-Moor wage gap among men is statistically significant in the private sector and insignificant in the others. Controlling for between-occupation inequality in the private sector reverses the sign of the gap, indicating that Moors earn more than Sinhalese *within* occupations, while Sinhalese men are in higher-paying occupations relative to Moor men. Unlike in the case of Tamil men, occupational stratification along ethnic

234 Gunewardena

Table 9.3   Mean Unconditional and Conditional (Unexplained) Ethnic Wage Gaps, by Sex and Sector

Sex and Decomposition	Unadjusted				Occupation-adjusted			
	All	Public	Private	Agricultural	All	Public	Private	Agricultural
Male								
Sinhala–Tamil wage gap								
Mean wage gap (raw)	0.299	0.307	0.203	0.126	0.046	0.130	0.101	0.120
Tamil reference	0.174	0.280	0.128	0.139	0.072	0.200	0.088	0.138
Sinhalese reference	0.152	0.209	0.114	0.105	0.035	0.098	0.068	0.098
Pooled	0.137	0.194	0.110	0.093	0.038	0.099	0.067	0.088
Equally weighted	0.163	0.245	0.121	0.122	0.053	0.149	0.078	0.118
Sinhala–Moor wage gap								
Mean wage gap (raw)	0.049	−0.074	0.037	−0.043	−0.028	0.024	−0.030	−0.048
Moor reference	0.017	[a]	0.002	[a]	−0.018	[a]	−0.030	[a]
Sinhalese reference	−0.001	[a]	−0.008	[a]	−0.033	[a]	−0.044	[a]
Pooled	0.001	[a]	−0.007	[a]	−0.032	[a]	−0.042	[a]
Equally weighted	0.008	[a]	−0.003	[a]	−0.026	[a]	−0.037	[a]
Tamil–Moor wage gap								
Mean wage gap (raw)	−0.250	−0.381	−0.166	−0.169	−0.074	−0.106	−0.132	−0.168
Moor reference	−0.175	[a]	−0.125	[a]	−0.078	[a]	−0.113	[a]
Tamil reference	−0.164	[a]	−0.137	[a]	−0.096	[a]	−0.127	[a]
Pooled	−0.148	[a]	−0.127	[a]	−0.082	[a]	−0.116	[a]
Equally weighted	−0.170	[a]	−0.131	[a]	−0.087	[a]	−0.120	[a]
Female								
Sinhala–Tamil wage gap								
Mean wage gap (raw)	0.316	−0.024	0.170	−0.084	−0.015	0.061	0.092	−0.109
Tamil reference	0.019	−0.043	0.004	−0.116	0.009	0.077	0.050	−0.145
Sinhalese reference	0.013	−0.104	0.035	−0.111	−0.066	−0.020	0.049	−0.141
Pooled	0.011	−0.098	0.021	−0.096	−0.024	−0.003	0.039	−0.120
Equally weighted	0.016	−0.073	0.020	−0.114	−0.028	0.029	0.050	−0.143
Sinhala–Moor wage gap								
Mean wage gap (raw)	−0.147	−0.151	−0.071	[b]	0.071	0.115	0.062	[b]
Moor reference	−0.107	−0.051	[a]	[a]	−0.009	0.137	[a]	[a]
Sinhalese reference	−0.123	−0.014	[a]	[a]	0.005	0.070	[a]	[a]
Pooled	−0.117	−0.013	[a]	[a]	0.003	0.069	[a]	[a]
Equally weighted	−0.115	−0.033	[a]	[a]	−0.002	0.103	[a]	[a]
Tamil–Moor wage gap								
Mean wage gap (raw)	−0.464	−0.127	−0.241	[b]	0.086	0.054	−0.030	[b]

Table 9.3   Mean Unconditional and Conditional (Unexplained) Ethnic Wage Gaps, by Sex and Sector *(Continued)*

Sex and Decomposition	Unadjusted				Occupation-adjusted			
	All	*Public*	*Private*	*Agricultural*	*All*	*Public*	*Private*	*Agricultural*
Moor reference	−0.148	*0.010*	*a*	*a*	*0.019*	*0.077*	*a*	*a*
Tamil reference	−0.058	*0.127*	*a*	*a*	*0.052*	*0.103*	*a*	*a*
Pooled	−0.059	*0.058*	*a*	*a*	*0.029*	*0.067*	*a*	*a*
Equally weighted	−0.103	*0.068*	*a*	*a*	*0.036*	*0.090*	*a*	*a*

Source: Author's computations based on data from DCS 1996–2004.
Note: All gaps that are not in italics are statistically significant at the 10 percent or higher level of significance.
a. Decomposition is not possible because at least one of the regressions is incompletely identified.
b. Wage gaps are not computed because the female Moor mean wage in agriculture is based on an extremely small (18) sample size.

lines between Sinhalese and Moor men appears to be explained by differences in productive characteristics, but the small but statistically significant advantage Moor men have over Sinhalese men within occupations appears to be completely unexplained (second panel, table 9.3).

Tamil-Moor male wage gaps favor Moors. Adjusting for between-occupation inequality in the aggregate wage gap reduces it considerably, which is consistent with Moors being in higher-paid occupations relative to Tamils. However, this is not the case when private sector Tamil wages are compared with Moor wages in the same sector. The reduction in the unexplained wage gap when occupational controls are included is very much smaller, indicating within-occupation inequality plays a greater role in wage inequality between Tamil and Moor males in the private sector.

Ethnic Wage Gaps among Females
Tamil females earn less than Sinhalese and Moor females overall but more than Sinhalese females in the agricultural sector. Mean wage gaps between Tamil women and Moor and Sinhalese women are insignificant, while Moor women in the public sector earn more than Sinhalese women and no less than them in the private sector. When the distribution is purged of inequality between occupations, Sinhalese women earn more than Tamil women in agriculture, no less than Moor women in the public sector, and Tamil women earn no less than Moor women in the private sector.

Wage gaps among women of different ethnic groups appear to be completely or largely explained by differences in productive characteristics. Wage gaps between Sinhalese and Tamil women are considerable (30 percent of the Sinhala wage) and favor Sinhalese women, but are completely explained by their higher productive characteristics (table 9.3, first column, fourth panel). Sectoral disaggregation indicates that there is no significant wage gap in the public sector, and that the private sector unadjusted wage gap (of about 17 percent) is completely explained. Controlling for occupation reduces the size of the overall wage gap to 9 percent, and yields a small unexplained gap of 4–5 percent, indicating that Sinhala women in the private sector are in higher-paying jobs relative to Tamil women and that part of this tracking of Tamil women into lower-paying occupations is explained by lower productive characteristics, while part is not. Wage gaps between Sinhala and Tamil women in the agriculture sector favor Tamil women and are unexplained by their productive characteristics. The gap occurs most likely because Tamil women with identical characteristics to their Sinhalese counterparts benefit from being in the unionized, regulated plantation agriculture sector.

Aggregate and public sector wage gaps between Sinhalese and Moor women favor Moors. Aggregate wage gaps appear to be unexplained, but disaggregation reveals that public sector wage gaps are either insignificant or completely explained by the higher productive characteristics of Moor women. There is some indication that Moor women are in higher-paying occupations within the public sector—controlling for between-occupation inequality turns the Moor-favoring unconditional wage gap into an insignificant unconditional wage gap.

Tamil-Moor unconditional wage gaps also favor Moors and are quite considerable at the aggregate level (46 percent). But the gaps are insignificant in the public sector and about half the aggregate magnitude in the private sector. Aggregate wage gaps are largely explained, and public sector wage gaps entirely explained, by the better productive characteristics of Moor women. The reversal in sign of the occupation-adjusted aggregate Tamil-Moor wage gap indicates that Moor women are in higher-paying occupations relative to Tamil women.

Conclusions and Policy Implications

Conclusions and policy implications apply to the sample used in this study. Gender wage gap decompositions indicate that in all sectors and for all ethnic groups, women are underpaid, even when unconditional wage gaps favor women. Conditional (unexplained) gender wage gaps are larger than unconditional wage gaps (except among Tamils in the private and agriculture sectors), indicating that in the absence of discrimination, all female employees (with the exceptions mentioned above) would earn more on average than all male employees, because of their better productive characteristics. The results are also consistent with occupational segregation of females in the private sector, but not in the public sector.

Tamil men (outside the North and East) were underpaid compared with Sinhalese men in the same regions. Larger unexplained wage gaps in the public sector compared with the private or agricultural sectors may be related to language ability or patronage. The results are consistent with occupational segregation of Tamil men in public and private sectors.

Ethnic wage gaps among women are largely explained by productive characteristics, indicating a role for policies to promote education among minorities with low educational attainment. Unexplained ethnic wage gaps in the agriculture sector that favor Tamil women most likely occur because Tamil women are in the regulated and unionized plantation sector, while Sinhala women are predominantly workers in the informal agriculture sector, which is not covered by any of the formal wage-setting mechanisms.

Moor men and women face no unfair disadvantage in wage determination. Moor men do well within occupations relative to Sinhala and Tamil men. Their poorer endowments relative to Sinhalese men track them into lower-paying occupations, but these occupations still pay better than those of Tamil men. Moor women receive higher wages than Sinhala and Tamil women, but this is mostly explained by their better productive characteristics and employment in higher-paying occupations.

These results indicate that while women have benefited from schooling and expanded employment opportunities, they are still underpaid, even in the public sector, where they appear to benefit from gender-specific policies. Sinhalese males appear to be the primary beneficiaries of labor market policies and civil service hiring practices, which appear to work against Tamil males. Collective bargaining protects the wages of Tamil females in the agriculture sector.

Existing wage-equalizing mechanisms appear to have no effect on the relative wages of Sinhalese females in agriculture or of females in the private (largely informal) sector. In addition, evidence of occupational segregation of females in the private sector and Tamil males in the public sector indicates that wage-setting mechanisms that only protect equal wages for equal work in the same job are inadequate to promote equity and prevent discrimination.

Policies that promote equal wages for work of equal value are called for. Other policies to reduce occupation-based wage inequality include eliminating patronage in civil service hiring and removing constraints that limit hiring in the regulated sector. An hourly or daily minimum wage that covers all sectors and occupations may be more successful in eliminating gender and ethnic disparities among lower wage-earners than existing wage-setting mechanisms are.

Notes

Data from the quarterly Labor Force Surveys are used by permission of the Department of Census and Statistics, Sri Lanka, which bears no responsibility for the analysis or interpretations presented here. The author is grateful to Milan Vodopivec, Ramani Gunatilaka, and an anonymous referee for comments and suggestions. Nanak Kakwani is gratefully acknowledged for suggesting the method for eliminating between-occupation inequality that is used in this chapter.

1. The evidence suggests that such legislation tends to protect prime-age workers and hurt younger workers and entrants into the labor force.

2. Ajwad and Kurukulasuriya (2002) find that the size of the gender wage gap and the extent to which it is explained by the stock of productive characteristics may vary by ethnic group.

3. Employment discrimination occurs when women (or members of the group being discriminated against) must possess higher productivity than the men (or favored group) in a particular job in order to be hired to the same position.

4. The QLFS survey series are not comparable in terms of geographical coverage. The 2003 survey included Eastern province for the first time in the series history (Northern and Eastern Provinces were previously excluded because of the civil conflict), and the 2004 survey includes both provinces except the districts of Mullaitivu and Killinochchi.

5. Defined by the DCS as those who worked for 26 weeks or more during the previous 12 months.

6. Owing to the omission of the Northern and Eastern provinces from the survey, the majority of the Tamils in the sample are those in the Central Highlands and in urban areas in the rest of the country. Similarly, Moors are also underrepresented in the sample, as they make up 41 percent and 28 percent, respectively, of the population in Ampara and Trincomalee districts in Eastern Province (DCS 2001). Their population share in the rest of the country ranges from 1 percent in Hambantota in Southern Province to 19 percent in Puttalam in North Western Province.

7. Wages are adjusted to eliminate between-occupation inequality by deflating by the ratio of the overall mean to the mean of the jth occupation, that is,

$$x_{ij}^{occ} = x_{ij} \left\{ \frac{1}{N} \sum_{i=1}^{N} x_{ij} \bigg/ \frac{1}{n_j} \sum_{i=1}^{n_j} x_{ij} \right\}, \quad i = 1, \dots N; j = 1, \dots m; \text{ for each } j, i = 1, \dots n_j,$$

where x_{ij}^{occ} is the occupation-adjusted log of hourly earnings of the ith individual in the jth occupational group, x_{ij} is the (unadjusted) log of hourly earnings of the ith individual in the jth occupational group, the term in the numerator is the overall mean of the log of hourly earnings, and the denominator is the mean of the log of hourly earnings in the jth occupation. Thirty-nine occupational categories based on 3-digit and 4-digit International Standard Classification of Occupations categories were used. A list is provided in Gunewardena (2008).

8. World Bank (2005) found that the 18 percent who did not complete compulsory schooling were likely to be from conflict-affected areas, the estate sector, and the rural hinterland. In addition, lower ordinary level (O-level) pass rates in North Eastern, North Central, Uva, and Central provinces indicate that minorities may have lower secondary school educational attainment than the Sinhalese majority.

9. However, Tamil women have lower endowments than Tamil men and Moor women have higher endowments than Sinhala women.

10. The number of private preschools was estimated to be between 11,000 and 12,500, exceeding the number of schools in the country.

11. This finding could imply different decision outcomes by ethnicity for married women's choice to remain in the labor force. It may reflect underlying differences in preferences, conditioned by culture, or a perception of differences in expected future income streams. It may also be related to other factors that influence the choice to remain in the labor force: a greater proportion of Sinhalese public sector women were located in Western Province, where transport infrastructure and child-care provision are likely to be better than in the outlying provinces. The share of married women is determined by the demand side of the market as well, but it is not clear why state sector employers would discriminate against minority married women.

12. The provision of crèches on tea estates was probably the earliest manifestation of preschool child-care provision in the country.

13. These wages are said to cover approximately 1 million workers in the private sector who are mainly manual workers. Workers not covered by wage boards are those in subsistence agriculture, cottage industries, and personal services (Navamukundan 2002).

14. I am grateful to Nanak Kakwani for suggesting this method of incorporating occupational structure in the model.

15. An alternative set of location variables (district dummy variables) were used and coefficients were found to be significantly different from the reference

(Colombo district), but not from each other. An alternative specification with year interactions with schooling and experience variables was also estimated. Coefficients on interacted variables were found not to be statistically significant.

16. Heltberg and Vodopivec (2004) use data from the 2000 Sri Lanka Integrated Survey.

17. Results and discussion of the regressions of the log of hourly earnings on these covariates are presented in Gunewardena (2008).

18. Gunewardena (2008) includes an appendix that provides numeric examples.

19. Four broad categories of occupation were defined in the agricultural sector— market-oriented agrarian workers, market-oriented fishery workers, subsistence agricultural and fishery workers, and agricultural, fishery and related labourers (unskilled workers).

20. The equally weighted decomposition indicates that women are underpaid by 15 percent, whereas the wage structure yielded by the pooled sample is closer to that of the male wage structure, indicating women are underpaid by only 10 percent.

21. Sector-specific decompositions of the gender wage gap are not conducted for the Moor sample because of small sample size and the related problem of perfect collinearity between variables.

References

Ajwad, M. J., and P. Kurukulasuriya. 2002. "Ethnic and Gender Wage Disparities in Sri Lanka." *Sri Lanka Economic Journal* 3 (1): 1–26.

Aturupane, Harsha. 1996. "Is Education More Profitable for Women? An Economic Analysis of the Impact of Schooling on the Earnings of Men and Women in Sri Lanka." *Sri Lanka Journal of Social Sciences* 19 (1 and 2): 27–45.

Blinder, Alan. 1973. "Wage Discrimination: Reduced Form and Structural Estimates." *Journal of Human Resources* 18 (Fall): 436–55.

DCS (Department of Census and Statistics). 1996–2004. *Quarterly Reports of the Sri Lanka Labour Force Survey.* Colombo.

———. 2001. *Census of Population.* Colombo.

Department of External Resources, Government of Sri Lanka. 2000. Sri Lanka Integrated Survey. http://www.erd.gov.lk/publicweb/ERDDOCS.html.

Gunewardena, Dileni. 2002. "Reducing the Gender Wage Gap in Sri Lanka: Is Education Enough?" *Sri Lanka Economic Journal* 3 (2): 57–103.

———. 2006. "Are There Disparities in Wages by Ethnicity in Sri Lanka and Why?" In *Does Inequality Matter? Exploring the Links between Poverty and Inequality,* ed. Prashan Thalayasingham and Kannan Arunasalam. Colombo: Centre for Poverty Analysis.

————. 2008. "Analysis of Gender and Ethnic Wage Differentials among Youth in Sri Lanka." Working Paper, Department of Economics and Statistics, University of Peradeniya (http://www.arts.pdn.ac.lk/econ/Analysis%20of%20wage%20inequality_revisedJuly28.pdf).

Heckman, J. 1979. "Sample Selection Bias as a Specification Error." *Econometrica* 47: 153–61.

Heltberg, Rasmus, and Milan Vodopivec. 2004 (July). "Sri Lanka: Unemployment, Job Security, and Labor Market Reform." Washington, DC: World Bank.

Mincer, Jacob. 1974. *Schooling, Experience and Earnings.* New York: Colombia University Press.

Navamukundan, A. 2002. *Wage Determination and Grievance Procedures in the Private Sector in Malaysia, Sri Lanka and South Korea.* Geneva: Global Union Research Network.

Neumark, David. 1988. "Employers' Discriminatory Behavior and the Estimation of Wage Discrimination." *Journal of Human Resources* 23 (3): 279–95.

Oaxaca, Ronald. 1973. "Male-Female Wage Differentials in Urban Labor Markets." *International Economic Review* 14 (October): 693–709.

Polachek, Solomon William. 1975. "Differences in Expected Post-School Investment as a Determinant of Market Wage Differentials" *International Economic Review* 16 (2): 451–70.

Rama, Martin. 2003. "The Sri Lankan Unemployment Problem Revisited." *Review of Development Economics* 7 (3): 510–25.

Reimers, C. 1983. "Labor Market Discrimination against Hispanic and Black Men." *Review of Economics and Statistics* 65: 570–79.

Rodgers, Yana van der Meulen. 1999. "Protecting Women and Promoting Equality in the Labour Market: Theory and Evidence." Policy Research Report on Gender and Development, Working Paper Series 6. Washington, DC: World Bank.

World Bank. 1998. *World Development Report.* Washington, DC: World Bank.

————. 2005. *Treasures of the Education System in Sri Lanka.* Colombo: World Bank.

————. 2006. "Social Protection Report." Colombo: World Bank.

CHAPTER 10

Concerns of Youth Affected by Civil Conflict in Sri Lanka

S. T. Hettige and Zindu Salih

Youth carry the dual and sometimes contradictory responsibilities of being carriers of tradition as well as agents of change. No longer adolescents but not yet adults, young people are often at the forefront of social and economic change. Such transformations are never easy and, as history shows, have many times resulted in social unrest and even armed conflict. That is particularly true in Sri Lanka, where youth have been affected by two decades of armed ethnic conflict that ended in early 2009.

This chapter explores the ways in which and to what extent Sri Lankan youth have been affected by those years of conflict. It draws on research conducted by both national and foreign scholars and looks at experiences documented in other parts of the world where young people have faced or are facing similar situations. The chapter begins by placing the ethnic conflict in Sri Lanka in its historical and political context, in particular looking at what this has meant and still means for the youth of the country. Specifically, it looks at the economic, social, and psychological effects of conflict on Sri Lankan young people.

In the national statistics of Sri Lanka, youth are defined as those ages 15–29 and make up about one-fourth of the population. Youth ages 15–19 make up about one-tenth of the population, closely followed by those ages 20–24 (DCS 2001). According to available statistics, the profile of the young in Sri Lanka gives mixed messages. On one hand, the population is highly literate, with a literacy rate of 90.7 percent and high enrollments in primary and secondary education. On the other hand, alcohol and drug use among youth is high, death rates are increasing, and unemployment rates remain very high (DCS 2001). These trends are even more worrisome when placed in the current situation facing youth in Sri Lanka, in which the years of conflict have given rise to new and challenging issues, discussed later in the chapter, such as the breakdown of normal familial and social networks.

Conflict-affected young people in Sri Lanka come from many different economic, sociocultural, and political backgrounds. Not only does conflict affect male and female youth in different ways, it also has different effects on youth from different economic backgrounds such as rich or poor, employed or unemployed, the educated and the less educated or uneducated. The term *youth* encompasses young soldiers and former soldiers, ex-army personnel, army deserters, militants or former combatants, the displaced, the homeless, and the disabled. In many cases young people experience several of these situations simultaneously. The distinctive characteristics of each of these subgroups and the different ways in which they are affected by conflict means that the experiences of each of these different groups must be taken into consideration in addressing the needs of conflict-affected youth.

Perhaps because the notion of youth as a research subject is still quite young, few studies are available, particularly in Sri Lanka, that specifically focus on the impact of armed conflict on young people. However, several scholars have addressed the ethnic divide around which the conflict in Sri Lanka revolved, youth's involvement and role in the war, and the ways socioeconomic circumstances have been instrumental in perpetuating conflict.

Furthermore, because of the cyclical nature of the conflict—that is, the adverse socioeconomic circumstances leading to conflicts involving frustrated groups, which in turn lead to further deterioration in social and economic conditions—it is difficult to distinguish the effects of conflict per se from the effects of economic and social circumstances that have a complex connection to the conflict. Therefore, much of the discussion here is necessarily based on issues that are affected by conflict but not specific to it, such as employment and education, while other issues raised are conflict specific, such as the psychological impact of the conflict on youth.

Youth and Conflict

Defining Youth

Depending on social, political, and economic landscapes and on cultural factors such as definitions of family, youth has different meanings in different countries and cultures, indeed even within one society. Therefore, generalizations regarding youth need to be treated with caution. As Atal (2005) points out, youth relates to an age group between childhood and adulthood that is in fact largely heterogeneous. This category consists of several groups of young people with diverse ethnic, religious, economic, and social backgrounds. As these factors change for each individual, the criteria and the period defining youth could also change. Thus, the population category of youth is not static; the perceptions, issues, aspirations, and responsibilities of youth may change with changes in the environment, and there is a need to continually assess the relevance of the youth profile against the realities on the ground (Atal 2005; Mayer 2005). For example, as Atal (2005) states, an increase in literacy and education could mean a rise in educated and employed youth and a decrease in uneducated, unemployed youth.

Conflict may also vary the span of what is normally regarded as adolescence and youth. During conflict young people may be forced to take on adult roles in caring for younger siblings, generating income, and going into combat (Kempner 2005). In other cases, such as in the north of Sri Lanka, an area devastated by the conflict, conflict may artificially extend adolescence by preventing young people from going to work and becoming financially independent and by delaying marriage (Mayer and Salih 2003).

Sri Lankan Youth and Conflict: A Historical Perspective

The ethnic conflict that ravaged Sri Lanka between 1983 and 2009 is largely attributed to youth unrest in the country. Two extremely violent youth uprisings have had historic significance, one known as the 1971 April Rebellion and the other during 1987 to 1989 after the Sri Lankan Civil War started in 1983; in addition, the major violent conflicts in the northeast and south of Sri Lanka were led by young people (Mayer and Galappatti 2005). It is thus most salient that policy makers and others try to understand the factors that drive these young people to use violence as a means of achieving their goals, whatever those goals may be.

Some of the causes of these violent expressions of frustrations were connected with postcolonial socioeconomic policies (Hettige 1998a,

1998b). In the 1950s the burgeoning of state services created many lower-level positions in the public sector that drew young people, especially from the "lower" rungs of society. Salaried state jobs rapidly became socially esteemed and highly sought. Meanwhile, the government introduced free education across the island. Because of ethnonationalist politics, however, schooling was subsequently restricted to the vernacular; Tamil and Sinhalese students were taught only in their ethnic language. There was a rapid increase in vernacular-educated youth who sought the social status and security of state employment, but they were barred from competing for higher public positions, which were reserved for those who spoke English—generally the urban elite whose families could afford private and foreign education. This situation gave rise to a group of educated rural young people with unmet expectations and aspirations, who began to express their grievances through political actions and to mobilize against the privileged, Western-educated elite.

Another factor was the discrimination and unjust policies, real and perceived, that disillusioned and frustrated youth groups in the north and south of the country (Mayer 2005). These frustrations led to increasing militancy and violence, and youth-led insurgencies became frequent in these areas. Sinhalese youth participated in the two insurgencies led by the nationalist Janatha Vimukthi Peramuna (JVP), and Tamil youth joined militant groups in the north and east. Many of these youth, mostly young men, lost their lives, while many who survived were exposed to various forms of violence such as torture, injury, trauma, imprisonment, and displacement. Youth who joined the government forces had similar experiences; they too were killed or injured, captured, tortured, and traumatized. When the war intensified in the mid-1990s, hundreds of soldiers deserted the government security forces. Because the prevailing regulations at the time did not permit them to return to their normal lives and jobs, many went underground, where they joined criminal groups to earn a living.

Perhaps the situation can be better understood set against the changes in the economy that followed independence. The state-dominated system that had prevailed since independence in 1948 began to give way in the 1970s to a more market-oriented economy. The expanding private sector, however, did not sufficiently absorb the unemployed, because here too, there was greater demand for the English-speaking than for workers who spoke only vernacular. As a result the increasing economic liberalization in the country contributed toward largely marginalizing the rural educated young people who did not speak English, keeping them out of the mainstream economy and its benefits. It is these rural youth who were at the forefront of the insurgencies, drawn into political movements in hopes of fulfill their aspirations (Hettige 1998b).

These youth groups were not only seeking redress of economic injustices; they also aspired to political leadership (Uyangoda 1996). It is of major concern, then, that young people in Sri Lanka have repeatedly chosen to deploy violence as a means of achieving their goals. The National Youth Survey of 2000 showed worrying indications of this: 86.7 percent of youth between the ages of 15 and 19 who said they had no interest in politics also said that violence is an acceptable means to fulfill one's goals. Fifty-one percent of the 20- to 24-year-olds and 31.8 percent of the 25- to 29-year-olds believed the same (Mayer and Galappatti 2005).

Whether young people were political leaders, perpetrators of violence, militants, victims, or nonaligned, they have all experienced life through the prism of ethnic conflict, and all aspects of normal life—their education, employment, health care, and future aspirations—have been affected. The following sections look more closely at how young people, particularly those living in conflict areas, have been affected directly and indirectly by the events and the consequent economic, social, psychological, and political conditions.

The Economic Effects of Conflict

Youth Employment and Livelihoods

Although the economic reforms in Sri Lanka since 1977 have expanded employment opportunities in the emerging private sector, for young people, the state continues to be the main employment avenue (ILO 2002). Overall unemployment levels have shown some improvement, but a significant number of youth cannot find jobs. In 1997, 35 percent of the unemployed labor force were teens and 39 percent were young adults. Moreover, chances of being unemployed in Sri Lanka are higher for the young and educated. Indeed, half of the unemployed have completed their Ordinary- or Advanced-level education qualifications (ILO 2002).

As in other developing countries, the majority of the employed are in occupational tiers such as factory work and agriculture. Data on wages show that real earnings and quality of employment have deteriorated since the early 1980s (ILO 2002). Furthermore, underemployment is an issue that needs further exploration. The underemployed tend to be counted with the employed, which could give an inaccurate picture of employment in the country. Underemployment seems to affect mostly

workers over age 25, a possible indication that youth who have been waiting for the ideal job are forced to settle for what is available or take up
self-employment.

Historically unemployment, particularly youth unemployment, has
been chronic in Sri Lanka. The state policies, which in the postcolonial era
were shaped by nationalistic and ethnic ideologies, brought a new face to
the unemployment problems. State schools and mission schools were
established along religious and ethnic lines, with many mission schools
bringing caste and class into their policies (Thangarajah 2003). The
emphasis on, and promotion of, monolingual education resulted in a society divided into the English-speaking and the vernacular-educated. This
was especially frustrating for the majority rural youth educated in their
ethnic tongues because the desirable jobs, such as those in the civil service, were available only to the minority English speakers (Thangarajah
2003). In today's context, Sri Lankan society is still facing the social and
logistical difficulties in bridging the barriers brought on by a whole generation whose members speak only one of the three main languages spoken in the country—Sinhala, Tamil, and English. Even though 90 percent
of the population is literate, most people do not speak a second language
and are therefore unable to communicate with other social groups (Hettige
1998b). Not only do these language barriers increase ethnic divides and ani-
mosities, they also make it extremely difficult for young people to attain
employment outside their ethnic-geographic demarcations.

At the same time as economic and demographic pressures forced
young people to leave their home areas to find work, their inability to
communicate in the language spoken in areas where jobs were available
made them unemployable. The expansion of the private sector opened up
opportunities only for the already advantaged English-speaking urbanites
and did not bring the jobs that rural job seekers had hoped for (Hettige
2005b). The effects of the civil war, such as loss of infrastructure, decreased
economic investment, and the ethnic animosity and suspicions that crys-
tallized into racism, exaggerated these problems. It became harder for
the young people, particularly those in the conflict-affected areas, to be
economically and socially mobile and to seek employment elsewhere.

Prejudice against youth as troublemakers and a threat to peace has
been a major obstacle for young people in Sri Lanka. In the context of the
conflict, this issue is even more acutely felt because youth are viewed as
the cause of the unrest on both sides of the ethnic divide. As Mayer and
Salih (2003) point out, in the economic and political context of war, the life
chances of youth in the conflict zones are significantly narrowed when

they are treated by warring parties as potential threats. Thus, young people's prospects of attaining particular social and economic goals are bleak.

Sri Lanka has suffered terribly as a result of the ethnic war; 30 percent of the territory and 15 percent of the population have been devastated by this conflict (Selvarajah 2003). Among the most affected in this situation are the country's young people, particularly those directly involved or affected by the conflict, such as ex-combatants; victims of kidnappings, rape, and other forms of violence; and those displaced by conflict. However, some of the main issues these young Sri Lankans face are not dissimilar to issues faced by the young population in general. Research shows that youth in the country's conflict areas have cited unemployment as their biggest problem (Mayer and Salih 2003; Siddhartan 2008). This is apparently the case in many parts of the world facing conflict, such as Sierra Leone (UNOWA 2005) and the Democratic Republic of Congo (Kemper 2005).

In the aftermath of armed conflict, some of those most affected by unemployment are young ex-combatants. These youngsters range from children to young adults, who generally gave up their education and livelihood opportunities to willingly or unwillingly take up arms, becoming perpetrators, and often victims, of violence. Reintegration of these combatants through employment is proving a difficult and sensitive task. In the Democratic Republic of Congo, it was found that ex-combatants resented and did not respond to being called children, and targeting individuals to retrain and reintegrate them was challenging (Kemper 2005). These young people have experienced a harsh adult world and their old links to parents and family have been broken, complicating their transition to peaceful civilian life. Finding economic and social space for ex-combatants is also hindered by the psychological problems many of them deal with. In Sierra Leone, development workers found it difficult to include ex-combatants in programs because fear and shame made them hesitant to identify themselves (Kemper 2005). Efforts in Sri Lanka to reintegrate young ex-combatants (which refers to fighters in the Liberation Tigers of Tamil Eelam) could run into difficulties similar to those experienced by government soldiers, most of whom are young people. Those who go back to their families have often missed out on education and training and face immense obstacles in finding employment.

Siddhartan (2008) captures clearly the negative impact of conflict on employment for young people and the lack of opportunities in the conflict-ravaged area of Batticaloa. First, displacement within and outside the region, along with voluntary and involuntary migration of people out of the conflict zone, makes it practically impossible for these people to hold a long-term job or find stable employment. Moreover, because of displacement and because security forces have occupied some agricultural lands, many cultivated lands and farming areas have been abandoned. Restrictions imposed on fishing and movement in coastal and so-called uncleared areas, and displacement in these areas, have led to mass unemployment as well as to the loss of traditional means of livelihood. The situation is exacerbated by periodic ethnic riots and violence, which discourage displaced persons from returning to their abandoned plots or fishing areas and dissuade them from investing in any economic activity. As a result, poverty in these areas is increasing, and fewer and fewer young people wish to become farmers or fishermen.

Even in the face of such adversity, young people have been and are active economic agents, struggling to make a living and to support their families. Even as the traditional systems to help young people find employment, such as directed education, inheritance, passing on of skills from father to son or mother to daughter, unravel in the face of conflict, young people are finding other ways to cope with the changing situations. As Siddhartan (2008) states, "One of the most striking coping mechanisms that I observed is that they engage in multiple employments. They (simultaneously) engage in farming, wage labor, fishing, casual state sector jobs, etc." This shows that although the element of choice may be absent, young people are taking up adult responsibilities. The concern is that the poverty and frustration caused by chronic or intermittent unemployment could exacerbate conflict, as it has done in the past.

Impact of Conflict on Youth Education

Sri Lanka has long held a reputation for a successful education system. Since independence in 1948, the country has had universal free education and increasing numbers of university graduates. Education became deeply rooted in the social psyche of Sri Lankan society as the ultimate equalizer. A person's education level was the determinant of mobility, esteem, and social status, and youth now perceive upward social mobility as an attainable goal. The sole objective for many youth is to escape from their socially "inferior" background, and education is seen as the tool that allows them to do so (Hettige 1998a, 1998b). At the same time that education was gaining such crucial importance in the social fabric, however, the national education policies and programs were developed in a way that heightened the ethnic divide and escalated tensions among cultural groups, particularly along linguistic lines.

Selvarajah (2003) has documented the links between the current education system and conflict as well as the impact of conflict on education. He points out that the failure of the education system is most evident in the existence of child soldiers who carry arms instead of attending school, in the youth-led JVP insurrections, and in the disruptions in university routines caused by young politicized groups. It is not the lack of good schools per se that contributes to violent conflict, but rather the educational system itself, which is structured along ethnic and economic lines and fosters ethnic divide. There is also a lack of specialized programs to reintegrate into the education system the many youth who left school to join the ranks of combatants (Hettige 2005b), which means that many young people who want to (re)gain an education simply do not have the institutional support to do so.

The impact of the conflict on education in Sri Lanka has been devastating. Again, Selvarajah (2003) provides a picture of these wide-ranging and alarming consequences. Armed warfare, riots, and violence have disrupted access to education. In many areas displaced children, including those living in camps, do not have the means or the opportunities to go to school. Moreover, the frequent movement of people from areas controlled by the military, the lack of daily security, and poverty discourage parents from sending children to school. For children who do go to school, the lack of facilities and shortage of teachers and staff greatly compromise the quality of education. This is reflected in the high dropout and repetition rates of Sri Lankan students. In addition to the conflict-enforced cessation of school life, the high dropout rates may be caused by the increasing competition that proves unbearable to some students and to the mounting costs connected with obtaining education. Moreover, more and more parents and students feel that education does not guarantee "proper" employment. Young people in school are not sure what is available or even what they want to do after school, and there is a lack of career guidance available for students (Hettige 2005a). Most schoolchildren seem to rely on their parents to guide them in this regard. This cannot be the best way to prepare for their future in a rapidly changing world of work.

In addition to the adverse effects on the psychosocial and cultural aspects of education, the civil war has severely affected tangible aspects such as infrastructure. In the conflict areas of the north and east, some schools have closed or temporarily moved elsewhere. What used to be schools are now refugee camps and temporary schools, where the environment is not conducive to learning. Schools generally show physical disrepair, and sanitary and hygienic conditions are poor (Selvarajah 2003).

It is no surprise, then, that student enrollments in conflict areas are low. For example, in Vanni district only a quarter of the potential student population actually attended school (Selvarajah 2003). Among the reasons given for low school attendance are poverty, which either makes school unaffordable or requires children to work rather than go to school, and sickness or disability in the family, which obliges children to help in domestic and economic activities. Moreover, in the unstable security situation, parents are reluctant to send children to school (Selvarajah 2003).

It is highly likely that there are gender differences in school attendance. For instance, during Mozambique's civil war, the disruption to community life meant that young girls not only did not attend school but that the traditional skills and informal education they received from the family also ceased (Maslen 1997). In addition, sickness and disability in the family caused by war add to the burden of the girl child, whose role is to assist in caring for family members and help with domestic chores, while boys are more likely to drop out of school to take on financial responsibilities for their siblings and adults (Siddhartan 2008).

The impact of conflict on educational personnel is also a major issue. Large numbers of teachers, as well as students, have been displaced; for example, in 2001, 10,000 children and 600 teachers lived in camps in Vavuniya (Selvarajah 2003). The teachers who are working in schools or educational institutions are stressed and overworked and must cope with a dangerous security situation and the lack of facilities. They also have to deal with students who are psychologically affected by conflict, even though they often lack the training to do so—a situation that points to a need for counseling and guidance programs for schools across Sri Lanka (Hettige 2005a).

Social and Psychological Impact of the Conflict

Young people in conflict-affected areas also experience severe psychological and social problems that can dwarf the problems of lost education and employment opportunities. The United Nations counted 111 reported armed conflicts in the world between 1989 and 2000. In the modern world, armed conflict has taken on a more sinister face, one that barely differentiates between military and civilian targets. Indeed, since the First World War, civilian casualties as a proportion of the total number of casualties have increased from 5 percent to a shocking 80 percent, most of whom are women and children. The youngsters killed, maimed, disabled, displaced, orphaned, rendered homeless, and psychologically affected number in the millions (UN 2003).

The situation was not different in Sri Lanka, where more and more civilians were drawn into the conflict. Displacement is a major issue affecting thousands of families belonging to all ethnic groups living in the north and east. Although many displaced persons found their way to foreign countries where they sought asylum, many others became internally displaced, living in refugee camps in and around conflict zones. According to the Ministry of Rehabilitation data, there were over 750,000 internally displaced persons in the northeast in 2000. Given that only a small number of the displaced have been resettled, hundreds of thousands of families continue to live in refugee camps with minimal facilities. Children and youth make up a large proportion of the refugees. They have no access to proper educational facilities and other requirements.

Impact of Conflict on Social Identity

Colonial and postcolonial policies have divided Sri Lankan society along seemingly obvious lines of region, language, religion, and ethnicity, often forcing people to choose a side and alienating one side from another. The policy of universal but monolingual education produced a younger generation unable to communicate with any group except those from their own linguistic and regional background. It also forced people to seek employment within areas that spoke their language, reinforcing the ethnicity of particular regions. Multiculturalism was truly available only to the English-speaking urban population, particularly those living and working in Colombo, the commercial capital.

Where ethnicity is a major factor behind identity politics, it is exploited by political groups who further reinforce ethnic identity and the construction of imagined history (Thangarajah 2003). War and conflict not only affect notions of ethnicity but also change people's perceptions of their role in society. This is particularly evident in the case of youth identity as ideas of what is childhood and adulthood change; childhood can end abruptly when children are forced to take on adult responsibilities as armed combatants or primary caregivers in the family (Kemper 2005). Siddhartan (2008) found that in Batticaloa, a conflict-affected district in the northeast, adults perceived young people as being irresponsible in general, while an increasing number of youth considered themselves to be adults assuming adult responsibilities, and many youth expressed the need to change the definition of youth.

Psychological Impacts

In conflict areas and for families affected by conflict, the psychological impact can be severe for children, youth, and society as a whole as they deal with anxiety, fear, neglect, exposure to violence and cruelties, and displacement. For young people sheer survival takes precedence over any other need such as education, recreation, or employment.

For today's Sri Lankan youth, the brutal armed conflict began when they were infants or very young children (Samarasinghe 1998)—this is a generation born into and brought up in time of war. Humans learn to negotiate with and navigate their external environment mainly through their relationship with their mother, so the emotional and physical situation of the mother plays a crucial role in the well-being of young people. In a conflict situation, as Samarasinghe (1998) observes, the mother is put in a position where she faces the external world with insecurity, lack of confidence, and fear, emotions that young children internalize and could later employ in their dealings with society and that can lead to anxiety, distrust, grief, uncertainty about the future, and feelings of persecution and distress.

Young people, particularly women, are also facing other forms of social dislocation, such as migration to the Middle East, which break the normal roles and routines of families (Samarasinghe 1998). The families and the youngsters left behind have to deal not only with the loss of the primary caregiver but also sometimes with the social stigma attached to migrant families. This phenomenon is not confined to the conflict-affected areas—migrant workers come from all parts of the country, so hundreds of thousands of families everywhere are affected.

Furthermore, a large body of research into experiences of combat soldiers and militants shows that they face serious psychological and physical consequences stemming from trauma. Victims exposed to violence show severe and durable symptoms, which can last for years after exposure to the disaster (Samarasinghe 1998). This is very concerning, given that thousands of Sri Lankan men, women, children, and young people have been exposed to violence and social dislocation over the last several decades.

The limited research into the numerous psychological issues generated by conflict reveal that young people find it difficult to deal with relationships, examination pressures, the pressures of poverty, unemployment, intergenerational conflict, and other psychological problems (Hettige 2005b). These issues have figured prominently in many cases of self-harm in Sri Lanka over the last several decades.

In the east of Sri Lanka, as in many parts of the conflict zones, the youth generally come from the rural poor and a highly marginalized section of society, and they have been excluded from the mainstream. Siddhartan (2008) describes how discrimination and institutional barriers have alienated Tamil youth from mainstream social and economic spheres. For example, Tamil youth face discrimination from security forces, who routinely round them up and hold them for hours at army checkpoints. At the same time displacement makes going to school and work difficult—conditions that reinforce their marginalization.

The conditions of war and the sheer difficulty of finding a "normal" life seem to contribute to demoralization and despair among the young in Sri Lanka. Noting how conflict affects the aspirations and motivations of young people, Siddhartan (2008) found in his research that "due to the war youth have lost their desires and opportunities for education and employment," while the structural constraints and displacement, ethnic issues, and cultural limitations also make it improbable that young people will be able to attain their goals.

Some evidence suggests that being subject to conflict situations gives rise to some positive psychological symptoms as well. As Samarasinghe (1998) explains, research shows that response to disaster also includes reactions such as valuing life more, seeing meaning and purpose in suffering, and valuing other people and relationships more.

Effects of Conflict on Society

The numerous ways in which armed conflict affects society are almost unimaginable. Increases in deaths, disabilities, the homeless and displaced, poverty, youth criminals, and criminal violence are just some of the manifestations—as are renewed and resurgent conflicts.

In the case of young people, in Sri Lanka as elsewhere, the disruption of social organization and interruptions in the "normal" life cycle of birth, employment, marriage, children, and death have been changing the role and place of youth in society. Moreover, youth are more susceptible to internalizing the implications and outcomes of social change, a phenomenon that makes them more vulnerable to conflict circumstances (Mayer 2005).

Conflict and war break down family social structures and institutions, casting young people into limbo as they struggle to redefine their place in the family and society. One of the issues highlighted by Mayer and Salih (2003) is the indeterminate extension of "youthhood" in the north as marriage becomes delayed or impossible. Even older youth are not recognized by society as actors in the decision-making process, which causes frustrations and distress among large numbers of young men and women. At the same time society is deprived of a valuable resource for social progress. In a study on youth in Jaffna, delay in marriage was a cause for much frustration and distress (Mayer and Salih 2003). For many women from economically disadvantaged backgrounds, the inability to marry caused much distress and humiliation because they were afraid of being a burden on their families and because of the social stigma attached to spinsterhood. The young women expressed feelings of hopelessness in their daily life. Similar experiences were evident among unmarried young women in the south in the aftermath of political violence in the late 1980s (Hettige 1994). The death or exodus of young men usually leads to a drastic change in the ratio of women to men, making it difficult for women to find marital partners, which could be one of the contributing factors to the high numbers of females migrating for work.

Because adulthood for the most part is a socially assigned marker in human life, it is also society that provides the preconditions such as education, social services, and basic security that would ensure acquisition of economic and social status that defines an adult. When conflict destroys society's means of providing these requirements, young people are left adrift with no guidance and no support in attaining their preconceived goals and aspirations (Kemper 2005). This is difficult for young people and the community to cope with as youth try to quickly define their position and status in society, perhaps in terms of financial status, that would lead to their ultimate independence from parents (Mayer 2005).

Conflict-prompted rupture of the normal social structures also can result in a loss of space for youth and their ambitions, contributing to the widening gap between youth aspirations and social expectations and available opportunities. The National Youth Survey revealed that while 90 percent of the youth interviewed in Jaffna wanted to engage in social service activities and "be of service to others," there were limited opportunities to do so and little adult encouragement (Mayer and Salih 2003). The survey also found that while young people felt obliged to provide for their family, they lacked the decision-making adult status that accompanied such responsibilities. Such structural breakdown needs to be urgently addressed. If youth are excluded from social and civil structures, society loses a potential and valuable peace-building and development asset (Kemper 2005).

In war-affected Sri Lanka, criminal violence among young people has recently increased (Mayer and Galappatti 2005). The causes for this are manifold and need closer analysis. However, judging from experiences in other similarly affected parts of the world, socioeconomic deterioration and long-term exposure to violence can have adverse effects on moral standards and values. In a study of conflict-affected Mozambique, for example, Maslen (1997) found that inadequate food security, vulnerability to attacks, physical and sexual abuse, dangers from land mines, and economic instability were everyday realities for millions of displaced children and youth that could be linked to the rising juvenile criminality experienced in that region.

Moreover, even when the situation becomes more peaceful or normalized, young people exposed to violence need to be reintegrated into society. Kemper (2005) draws attention to the fact that for young people who have been trained and deployed as combatants, the traumas and "vengeful mindset" that go with the situation are psychologically damaging. Such young people need specialized treatment and long-term interventions for reentry into society. According to her, "youth have to re-learn normal cultural and moral values after having passed through a process of 'a-socialization.'"

Another negative consequence of conflict is the intensification and spread of poverty. As a group youth are prone to fall through the cracks of poverty alleviation programs and socioeconomic interventions and are thus particularly vulnerable to the ramifications of poverty. They tend to get caught in the vicious cycle of poverty brought on by lack of access to education, training, employment, funds, and capital for self-initiatives and by lack of political influence (Siddhartan 2008). Poverty is a global problem for young people—out of the 3 billion people surviving on less than $2 a day, around half are below age 24 and live in developing countries (UN 2003). Violent conflict inevitably increases poverty (Mayer and Salih 2003). In the context of conflict in Sri Lanka, militarism and the resources spent by both the government and the armed militant groups undoubtedly channeled valuable resources away from the local economy, while paradoxically the consequent economic decline encouraged militarism (Bandarage 2000).

Gender Dimensions of Conflict

As Emmanuel (2005) highlights, the actual impact of conflict on women in the long term has yet to be fully studied. But it is clear that conflict affects young women in different ways from men. As in other social phenomena, conflict tends to deepen gender discrimination and disadvantages faced by women. It is evident that girls and young women, both as combatants and as civilians, have generally endured especially harsh treatment during wars (Maslen 1997).

This can be seen in several cases in Sri Lanka as well. As Siddhartan (2008) points out, the increasing number of widows and female-headed

households leads to increasing levels of social ostracization and marginalization. This in turn leads to greater levels of vulnerability. For example,
Siddhartan reported that widows were sometimes labeled as prostitutes
and that sexual harassment and violence against women increased.

On the other hand, conflict also provides a glimmer of opportunity for
women's empowerment. In households where men have died in the
conflict or moved to find employment, women take over the decision
making (Siddhartan 2008). This increase in the economic participation of
women does not necessarily translate into broader empowerment, however, because they are still often left out of community-level participation
and decision making (Siddhartan 2008).

Conflict and Youth Politics

Despite high political awareness and participation in Sri Lanka (Hettige
1998a, 1998b), national politics is divided and perpetuated along ethnic
lines. As Uyangoda (1996) points out, that same ethnic differentiation
defines youth politics in the country, but he also notes that within the
main ethnic groups of Sinhala, Tamil, and Muslim, youth end up being
largely sidelined from the decision-making process. Each of these ethnic
groups has tended to recruit its top leaders—what Uyangoda calls the
"inaccessible elite"—from the social intermediate class, or "subordinate"
elite, such as members of parliament, powerbrokers, and academics. This
tendency has left large groups of youth from rural farming backgrounds
and urban working-class families marginalized and underrepresented in
the power structures and mainstream politics. As a result, youth have
been politicized along ethnic lines, a situation that, in light of the conflict,
will only be further reinforced.

Conclusions

Despite the limited research on the topic, it is increasingly clear that conflict renders young people particularly vulnerable: they are often alienated
from socioeconomic structures and support such as adequate education,
training, and job opportunities; they are overlooked in national planning
and policies; they face discrimination on both sides of the war; and they
experience immense psychological trauma and social marginalization.

The most urgent issue facing young people in Sri Lanka is the lack of
desirable jobs. This has been the case for several decades; however, it is
still a situation that development interventions and state policies have
been unable to resolve. Indeed, the violent conflicts in Sri Lanka, although

running along ethnic lines, are believed to have their roots in the frustrations of young people who do not have access to employment and are left on the margins of society, creating a vicious cycle of unemployment, poverty, and conflict.

Despite the ethnic differences, Sinhalese and Tamil (and to an extent Muslim) youth experience similar socioeconomic circumstances and marginalization. This is an aspect of the problem that seems to get lost in the attention paid to the ethnic, social, and cultural divisions among the young people of the country, and it perhaps could be used to help transform conflict into dialogue and trust.

Still, it is clear that different groups among the conflict-affected youth have experienced the effects of war in different ways. There are specific issues for each of the groups. Different approaches for reintegrating youth into society will be needed for former and current combatants and soldiers, widows, orphans, refugees, the displaced and the homeless, the unemployed, the educated and uneducated, the disabled and sick, and the poor. Moreover, even within these broad categories different approaches will be needed. While some ex-combatants are physically disabled, others are psychologically traumatized. Some could find alternative livelihoods, while others are likely to remain unemployed because of lack of skills.

The issues facing different subgroups of youth affected by conflict need to be addressed at all levels of society—at the national and policy level, in institutional interventions and institutional policies, at the community level, and by various elements of civil society. Moreover, war not only affects those who experience it directly but can echo in future generations as well (Samarasinghe 1998). Thus, it is imperative that further research be done on the effects of war on Sri Lankan society.

References

Atal, Y. 2005. "Youth in Asia: An Overview." In *Youth in Transition The Challenges of Generational Change in Asia*, eds. Fay Gale and Stephanie Fahey. Bangkok, UNESCO.

Bandarage, A. 2000. "The Sri Lankan Conflict: Broadening the Debate." Speech given at the Sri Lanka Symposium held by the Carnegie Council on Ethics in International Affairs and Asia Society, New York, June 13, 2000.

DCS (Department of Census and Statistics, Sri Lanka). 2001. "Census of Population and Housing 2001." Colombo (http://www.statistics.gov.lk/).

———. 2004. "2004 Annual Report of the Sri Lanka Labour Force Survey." Colombo (http://www.statistics.gov.lk/samplesurvey/annual%20report-20041.pdf).

Emmanuel, S. 2005. *Dealing with Women's Militancy: An Analysis of Feminist Discourses from Sri Lanka,* Colombo: Social Policy Analysis Research Centre.

Hettige, S. T. 1994. "Impact of Political Violence on Women in Southern Sri Lanka." Colombo: University of Colombo.

———. 1996. "Youth Unrest in Sri Lanka: A Sociological Perspective." In *Unrest of Revolt: Some Aspects of Youth Unrest in Sri Lanka,* ed. S. T. Hettige. Colombo: Goethe Institute and American Studies Association.

———. 1998a. "Global Integration and the Disadvantaged Youth: From the Centre Stage to the Margins of Society." In *Globalization, Social Change and Youth,* ed. S. T. Hettige. Colombo: German Cultural Institute.

———. 1998b. "Pseudo-Modernization and the Formation of Youth Identities in Sri Lanka." In *Globalization, Social Change and Youth,* ed. S. T. Hettige. Colombo: German Cultural Institute.

———. 2005a. "A Concept Paper on Counselling and Guidance within the School System in Sri Lanka." Paper submitted to the Ministry of Education, Colombo.

———. 2005b. "Demographic and Economic Pressures to Move: Youth Aspirations and Livelihood Opportunities for Youth in the Liberal Economic Environment of Sri Lanka," In *Youth in Transition: The Challenges of Generational Change in Asia,* eds. Fay Gale and Stephanie Fahey. Bangkok, UNESCO.

ILO (International Labour Organization). 2002. *Employment and Unemployment of Youth in Sri Lanka: Country Study.* Colombo (http://www.ilo.org/public/english/region/asro/colombo/download/ptlppr02.pdf).

Kemper, Y. 2005. "Youth in War-to-Peace Transitions Approaches of International Organisations." Berghof Research Center for Constructive Conflict Management, Berlin.

Machel, G. 1996. *Impact of War on Children.* New York: Palgrave.

Maslen, S. 1997. "ILO Action Programme on Skills and Entrepreneurship Training for Countries Emerging from Armed Conflict: The Reintegration of War-affected Youth: The Experience of Mozambique." ILO, Geneva.

Mayer, M. 2005. "Reflection on Social Development in Sri Lanka." In *Perspectives for Social Development in Sri Lanka,* ed. S. T. Hettige and M. Mayer. Colombo: Social Policy Analysis Research Centre.

M. Mayer, M., and A. Galappatti. 2005. "Democracy's Future? Youth Attitudes toward Governance in Sri Lanka." Democracy-Asia, Colombo.

Mayer, M., and M. Salih. 2003. "Poverty Alleviation and Conflict Transformation: The Case of Youth Integration in Jaffna, Sri Lanka." In *Building Local Capacities for Peace: Rethinking conflict and Development in Sri Lanka,* ed. M. Mayer, D. Rajasingham, and Y. Thangarajah. New Delhi: Macmillan.

Samarasinghe, G. 1998. "Some Thoughts on the Sri Lankan Family Exposed to Armed Conflict and the Impact on the Psychological Well-Being of Youth."

In *Globalization, Social Change and Youth*, ed. S. T. Hettige. Colombo: German Cultural Institute.

Selvarajah, M. 2003. "Education in the Conflict Areas in Sri Lanka: A Case for Capacity Building at Local Schools in Batticoloa." In *Building Local Capacities for Peace: Rethinking conflict and Development in Sri Lanka*, ed. M. Mayer, D. Rajasingham, and Y. Thangarajah. New Delhi: Macmillan.

Siddhartan. 2008. "Youth Voices: 'I Do Not Want Anything from Anybody, I Will Re-build My Family.'" In *Youth, Peace and Sustainable Development*, ed. S.T. Hettige and M. Mayer. Colombo: CEPA.

Thangarajah, Y. 2003. "Ethnicization of the Devolution Debate and Militarization of Civil Society in North-Eastern Sri Lanka." In *Building Local Capacities for Peace: Rethinking Conflict and Development in Sri Lanka*, ed. M. Mayer, D. Rajasingham, and Y. Thangarajah. New Delhi: Macmillan.

UN (United Nations). 2003. *World Youth Report*. New York.

UNOWA (United Nations Office for West Africa). 2005. *Youth Unemployment and Regional Insecurity in West Africa*. Dakar.

Uyangoda, J. 1996. "Political Dimensions of Youth Unrest." In *Unrest of Revolt: Some Aspects of Youth Unrest in Sri Lanka*, ed. S. T. Hettige. Colombo: Goethe Institute and American Studies Association.

Index

Boxes, figures, notes, and tables are indicated by *b, f, n,* and *t* following the page number.

Enterprise for Pro-Poor Growth. *See*
International Labour Organization
(ILO)
Entrepreneurial Studies course, 185, 187
entrepreneurship, 10–11, 167–98
    access to business support, 190
    access to finance, 189, 195n18
    conceptual issues, 168–72, 193n3
    economic environment to foster,
        189–90
        promotion of, 192
    methods of study, 172–73
    opportunity-driven vs. necessity-driven
        youth, 170–71
    policy recommendations for, 13,
        169–70, 190–93
    promotion of enterprise culture, 13,
        190–91, 193n3
    regulatory environment to foster, 190
        promotion of, 192
    returning migrant workers and, 159
    sociocultural environment to foster, 168,
        172, 186–89
    training programs for, 11, 167, 173–76
        accessibility of, 184
        after-training services, 181–82, 191
        availability in local languages, 183–84
        gender equity and sensitivity, 178
        geographical scope, 182–83
        goals of, 168–69, 185–86
        lack of data on, 167, 171–72,
            177, 192–93
        monitoring and evaluation, 181,
            192–93
        promotion of, 13, 191
        providers of, 173, 174–76t
        sociocultural grounding, 184–85,
            186–89
        strength and weaknesses of, 177–85
        success rates, 178–79, 194n16
        sustainability of, 179–81
        youth focus, 177
    youth attitudes toward, 170–71,
        184, 186–88
EPF. *See* Employees' Provident Fund
equal opportunity, 11–12, 15, 16. *See also*
    discrimination and social exclusion
ethnicity. *See also* Muslims; Sinhalese;
    Tamils
    discrimination, 15, 213–14
    language education and, 14
    similarities among ethnic groups, 259

wage gaps, 218, 221–23t, 233–36,
    234–35t
    females, 234–35t, 235–36
Expand Your Business program
    (ILO/SIYB), 171
experience
    of female migrants, 152
    job vacancies, requirement for, 76–77
exploitation
    of female workers, 212
    of overseas workers, 147–48
Export Processing Zones, 63
export sector, 142

F

field of study, effect of, 9, 129, 134, 206
first-time job seekers, 77
foreign employment trends. *See* mobility
    and overseas migration
foreign investment, 43
formal employment, 37–38
Fournier, M., 120

G

Gamburd, Michelle Ruth, 152–53
GDP. *See* economic growth
gender dimensions
    of civil conflict, 256, 257–58
    discrimination, 211–13
    of educational attainment, 4–5, 28,
        206–7, 211
    of entrepreneurship training, 178
    of informal vs. formal workers, 38
    of job duration, 84
    of job vacancies, 75–76
    of labor force structure, 22, 26–27t, 28
    married women and wages, 224–25,
        239n11
    of occupational preferences, 81, 81t
    of overseas migration, 10, 75, 140, 145,
        145t, 147, 151–52, 154, 158, 254
    of private sector jobs, 36
    of school-to-work transition, 122–23t,
        125–27t, 129, 134
    of suicide, 212–13
    of TVET, 91, 96–97
    of underemployment, 38
    of unemployment, 4, 40–41,
        41f, 42, 111n5
    of wages. *See* wage differentials
Generate Your Business program, 179

ECO-AUDIT
Environmental Benefits Statement

The World Bank is committed to preserving endangered forests and natural resources. The Office of the Publisher has chosen to print *The Challenge of Youth Employment in Sri Lanka* on recycled paper with 50 percent post-consumer waste, in accordance with the recommended standards for paper usage set by the Green Press Initiative, a nonprofit program supporting publishers in using fiber that is not sourced from endangered forests. For more information, visit www.greenpressinitiative.org.

Saved:
- 11 trees
- 3 million BTU's of total energy
- 1,018 lbs of CO_2 equivalent of greenhouse gases
- 4,905 gallons of waste water
- 298 pounds of solid waste

green press
INITIATIVE

www.ingramcontent.com/pod-product-compliance
Lightning Source LLC
Chambersburg PA
CBHW071842270326
41929CB00013B/2080